D0881002

THE LONG ENGAGEMENT

THE LONG ENGAGEMENT

MEMOIRS OF A COLD WAR LEGEND

JOHN PEET

With an Introduction
by
LEN DEIGHTON

FOURTH ESTATE · LONDON

First published in Great Britain in 1989 by
Fourth Estate Limited
Classic House
113 Westbourne Grove
London W2 4UP

British Library Cataloguing in Publication Data
Peet, John, *1915–1988*
    The long engagement: memoirs of a cold war legend.
    1. East Germany. Journalism. Biography.
    I. Title
    070'.92'4

    ISBN 0 947795 64 2

Typeset by York House Typographic, London W7
Printed & bound by WBC Print Ltd, Bristol

Contents

Introduction

by
Len Deighton

When in June 1950, Reuters man in Berlin, a highly respected thirty-four-year-old reporter with world-wide friends and contacts, went over to East Berlin to work for the communists the story was something of a sensation. The news conference took place in the old Propaganda Ministry, using the room in which Dr. Goebbels gave his press briefings. Peet filed the announcement to Reuters London office as his last task before crossing the border. Even now, when old time newspaper men get together, the story of John Peet's defection is told and retold.

Peet was a newspaper man of the old school, a type now virtually extinct. Such men were doubters, their hard-nosed disbelief based upon years of news gathering and wide-ranging knowledge. For them the story was a means to an end. What they despatched to editors and wire services was only the hard facts. The rumours and guesses – often defamatory and far more illuminating – were exchanged over drinks at the nearest bar, and that was what made such men rewarding to be with.

It is over a quarter of a century ago that I first met John Peet. I'd driven up from Prague through Leipzig in a battered VW beetle with a crash gearbox that worked only for me. My travel papers were not in order and I was flagged down by a Russian Army military policeman and taken to a grim-looking transit barracks surrounded by an ocean of soft mud in which the Russian army parked its trucks. That I was detained there for a long time was partly my own fault. Had I agreed to drive all the way to West Germany and then try to sort out my paperwork over the phone to Prague they would have let me go. I refused to do that and I spent most of the night being quizzed by a cheerful young Russian officer who showed only passing interest in my paperwork. We talked about my suit, my car and my typewriter. I had to tell him what they cost and how much I earned. I was determined not to show anger. Finally, as a reward for my patience I suppose, he phoned his chief and lied. He said that now he had looked more closely at my papers they were in order. There was no problem: I was free to leave. It was an interesting insight into the way things were done in the Russian army. I used the incident later in a story.

In Berlin at that time I knew only one person. Kurt Jung-Alsen, a genial man who had a prewar reputation as a Berlin stage director. In the post-war period he had directed some rather good films, including one about a Waffen SS atrocity against British troops in the Dunkirk retreat. I'd been with him one memorable Sunday morning when, on TV, we watched the Wall being erected. Now, while I was enjoying his hospitality in East Berlin, Kurt uttered those words that are calculated to make any Englishman's heart sink. *'There's an Englishman living here,'* he said. *'I'm going to get the two of you together.'* That was how I came to meet John Peet.

It has always been my policy in Communist countries to declare my position as a non-believer. (People living in the East are otherwise likely to assume that any foreign visitor might be a dedicated Communist ready to report any divergence from the Party Line.) I did this with John and I must say that although over the years we never avoided political discussions, we never had an argument of any kind.

It was difficult to argue with him since what he liked best was to exchange information: historical, political, social, mechanical, mystical. There was no argument or point of view – however extreme or dotty – that he wouldn't listen to with interest (the only comparably open-minded person I ever knew was Bertrand Russell). Peet was not an evangelist and I certainly am not one. He would bombard me with questions and answers too. One typical letter from him began

'Dear Len, Your thirst for information is unquenchable, and you know exactly which button to press to allow me to display expertise (which in my case means having a fairly good recollection of the broad outline, and where to go to look up details).

There followed a description of the law pertaining to the payment, or rather non-payment, of life-insurance policies in the Nazi period (with particular reference to deaths in concentration camps) but it might have been about some of the curious words of Berlin German (a particular passion with him), a Volga–German woman who was a Russian Army major, the use of postage stamps as currency during the Spanish Civil War or the latest communist joke. And returning always to our mutual passion, Berlin, where he lived for most of his adult life, having first visited the city in the Easter vacation of 1933.

His knowledge was nothing short of encyclopedic except that the things he told could not be found in any encyclopedia. Anyone wanting to know what was really happening in Berlin went to him. Freddie Forsyth, a splendid researcher and a mutual friend, would I'm sure be ready to acknowledge John's help. Peet corresponded with Jessica Mitford whom he'd known in 1939. And yet he was never a name-dropper and regarded such consultations as confidential. I readily concede my enormous debt to him and I especially liked being with him when things happened. He once wrote . . . *the way you weave into the fabric the sights and sounds from some of our outings give it a special charm for me* . . . . He told me how much he enjoyed reliving incidents or escapades we had shared. John combined a wonderful disrespect for rules and regulations with a happy knack of getting you to the right place at the right time. And then look out!

But what was John Peet really like? He was tall and thin and latterly wore a rather long wispy grey beard that even on a Berlin street could make heads turn. He was a quietly spoken man with a public-school voice and a rewarding sense of humour. He was wonderful with children and willingly took my sons off for a sightseeing tour of Berlin. Some said he was inscrutable, and once he wrote to me saying, *I find it extremely hard to get this story down on paper. Marginal and silly though the story is, my inner censor works hard to try to stop me calling a spy a spy.* But inscrutable or not, to marry four times surely reveals a touch of romanticism as well as optimism. He describes his background as 'suffragettist, pacifist, Christian Socialist', although he once told me how much he enjoyed teaching Monopoly to his Communist friends and watch them becoming adept at unbridled capitalism. Both his parents were Quakers and his father's suffering in prison, at a time when 'hard labour' meant exactly that, undoubtedly had a great effect upon his thinking, more perhaps than he acknowledges.

Radical, and ascetic, he remained essentially and enthusiastically English in a way that only expatriates can. Perhaps, like so many romantics, he expected too much of human nature. Certainly at war's end he expected West Germany to expunge Naziism from political life, instead, prominent Nazis rose to high positions. He believed that the Allies would implement their Potsdam promise to do something about *the present excessive concentration of economic power as exemplified by cartels, syndicates, trusts and other monopolistic arrangements.* In fact it was these very ingredients that were nourished to produce what is either the West German miracle or the unacceptable face of modern Germany (and modern Europe too) according to your point of view.

I am pleased to write a foreword for the autobiography of one of the most intriguing men I have ever met. Public schoolboy, Communist, Grenadier Guardsman, down and out in Vienna and Prague, veteran of the International Brigades fighting in Spain (I found his excerpts from letters written during the war particularly interesting and moving), agony aunt for a weekly magazine, rejected by an RAF aircrew selection board, sought by a Soviet spy recruiter, he not only joined the Palestine Police but as a

CID detective tried to understand what the Holy Land conflict was all about. A task made difficult when he found himself in Bethlehem's Church of the Nativity on Christmas Eve trying to keep the peace between Roman Catholic and Greek Orthodox clergy while in the cellar below a baton-wielding Muslim and British constable guarded the site where Jesus was born.

Born immediately before the Russian revolution his life provides unfamiliar historical footnotes for our lifetime, a period dominated by brutal religious and political intolerance. Although he disliked the old school tie, his combat role in the Spanish Civil War made him one of a very special elite, recognized in the West but of even more account in Eastern Europe. His life is a puzzle, but then to some extent everyone's life is a puzzle. Read this book; it is essential reading for anyone trying to understand the contradictory world in which we live.

Publisher's Note: It was a point of principle in John Peet's writings never to capitalise the word 'nazi', or any word containing it. In deference to his lifelong stand against fascism in all its forms, the publishers have adhered to this style.

1

Transformation Scene

T he message which came hammering out on the telex in Reuters' office in London on the morning of 12 June 1950 later became a minor Fleet Street myth. It ran like this:

By John Peet, Reuters Correspondent, Berlin, June 12 – Reuters chief correspondent in Berlin, 34-year-old John Peet, today made a public declaration that he 'could no longer serve the Anglo-American warmongers'. Mr Peet made the declaration to more than 200 German and foreign correspondents at a press conference in the East German Information Department.

In all modesty I must describe the despatch as a good workmanlike story in the best news-agency tradition: short, impartial and to the point, complete with a short biography of the main character and name and address of next of kin.

Reuters had always treated me well, and I felt a professional obligation to finish up my agency career with an elegant exit. My only regret was that, since I myself was giving the press conference in East Berlin, I could not well dodge out of the room – as the men from the rival wire services did – to phone in a first short snap on the news. So I was scooped on my own story. Regrettably, Reuters in London decided that my nicely rounded 'obituary' was not suitable for publication, and they spiked it.

When I had finally decided, a few weeks earlier, to leave Reuters and move to East Germany if the authorities there would have me, I had, in my innocence, imagined that I might make a short public statement, in either

West or East Berlin, and then proceed to my West Berlin flat to pack up in leisure and drive over to East Berlin to start a new chapter in my life.

Through an old friend in East Berlin I contacted the proper quarters. After an initial period of deep suspicion, a grudging OK was given; but it was made clear to me that I would have to play the cross-curtain move their way. I was then introduced, suitably mysteriously, to my mentor in such clandestine business. He turned out to be an affable man of about my age, who had been in and out of gaol for revolutionary activities all over Europe since his teens.

My plan was far too straightforward for him; old traditions of the revolutionary movement apparently demanded that any such operation had to be conducted with a major degree of vigilance and mystification. He painted for me in drastic colours what might happen to me if the ENEMY (he always said this in capitals) got wind of my switch before I was out of their area of control. This step would be such a blow to the warmongers that they would go to any lengths to prevent it. Arrest on a trumped-up charge, he suggested; detention in a mental hospital; lie-detectors; possibly even a carefully arranged fatal accident. Once I had made my statement, in the most sensational way possible, I would have to remain firmly in the socialist sphere, protected by the massed phalanxes of proletarian vigilance.

(His suggestions seemed a little hysterical at the time. With later knowledge of some of the things done by the spooks of the CIA and other organisations, they seem rather more credible, though even today I find it hard to believe that anything drastic would really have happened had we conducted the move in a less dramatic manner.)

My mentor's proposal was that I should, for a start, avoid doing anything to indicate in the slightest degree that I was contemplating leaving my job and home in West Berlin. If possible I should give active and visible evidence that I intended to stay on the job and in my flat for ever. 'Order new curtains and tell all your friends,' he suggested. 'Start an argument with Reuters' head office about holiday plans for the next twelve months. Ask for assurances that you will retain your present appointment for several years to come.' Instructions to change fronts would come at short notice, he said, and I should thus hold myself ready to cut and run at the drop of a hat.

The following period was a little trying. On the one hand, I tried to comply with instructions and create the impression that I was in West Berlin to stay; on the other, I wanted to leave my affairs in order when I went. In particular I was plagued by the idea that I must not leave any debts behind, and I had no cash handy to deal with this, in particular a largish advance I had had from Reuters to buy a new car.

The only way I could see of raising the money unobtrusively and quickly was to sell off large parts of my considerable library, accumulated in the early post-war years in Vienna, Warsaw and Berlin. In any case, it appeared unlikely that I would be able to take many books with me when I disappeared, and I was doubtful about the attitude of the East German authorities if I arrived there with cases full of *Mein Kampf* and other nazi volumes, let alone most of the works of Trotsky, obviously more dangerous than Adolf. The books were sold, and in a few days I was able to pay off my debts.

Simultaneously I continued to provide Reuters with a good service, staying well away from stories which might look 'Red-slanted', even if true. Then, suddenly, when I had begun to wonder whether the whole operation had been abandoned, the vital message came.

A certain amount of discretion on the telephone was undoubtedly necessary. In many states phones are regularly tapped by some government agency or other, but in the four-power city of Berlin in 1950 any sensible person reckoned with the possibility that one of the several competing intelligence services of the four occupation powers might be listening. And apart from the Allied tappers, there were a considerable number of freelance ears, mainly German, ready to sell their intercepts to the highest bidder.

But in this case, the discretion shown by over-vigilant Communists might easily have defeated its own ends. My contact man – not my mentor, for conspiratorial protocol demanded that there must be a cut-out – was a well-known East Berlin professor who had been a frequent visitor at my West Berlin flat. If MI6, or the CIA, or whoever was really keeping an eye on me had been listening in, a straightforward invitation from the professor would have raised no eyebrow. But the professor had been properly briefed by the experts, who had apparently studied their conspirators' handbooks all too well. Instead of saying, 'Professor X here. I was wondering whether you could come and have a cup of coffee with me on Sunday', he said, in an unnaturally high voice, 'Primrose has a message for daffodil. 1600 hours on Monday. I repeat, 1600 hours on Monday.' This meant, of course, as any student of spy stories will know, not a meeting at 1600 hours on Monday, but at 1500 hours on Sunday. Having convinced any possible tappers that something fishy was going on, he rang off.

So take-off date was tomorrow. I still had a lot to do. Personal property had to be sorted and loaded into my car; superfluous papers had to be disposed of. I had nothing remotely compromising to myself in the flat,

3

but I had to assume that after my move to the East all sorts of friends and acquaintances might be harried to some degree by the spooks of various nations. As I had no particular desire to make their job easier, I thought it better to destroy things like address books and Christmas card lists.

It had not struck me earlier how difficult it might be to destroy things in a modern centrally heated apartment with no grates or stoves, and readers contemplating flitting for any reason should bear this in mind. Sheets of ordinary paper can be torn up and flushed down the lavatory; but what do you do with your telephone book if it happens to consist of thick sheets of almost untearable cardboard which, even if hacked into small pieces, would be bound to choke the plumbing? This problem was finally solved by constructing a provisional grate inside the lavatory basin, on which the incriminating names and numbers could be burned. A first daylight attempt with closed windows nearly asphyxiated me, so I had to postpone the burning until dark, when clouds of bilious smoke from the windows would not be so obvious.

When the tearing and burning were all over, I took the further step of disconnecting and inspecting the U-bend under the lavatory to make sure that no evidence had stuck damply in hiding.

(Somebody, some time, should write a book, or at least a thesis, on fact imitating fiction in this field. I have a theory that most intelligence operatives gather their know-how from the books of John le Carré and Len Deighton and not vice versa. The only case of which I have personal knowledge concerns a German anti-fascist in Berlin during the war years, who suddenly, and without preparation, found himself running an important intelligence net for the Allied cause. Since he had no idea of the techniques, he bought or borrowed all the First World War spy books he could lay hands on, including the works of Somerset Maugham and Compton Mackenzie. He told me, many years later, that he had found them quite useful.)

Having finished the job of wiping off the fingerprints, so to speak, I loaded the boot of my car, gave the flat a final check to make sure nothing had been overlooked and then popped around to the British Press Club for a farewell drink with my colleagues. Here I scattered at the bar some more camouflage in the form of hints about my orthodox plans for the coming weeks and months.

On Sunday morning I took the morning shift at the office as usual and then told my assistants that I would be 'not available' for the next twenty-four hours, promising to ring in at intervals to check whether anything big was happening. Without saying anything specific, I think I conveyed the impression that I was taking off for a very private weekend.

And then into my car for a new life.

The whole thing went like clockwork. Through the Brandenburg Gate on the then invisible border – this was long before the Berlin Wall made cross-curtain trips rather more of a problem – and off to the rendezvous. Since all such conspiratorial meetings are arranged on the assumption that you must never loiter and must arrive on the dot, I drove to the general vicinity of my target and then cruised until one minute before three, trying to make sure I was not being followed, but acutely aware that I did not really know the tricks of the trade. At three precisely I drove down a quiet tree-lined street in East Berlin and, as instructed, turned sharply into a garage entry. As I drove in, the garage door opened, closing behind me as soon as I was inside.

And there stood my mentor, rather incongruously bulging in the cornflower-blue shirt of the Free German Youth movement. At our clandestine meetings in previous weeks he had confused me somewhat by claiming variously to represent the East German trade unions, the anti-fascist association and the East Berlin municipality, having apparently forgotten what he had said last time. It turned out later that he was simply an official of the Government Information Office.

But why had I, at the age of thirty-four, abandoned the moderate security, the congenial work and the fair prospects of my job as head of the Reuters Bureau in West Berlin to plunge into the uncertainties of a very different life in the young German Democratic Republic, which was at that time regarded by most of the world as a ramshackle nonentity, likely to disappear at almost any moment?

It is a long story, and I had better begin at the beginning.

2

Missionary Stew

Looking back, it appears that the thickness of the butter on the Peet family bread in my youth depended directly upon the state of the complicated civil wars in China in the 1920s. As we lived in Penge, a part of south London completely devoid of any links with Chinese warlords or civil conflicts of any type, and since nobody in our family was involved in gun-runninig or the opium trade, the connection may appear obscure.

But the explanation is really quite simple. My father, Hubert Peet, a talented journalist, had fallen on sparse days after the First World War, in which he had done time as an absolutist conscientious objector. Unable to obtain suitable work on a Fleet Street paper in 1919 – prejudice against COs as 'shirkers' was still rife – he went to work for a minuscule outfit calling itself the Far and Near Press Bureau, which had been established to organise publicity for various London-based missionary societies.

Until Hubert Peet took over, the Far and Near Press Bureau appears to have confined its activities to circulating dull routine hand-outs on rather boring missionary activities which were rarely used by the newspapers. He had other ideas; he knew from experience that newspapers would only use the material offered if it were presented as news, and if it had to be paid for. He put his ideas into practice, and suddenly missionaries became news.

The information was there for the taking. For the good souls who ran the offices of the London Missionary Society or the Society for the Propagation of the Gospel had totally failed to grasp the fact that the news that a crocodile in the Limpopo River had swallowed the bible of

6

Missionary Thistlethwaite was worth pounds, shillings and pence – or at least shillings and pence – to a struggling journalist who knew how to sell it properly. And if the crocodile had considerately gone on to take a bite out of the missionary too, then the Peet family could perhaps consider buying new curtains for the front windows.

So through the early 1920s Hubert Peet bustled from missionary society to missionary society in London, compiling card indexes of names, biographical details and postings and watching out patiently for the rather rare missionary who did something newsworthy or, more frequently, the missionary who had something done to him.

And this was where civil war in China came in. In the 1920s China was torn by strife, and since it was well peppered with missionary stations of all brands, the statistical chance of a missionary being cut off, besieged or even murdered became interesting. Kidnapped missionaries apparently had a particularly favourable effect on the family income. With a bit of luck a missionary, preferably female, kidnapped by a Chinese warlord would be in the news for months as ransom sums were discussed, and leader writers in the *Morning Post* muttered about sending in the gunboats.

Some autobiographies dither on for chapter after chapter about the family tree. Let me try to tick off this chore in a few paragraphs. There was a vague and possibly mythical forebear who was supposed to have introduced watercress to the London market; and an even mistier one, a jeweller, was said to have been knocked up in the middle of the night before Queen Victoria's coronation in 1837 to fix a loose diamond in the crown. An even more intriguing family legend had it that some great-great-granddad had been hung for stealing sheep. Recent research by a member of my family seems to show that the man actually existed, was in fact condemned to death for fiddling his flock – he was a shepherd – and was then grandly reprieved by King George III, who had met him on a country ride, and sent off to fight George Washington's National Liberation Army.

But more visible forebears were sturdy Victorian gentlemen, who never accumulated much in the way of riches, but appear to have been comfortably well off. My paternal grandfather, William Peet, worked for the publishing firm of Longmans, and made a minor but long-lasting name for himself by compiling the first bibliography of publishing, which still turns up in the footnotes to works in this field. My grandfather on my mother's side, the Reverend Harry Scott, was the son of a Walsall craftsman. He entered the ministry of the Congregational Church at an early age, and promptly sailed off with his bride to the Torres Straits, between New Guinea and Australia, where my mother was born.

With admirable Victorian self-confidence he taught himself the language of Murray Island, where he was stationed, and then proceeded to translate one of the Gospels and innumerable hymns into this language. I have a copy of his hymn-book, and would love to have a retranslation into English to see how the old boy tackled words like 'glory' and 'salvation', which you cannot easily point at when you are teaching yourself a language with the help of an illiterate Stone Age man. Since apparently nobody in the world speaks the Murray language except the three hundred inhabitants of the island, I shall probably never know.

My mother, after making news back in 1884 by being, we were told, the first white baby born in New Guinea, never made news again. Even this was strictly speaking a myth, since as far as Murray Island belonged to anyone except the islanders it formed part of Queensland, Australia. Both my mother and father had been brought up as Congregationalists, and they appear to have met at the Congregational Church in Purley. They were married there in 1910, but soon both joined the Society of Friends (Quakers), and this had a very considerable influence on their lives and the lives of their children.

At the time of the marriage my father had been working for several years as a journalist in Fleet Street, first on the *Daily Sketch* and then on the *Daily News*. I have some vague memories of his anecdotes about his Fleet Street days: how on the *Daily Sketch* he had been responsible for checking the captions on the photos of Ascot races and society balls, which accounted for his out-of-character familiarity with the names in Debrett; and how on the *Daily News* he had once been pressed into service to sub the Household Hints corner and had approved for publication a recipe for toffee which had involved nearly as much pepper as sugar.

He must sometimes have been engaged on straight reporting, for he had been present at the notorious 'Sidney Street Siege' on 3 January 1911, and had kept a number of press photos of the incident which lie before me as I write.

I must trust my memory for what he told me about the battle. Early on that January day in 1911, two policemen had gone to a tenement in Sidney Street, Houndsditch, to arrest a man known as Peter the Painter, believed to be a dangerous eastern European anarchist agitator. Shots were fired through the door, and one of the policemen was killed.

On the authority of Winston Churchill, then Home Secretary, the local police were armed with shotguns, and a company of the Scots Guards were called in, armed more effectively with Lee-Enfield rifles; Churchill hurried to the spot to take personal command.

One of the old press photos lying before me is captioned: 'Mr Winston Churchill surrounded by detectives and armed police'. It was this picture which intrigued me most when I was very young. There stood Mr Churchill, in a very shiny top hat, and next to him, large as life, were two perfectly ordinary London bobbies with guns tucked under their arms. It was this extraordinary fact which impressed me, for everybody knew at the time that the British constabulary never carried arms; that was something left to uncivilised foreigners.

The besieged house was set on fire, and two of the alleged anarchists perished in the flames. Peter the Painter is believed to have escaped. I recall a few odd nostalgic newspaper articles in the 1930s suggesting that Peter the Painter had really been Stalin; just for the record, Stalin was at the time in Tsarist exile in Vologda, 500 kilometres north of Moscow.

I have only scraps of information on the activities and interests of my parents in those days. They were active in the movement for votes for women, were politically on the fringes of the Independent Labour Party and apparently experimented with vegetarianism. In 1913 Hubert Peet took over the editorship of *Sells World's Press*, a bulky annual register of newspapers and magazines all over the world, mainly intended for advertisers.

In mid-1914 plans had been made for him to visit the United States in the firm's interest. The outbreak of the First World War in August made no difference to the plans, since everybody expected hostilities to be over in a few months at the most, and so in late 1914 he made his first trip to America. Apart from his work there for *Sells World's Press* he made extensive press contacts and became friendly with Oswald Garrison Villard, president of the *New York Evening Post* and editor of the radical weekly *The Nation*. There are some indications that it was during this visit that he first became interested in the problem of race relations. He returned to Britain early in 1915.

My mother must have had a trying time during his absence. For she was not only looking after two daughters aged three and two, but was also caring, with Quakerly concern, for a German couple trapped in England by the outbreak of war. For harbouring 'Huns' she was booed in the streets.

By 1915 it had become clear that the war would last for a long time, and conscription seemed inevitable. The Society of Friends therefore established the Friends Service Committee to help young men, whether Quakers or not, who had conscientious objections to military service.

Hubert Peet became the executive secretary of this body and, a few months later, one of the editors of *The Ploughshare*, a monthly journal associated with the Quaker Socialist Society. Going through the back numbers of this journal today, I find it a curious mixture: serious articles on social subjects by writers such as Bertrand Russell and Fenner Brockway (the latter amazingly still politically active when I write these lines in 1987, over sixty years later); news of conscientious objectors (COs); a long article on Karl Liebknecht, the anti-war German socialist who later founded the German Communist Party; letters from Russian Bolsheviks in exile in England; and mixed up with all this some items called 'Little Chapters of Meditation' which I must confess I find mystifyingly insipid.

The imposition of conscription in February 1916 meant that those opposed to military service had to make up their minds whether they would opt for some form of non-combatant service or become absolutist COs, who were almost all imprisoned. Before Hubert Peet received his call-up papers – as a married man of thirty he was not in the first draft – he was concerned in an almost forgotten incident which indicated that perhaps prison would not be the worst which COs had to face.

In May 1916 the military authorities took very drastic action to dissuade young men who were claiming exemption on grounds of conscience. Seventeen COs held in the military barracks at Felixstowe were suddenly transported without warning to the war zone in France. There, under military law, they could be court-martialled and shot for disobeying orders on active service.

By a lucky chance they were able to pass on news of their plight. Their train passed the garden of the parents of one of their number, and they managed to throw out a scribbled appeal for help. The parents telegraphed Professor Gilbert Murray, who immediately bearded Prime Minister Asquith in the House of Commons and got his promise to order the military not to execute COs.

It soon emerged that more COs had been sent to France, and some had already been sentenced to death. Dr F. B. Meyer, secretary of the influential Free Church Council, insisted on going to France to determine the facts, and he picked Hubert Peet to accompany him. When they got there they discovered that all death sentences had been commuted to ten years' penal servitude, and they interviewed fourteen of the COs in a military prison where, *The Ploughshare* reported, 'they were undergoing the rigours of No. 1 Field Punishment, including periods of bread and water diet, and had been subjected to periods of "crucifixion" with the hands tied to a rope stretched at the level of their shoulders between two pillars'.

The publicity given to the case meant that all the COs put in peril were returned to civilian prisons in Britain, where they were held until a few months after the war had ended.

Soon Hubert Peet himself got his call-up papers, and the subsequent events can be followed from a few contemporary newspaper cuttings:

Hubert William Peet, thirty, describing himself as a Quaker, Socialist and journalist, was today handed over to military custody by the Croydon magistrates . . . He had refused non-combatant service.

Addressing the court, Mr Peet said: 'I am a Quaker and a Socialist, and I believe that the teaching of Jesus means that I must confront violence with gentleness, anger with reason, hatred with goodwill. Though I may be technically a soldier I cannot be one actually and morally, and therefore I cannot recognise any military order.

Westminster Gazette, 14 November 1916

At Hounslow Barracks yesterday Hubert W. Peet was court-martialled for refusing to obey an order to parade. He declined to plead, declaring that though he might be technically a soldier, he was not one in reality and could not be made one against his will. He must disobey all military orders because of his conviction that all warfare, and not merely killing, was wrong. The court's decision will be promulgated in due course.

Morning Post, 24 November 1916

H. W. Peet has been sentenced to 112 days' hard labour for refusing to obey the commands of his superior officer.

Morning Post, 29 November 1916

Having completed his sentence of 112 days' hard labour for refusing to obey military orders, Hubert W. Peet was released from Wandsworth Prison on Saturday and returned to his unit at Hounslow. He will be court-martialled for the second time in the course of a few days.

Manchester Guardian, 26 February 1917

Hubert W. Peet was sentenced by court-martial at Hounslow Barracks yesterday to two years' hard labour for refusal to obey military orders. He had already served 112 days for a previous offence.

The Times, 15 March 1917

In February 1919 *The Ploughshare* noted that Hubert Peet, still in prison,

is by no means as well as we could wish. The senseless work and galling idleness to a man of his active nature is telling badly on his constitution and his nerves. Recently he was surprised and delighted to receive a visit from Oswald Garrison Villard, who stands alone in America for a cause like ours. Our visitor was distressed to find our colleague so situated. It was good to hear him say, however, that the atmosphere over here which we have been thinking to be rather stifling, was refreshing to Mr Villard, who reports a much more cruel, tyrannical attitude towards all pacifist thought and work in America, from East to West.

Two months later, in its April 1919 issue, *The Ploughshare* was able to report that Hubert Peet had been released: 'He has been in Pentonville since November 1916, and the long period of isolation, poor food, cold and confinement has had its inevitable effect on his physique. He will require careful nursing and a long period of rest before he is able to resume his work.'

I was only one year old when my father was imprisoned. Although I had been taken to Pentonville Prison once on a visit, my first memory of him must be dated immediately after his release, when I was three years and three months old. The memory is vivid: we were sitting round the table in the nursery in my grandfather's house in Shanklin, Isle of Wight – the total stranger who was said to be my father, my mother and my two sisters. My father, who was no good with his hands (a trait which I have inherited), was trying very hard to construct, with the aid of some pieces of cardboard and sealing wax, a model of his prison cell.

After that one sharp image, I have no further memories of him for several years.

Family life at home in Penge in the early 1920s appears in retrospect to have been fairly smooth. There was a pervasive but not oppressive Quakerly atmosphere of tolerance and goodwill towards all men, and a deep conviction that everybody would be good if they only had the chance. My parents treated us children – by this time there were four of us, two girls and two boys – in a way which was probably ahead of the times. Prohibitions and punishments were few. Domestic jobs were shared according to age and ability, and my father set an example by helping with the washing-up. We were encouraged to read what we liked.

Few mental snapshots of family life in the Peet family in the 1920s linger in my mind, but I can see a typical family evening in the living room: my mother knitting on one side of the fire, my father reading or correcting proofs on the other, and my sisters and possibly myself doing homework on the dining table. My younger brother is off-screen; he had presumably been sent to bed.

When homework was completed, and there was something suitable on the BBC, we gathered round a three-tiered wooden cake-stand which was crowned by our tiny crystal set. From the set a tangle of wires led to six pairs of headphones. My parents were strongly opposed to loudspeakers, and even when we had progressed to a wireless set with valves, or at least one valve, the headphones were retained for a number of years.

It was almost certainly the insidious influence of wireless – nobody called it radio in those days – which led to the sad decrease of the Victorian and Edwardian pleasures of family music. I begin to feel my age when I recall my mother seated at the black upright piano, and my father standing to the left, singing and turning the pages of the sheet music. He probably had a fair repertoire, but I remember only two of his songs. One was 'The Two Grenadiers' by Heinrich Heine with music by Franz Schubert, an unexpectedly martial song for a pacifist. The other, my favourite, which must have been a music-hall song in my father's youth, went like this: 'How does the little liver pill, when you're ill, know where your liver is, eh?' Today it still seems to me a logical question.

I cannot recall any intrusive religious or other indoctrinations. My parents were always ready to explain their convictions, but refrained from pushing them down our throats. When, probably at the age of thirteen or fourteen, I declared that I had become an atheist, and did not intend in future to attend Quaker meeting on Sundays, they were pained but made no attempt to talk me out of it.

Both my mother and my father were very patient in answering our questions and showing us how to do things for ourselves. As soon as we could read fluently my father made a great point of introducing us to encyclopaedias and other works of reference. I can remember very clearly one instance of this when I must have been about ten.

Entering Liverpool Street Station with my father, we passed a legless beggar holding a tray of matches decorated with a board saying 'Crippled in the Fenian Bomb Outrage at Clerkenwell in 1867'. What was a Fenian, I wanted to know, and why had he thrown a bomb?

My father suggested I should look it up when we got home. So I started with *Chambers's Encyclopaedia*, which told me who the Fenians were and mentioned various 'outrages' but gave me no information about the bomb in Clerkenwell. My father then pointed out several books on Irish history – his fairly large study at home was stuffed with books from floor to ceiling – and after a bit of a search I was able to satisfy my curiosity. Back in the

1860s the Fenians, also known as the Irish Republican Brotherhood, the direct forefathers of the IRA of today, had been very active. In November 1867 three Fenians were sentenced to death in Manchester for killing a policeman when they attacked a prison van to release some of their comrades. Even today a ballad about the incident, 'The Smashing of the Van', is sung in IRA circles. In retaliation for the death sentences the Irish underground organisation exploded a bomb outside Clerkenwell Prison in London, where other Fenians were being held. The bomb attack, staged on 13 December 1867, was badly bungled. The prison remained almost undamaged, but a number of surrounding houses were smashed, several people were killed, and over a hundred were injured.

Perhaps because this was the first, or the most interesting, bit of historical research which my father urged me to undertake, the main facts about the Clerkenwell bomb are still clear in my mind sixty years later; but when I came to write the story down I realised I had forgotten some of the details. Our flat in East Berlin is furnished with wall-to-wall bookshelves, but there is little there about the Irish troubles of the last century. Then I remembered that Karl Marx and Friedrich Engels had been very interested in Irish affairs (Engels was married, consecutively, to two Irish girls with strong Fenian connections), and looked up their correspondence. There, of course, it all was. On the day after the Clerkenwell bomb, Marx in London wrote to Engels in Manchester:

This latest Fenian exploit in Clerkenwell is very stupid. The London masses, which have shown much sympathy with Ireland, will be enraged by this, and driven into the arms of the government party. You cannot expect the London proletarians to allow themselves to be blown up in honour of Fenian emissaries.

My father's journalistic and public relations work soon spread from the strictly missionary sector into such fields as race relations and international peace. In the 1920s he travelled a lot, to a world YMCA conference in Helsinki, a conference on African education in Brussels and a meeting of the International Missionary Council on the Mount of Olives in Palestine in 1928. (Looking up the scanty records, I have just discovered to my dismay that he also attended two meetings of the League of Nations Opium Commission in Geneva, thus shattering my light-hearted assertion at the beginning of this chapter that nobody in our family had anything to do with opium.)

All this international activity brought a whole series of exotic guests to our home, guests of a type rarely seen in Penge in those days. There was a stately stout Indian lady in a sari who stayed with us for a month or two. She and a number of other Indian guests spoke very highly of Gandhi, notorious in the British newspapers of that time as a rather comic, though possibly sinister, bare-legged agitator. Then there was a suitably inscrutable Japanese Christian leader whose name I recall as Kagawa who fascinated me by folding little paper animals; and a large and handsome African from the Gold Coast named Dr Aggrey, later regarded as the grandfather of Ghanaian independence.

Some of those who visited us were a great disappointment to a small boy. When the splendidly named Bishop of the Arctic came to tea he had left his fur parka and his huskies at home, and he did not even wear bishop's gaiters.

The only genuine show-stopping name among my father's far-flung acquaintances, Albert Schweitzer, apparently never came to tea in Penge. Hubert Peet first encountered Schweitzer in 1922, on his first visit to Britain, where he was practically unknown at the time. Because of the missionary angle my father went to interview him; they got on well together, and Schweitzer asked him to act as his guide round London for a few days. From that time on they corresponded regularly, and for twenty-five years Hubert Peet edited the bulletin of the Dr Schweitzer Hospital Trust.

Some years later, in about 1930, I organised a collection for this hospital fund at my boarding school in Saffron Walden. My father suggested that I might personally present the money to the doctor, who was scheduled to give an organ recital in Norwich Cathedral not very far away. I duly travelled there and handed the proceeds over to him, and he insisted that 'the son of his great friend Hubert Peet' should lunch with him. My only memories of him are that he wore remarkably un-English clothes, in particular a flowing black cloak; that he had a very bushy moustache; that he ate his soup very noisily indeed; and that I understood practically nothing of what he said, although I had been learning French for years.

The doctor was very hospitable to our family. In 1931 he invited my parents, my brother and myself to spend several weeks at his family home in Gunsbach in Alsace. He himself was off in Lambarene in Africa being great and good, but we were well looked after by an assortment of his relations, friends and old family retainers. This was my first taste of 'abroad', and life in a small Alsatian village where most of the peasants wore wooden shoes and the farm carts were drawn by oxen was very exotic indeed.

As I mentioned earlier, my parents held that people would be good if they only had the chance. I recall that when we had a minor burglary, in which nothing of value was stolen, they discussed what they would have done if they had unfortunately interrupted the burglar at work. There was general agreement that the police would not have been called in – though as I recall it my mother threw into the discussion the argument that if the man had been removed from circulation he would at least have been unable to sin any more for a certain period.

In accordance with the admirable egalitarian ideals of the family, it was planned that I should attend the local council school, rather than one of the private schools to which most non-working-class parents sent their children. 'I didn't see why our children should be privileged,' my father told me long afterwards, 'but I took the precaution of going to take a look at the school first. It was disturbing enough to learn that the average form numbered about sixty, but it was the general atmosphere which really deterred me. The greasy institutional wall-paint, the echoes and particularly the smell. I suddenly remembered what it reminded me of: Pentonville Prison. I couldn't send you there.'

The alternative was a dame school in a large private house, run by a couple of old maiden ladies for the 'sons and daughters of gentlemen'. Although I must have attended this school for four years, it has left so little impression that I have had to think hard to recall whether it was a mixed school or for boys only. It was only when I recalled fat Yvonne, always sucking sticky sweets, that I could fix with certainty that the pupils included girls.

The school must have taught us all to read and write and reckon with some success, but the only thing which I quite certainly learned there was that since the Bible is a holy book it must always be treated with superstitious respect; in particular, nothing whatsoever may be placed on a bible lying on a table. I don't think we were told that we would go straight to hell if we laid a pencil on Holy Writ, but this was certainly the impression given. And it was a lasting impression: even to this day I feel a vague unease if I see somebody casually drop a newspaper or a box of matches on a reclining bible. In moments of extreme dauntlessness I sometimes try a sort of exorcism by placing a cup of coffee or even the works of Karl Marx on top of my bible, but it does not work. Subconsciously I wait for the clap of thunder and the smell of sulphur.

3

When the Red Revolution Comes

With a 'suffragettist', pacifist, Christian Socialist background, it was probably inevitable that I took a political stance at an early age. My first political clash can be dated with some accuracy as coming in 1924, the year of the general election which brought the first-ever Labour Government in Britain. I was just about eight years old.

On the long walk to my dame school with a group of other boys, talk turned to the election. One or two of the boys declared themselves Liberal supporters; rather more were Conservatives. When my turn came I said harmlessly, 'I'm Labour.'

The result was stunning, rather as if I had told a congregation of Fundamentalists that I regularly sacrificed to Baal. 'You can't really mean it,' said the oldest boy, all of nine.

'Of course I do. My pater is Labour, and so am I.' (Whether the word 'pater' was actually used is doubtful, but it gives the right period flavour.)

When the other boys had convinced themselves that I was not making a tasteless joke, they all punched me quite hard. A teenager in Scout uniform who was passing intervened, obviously as his good deed for the day. 'You can't all hit him at once: fight fair.' They explained breathlessly that I supported Labour. 'Oh, that's different,' said the Scout, and walked by on the other side.

There were apparently no after-effects, for I cannot remember being sent to Coventry or anything of that sort. Having been brought up on tales of missionaries abused by the heathen for bearing witness for their Saviour, I probably felt a certain smirking quiet satisfaction at my minor martyrdom for bearing witness for Ramsay MacDonald.

Active involvement in politics appears to have lain fallow for the following six years, though I began to read a lot, ranging from many of the dailies through the ILP weekly *New Leader* to the radical New York *Nation*, which baffled me continually with its details of US politics. All this political reading was mixed up with the usual juveniles. It was only recently when a friend gave me a boxful of old English books for boys that I noticed how crammed many of the volumes were with the calm assumption that the white man in general, and the British Empire in particular, had been selected by the Almighty to rule over the lesser breeds without the law.

At some point along the line I must have become conscious that, off to the left of the broad political panorama which I surveyed rather undiscriminatingly, there were some people called Communists with whom everybody else disagreed, sometimes mildly like the writers in the *New Leader* and *The Nation*, but often violently as in most of my other reading.

By chance, there appear to have been no Communists in my father's catholic range of acquaintances, though I feel sure they would have been treated with the usual Quakerly friendly tolerance if there had been. But then, in 1930 or 1931, when I was fourteen or fifteen, I finally came into contact with communism.

Since 1927 I had been a pupil at Friends School Saffron Walden, a very liberal Quaker boarding school in Essex where mild non-conformity was quite normal. One of the older boys was the grandson of George Lansbury, the saintly and picturesque Labour politician much revered in the Peet family, and one of my contemporaries actually turned out to be the son of a Communist, though he kept this very quiet for a long period.

With my background, I had always considered myself a Labour supporter. When the Labour Party won a parliamentary majority for the first time in the general election of 1929, I think I probably assumed that Prime Minister Ramsay MacDonald would take the first steps towards building a new Jerusalem in England's green and pleasant land. It soon became apparent, even to a callow schoolboy, that the new pilot was unable or unwilling to set course for a new Utopia.

But the MacDonald Government was not only dilatory and undecided; it was also unlucky. It took office in June 1929, and only four months later, in October, came the Wall Street Crash and the beginning of the world crisis. The effects of the US slump soon became apparent in Britain, making impossible even the mild social reforms which the Labour Government planned. Unemployment in Britain, which had been running at something over one million through the 1920s, suddenly shot up to 2,500,000 in 1930. In Britain and all over the world the crisis grew, and nobody appeared to have an answer. All the old-line politicians, from right to left, delivered speeches about pulling up socks and seeing light at the end of the tunnel, but that was that.

It was in these circumstances that my Communist-connected fellow-pupil noted that I not only read the newspapers but also appeared to ponder on what I had read, and he started lending me pamphlets and books. Suddenly everything seemed to fall into place. The Communists could explain the whole thing; they had foreseen the 1929 slump, enormous unemployment, widespread impoverishment, the threat of new imperialist wars.

The Communists could not only explain what was wrong with capitalism, but could present a logical alternative – scientific socialism. Not only was this logical, but the founding fathers had proven to their, and soon to my, satisfaction that it was inevitable. I was particularly impressed by the *Communist Manifesto*, written by Marx and Engels back in 1848. This gave a concise survey of human history which I found much more logical and illuminating that the school history books. Through the ages the ruling groups had superseded one another – slave society, feudalism, bourgeois capitalism – and now, inevitably, the proletariat would take over.

Soon I became an avid and addicted reader of the *Daily Worker*, which proudly announced under the title that it was 'Official Organ of the Communist Part of Great Britain, Section of the Communist International'. I had to take out a postal subscription, since the wholesale distributors boycotted the newspaper, and no shop in Saffron Walden stocked it. (The British Post Office worked well in those days, and the current issue reached me regularly by the second, the midday, delivery.)

In the *Daily Worker* I discovered a whole and fascinating new world.

It is perhaps a little difficult for later generations to understand what was so attractive about communism and the Soviet Union for a youth of fourteen or fifteen nearly sixty years ago. Trying to regrasp the flavour of the period, I discovered among some tattered pamphlets a copy of the message sent by the Executive Committee of the Communist International to the Congress of the Communist Party of Great Britain held in November 1929. Here is the opening passage:

> Your congress meets at a decisive moment in the history of your party and the British working class. It is taking place at the commencement of a world economic crisis, in the period of a new rising revolutionary tide in the international labour movement, in the period of the victorious fulfilment of the Five Year Plan of socialist construction in the USSR which is the most powerful factor of destruction of capitalist rationalisation. In these

circumstances, the ascension to power of the British 'Labour' Government, which is the government of capitalist rationalisation, of preparation for war against the Soviet Union and for the suppression of the colonies, opens a new page in the history of the struggle of the British proletariat.

The message continued with a flaming appeal for the Communist Party to transform itself within the shortest possible time into 'a mass bolshevik party . . . in the vanguard of the class struggle'.

Perhaps it is necessary to recall that at that time, according to figures published later by the Communist International, the Communist Party of Great Britain had shrunk from a high of 10,000 members in 1926 to some 3,000 in 1930 and was still sinking. Yet even if I had known these figures I do not think I would have been dismayed. Here was a cause, a good fight, and other movements with small beginnings had swept the world: look at Jesus and his paltry twelve disciples.

Part of the fascination was undoubtedly the fact that news of what was happening in the Soviet Union was at that time practically forbidden fruit, at least in Britain. None of the mainline British newspapers appear to have had Moscow correspondents. *The Times*, for instance, relied on a correspondent in Riga in Latvia who gleaned his information from newspapers and White Russian emigrants. The general tendency of most of the information which got into print was that the USSR was on the verge of breakdown.

But the *Daily Worker* and other Communist publications gave quite a different picture: socialism was obviously working there – no unemployment, no slump, no capitalists grinding the faces of the poor. Any doubts I might have had about the reliability of these reports were dispelled by the New York *Nation*, the radical weekly edited by Oswald Garrison Villard, who had visited my father in prison back in 1919. *The Nation* had a Moscow correspondent, Louis Fischer, who week by week reported much the same news, though in a rather more restrained and sedate fashion, and with reminders that there were still some shortages and shortcomings. A minor story in *The Nation*, which was one of the far-flung periodicals which piled up in my father's study (I recall the *South Australian Christian World* and the *Calcutta Guardian* as other titles) may well have been a decisive factor in convincing me that the Communists were the right people to be associated with.

There must have been plenty of other factors, but this single short comment in a New York periodical nearly six decades ago remained trapped in my memory like a fly in amber.

I read it in my father's study, probably in the Easter holidays of 1931.

Downpage in the right-hand column on a right-hand page, probably page 5 or 7, was a short editorial comment entitled 'The Yokinen Case'. August Yokinen was a Finnish member of the Communist Party in New York who worked as a janitor at the Finnish Workers' Club there. At a dance in the club, three Negro guests had been 'shunted aside' when they started to dance with white girls, and Yokinen had failed to intervene on behalf of the Negroes. As a result he was expelled from the Communist Party after a public hearing. Some New York daily newspapers had made fun of the case, *The Nation* commented, but in fact the case showed that the Communists took racial equality seriously and were ready to stand up for it. (If some eager-beaver reader looks up the files of *The Nation*, they may find the story on another page or under another title; but find the story they will, and I am only guilty of straining my memory too hard.)

Some years later in Spain, the first officer of the International Brigades I encountered was an American Negro at a time when a black officer commanding white troops was sensational. It confirmed my opinion that Communists took racial equality seriously.

Some time in this period I must have discussed, during school holidays, my new enthusiasm with my father, but no memory lingers. He was in any case very adverse to criticising the faiths of others, and I had obviously been converted. (I am reluctant to use religious jargon in this connection, but 'conversion', 'apostasy', 'faith', 'infallibility', 'dogma' and dozens of other such terms sometimes fit uncomfortably well.)

I must assume that my father tried to explain to me his belief that the use of force was never justified, even for such an admirable end as the establishment of a just society. But on the whole he probably took the view that I had the right to arrive at my own convictions. He may well have recalled his own youth, when his socialist loyalties and his doubts about some aspects of conventional Christianity almost certainly met with opposition in his conventional middle-class Victorian surroundings.

The year 1931 was certainly a fitting one to strengthen my new-found faith. I was already convinced that the Labour Party was a broken reed – though I found it a little hard to accept the current Communist dogma that the social democrats were really 'social fascists', often more dangerous than the real fascists. My conviction was stunningly confirmed at the end of August 1931 when Ramsay MacDonald and a large portion of his cabinet, elected two years earlier on a mildly progressive ticket, suddenly turned a double somersault and formed what they called a coalition 'National Government' with the Conservatives and Liberals.

This new government immediately took measures announced as necessary to 'save the pound'. The military budget was cut by £5 million, and unemployment payments were slashed by £25 million, which meant that the dole paid out to a single man was cut from 17 shillings weekly to 15 shillings and 3 pence.

A few days after this special budget, on 15 September 1931, came news which convinced a large part of the world that Britain was on her last legs. The Royal Navy mutinied at its Invergordon base. The cause of the mutiny was simple: sailors' pay had been cut by 20 per cent, from 5 shillings to 4 shillings daily. Officers' pay had also been cut, but by a much lower percentage. The mutiny, apparently the first in the Royal Navy since 1797, ended a few days later when the Admiralty halved the cuts.

Then, on 20 September, Britain abandoned the gold standard. I certainly did not understand what this meant, and neither did most other people, but it obviously showed that capitalism was on its way out.

In the meantime I had been forced to break off contact with my schoolboy comrade, the only person with whom I had been able to discuss things frankly, as he had admitted that his mother was a Trotskyite. I was not very clear what a Trotskyite was, but all the current Communist papers and pamphlets warned that they were insidious deviationists with whom no serious Marxist-Leninist and friend of the Soviet Union should have anything to do. Trotsky's conduct had become so unbearable that the Soviet authorities had been forced to expel him from the Soviet Union a couple of years before, and thirty years earlier he had had some serious disagreements with Lenin. So supporters of Leon Trotsky were beyond the pale.

About this time, probably in late 1931, the *Daily Worker* started printing a coupon urging readers to enrol in the Communist Party, a coupon which I promptly filled in. I had a vague idea that I would be summoned to a clandestine meeting of steeled and dedicated revolutionaries who would grill me to determine whether I was fitted to serve the cause (and perhaps whether I had any contacts with Trotskyites), but for some weeks nothing at all happened. Then a rather blotchily duplicated letter arrived from the CPGB (Communist Party of Great Britain) HQ in King Street, London, informing me that I had been duly enrolled, and that since I was a student (I had shied at writing 'schoolboy' on the form) my party dues would be one penny a week. That was all: no summons to appear before a selection committee, no blare of trumpets, no party card, nothing, not even the address of the nearest party branch.

It was all very disappointing, and nothing at all happened for nine more months. Then I got another blotchy duplicated letter stating: 'The first duty of a Communist is to pay party dues. Please pay up immediately your back dues, now amounting to three shillings.'

Coupon-filling had not proved a satisfactory method of enrolling in the world-wide army of the proletariat, and I decided to skip it for a while.

(If Britain had a Freedom of Information Act like that existing in the USA, I would long have put in an application to the competent authority – presumably the Special Branch of Scotland Yard – to see whether they managed to open my first file on that far-off date.)

Since Saffron Walden was a Quaker school, religion was not intrusive, but scripture was one of the regular subjects, and I am grateful for the good grounding in the Bible which this gave me. This has struck me particularly in the German Democratic Republic, where I have been living now for over thirty-five years. One of the disadvantages of the strictly non-religious education given there is that the Bible has no place in the schools, even as literature. Martin Luther's translation of the Bible fixed the German language in its modern form, just as the King James Bible standardised English. But most young GDR citizens look blank at references to even such legendary biblical figures as Noah or Cain and Abel, and the biblical allusions in the whole body of European literature are for them much of a riddle.

Apart from the Sunday-morning Quaker meetings at Saffron Walden, with their long silences (out of boredom I used to practise holding my breath for longer and longer periods, something which I had to tone down when one of the masters noticed me going blue in the face, and hurried me out fearing an apoplectic fit), one of the few religious exercises was a half-hour of hymn singing on Sunday afternoons. This song period gave me the opportunity for the only overt act of rebellion I can recall at that stage.

It came about like this. One of the favourite hymns was 'All Things Bright and Beautiful' by Cecil Francis Alexander (1818–95). As my political consciousness developed, I suddenly noticed that the third verse of the hymn was of a blatantly reactionary character. The first two verses of the hymn are in a rather cloying nursery tone, prattling harmlessly on about how the Good Lord made the little flowers that open and the little birds that sing, but the third verse suddenly changes gear, and tells us firmly that rich and poor had been made that way by God, and should damned well stay that way. This third verse stands quotation in full, since it may have been phased out of the hymn-books by now:

> The rich man in his castle,
> The poor man at his gate,
> God made them high or lowly,
> And order'd their estate.

Reading these lines all these years later, a vague feeling plagues me that the author was really some sort of premature crypto-Christian-Socialist provocateur, who wanted to plant the seeds of protest in his hymn-singing congregation by presenting them with something really outrageous: a nice theory, but without supporting evidence.

At that time, however, back in school, it seemed like a good case for mass protest. I drew the attention of our Trotskyite to the blatant anti-class-struggle nature of the hymn – even a suspect Red seemed a better ally than none – and we rallied a small band of supporters: several Liberals with principles, and a number of other pupils who were anti-authoritarian for the hell of it.

We decided that a public boycott was the right thing. Next time 'All Things Bright and Beautiful' was announced, we stood up with the rest of the school and belted out the first two verses even more loudly than usual. When the third verse came round, we suddenly shut up, and the volume of sound dropped with a jolt. Masters and mistresses looked mystified, and a large part of the assembly trailed away into silence as they peered round to see what on earth was happening. After the hymn had limped to an end, the headmaster announced in a very quiet, concerned, Quakerly fashion that he would like to see in his study whoever had organised this unusual demonstration.

The Trotskyite and I sloped off rather timidly to see him, and explained our case. To our astonishment, when we had explained he said that he had never seen it like that before, and he quite agreed that there were valid objections to the phrasing of this verse, though we should realise that it had been written during a different historical period and should be regarded in this light. He added to our confusion by actually congratulating us for examining things for ourselves instead of accepting them uncritically. But, he added, the manly thing would have been to come and see him about it, instead of staging a demonstration which might have upset school discipline.

At subsequent hymn periods, only the first two verses of 'All Things Bright and Beautiful' were sung.

Stories of schooldays at British boarding schools tend either to stress the sex life of the adolescent or to ignore the question entirely. Possibly because Friends School Saffron Walden was coeducational, I have to render a nil report on the subject. The boys and girls, aged between eleven and sixteen, mixed or did not mix according to taste. The staff looked with some favour on the activities of mixed groups, but showed some concern when couples emerged. The only scandal of which I was aware came when a senior boy and girl were observed exchanging a shy kiss. There was initial talk of expulsion, but this was modified to a ban upon them ever being alone together again.

I may have been, and may still be, unusually naïve, but I only heard that such a thing as homosexuality existed at the age of fifteen when I came across, in the school library, a copy of *The Loom of Youth* by Alex Waugh, a book which had caused a widespread scandal by dealing fairly openly with the subject of public-school sex. For a few weeks after reading the book I looked and listened apprehensively in the school dormitories and the bicycle shed, but could discover no signs. Possibly Quakers, though so admirable in many ways, are under-sexed.

School for me would probably have ended at the age of sixteen when I failed to pass Matric, owing to the fact that my grasp of French and Latin was minimal. At that time one of the masters announced that he had never seen a child with so little ability to learn a language. He may have been right to some degree, for even today, after spending most of my adult life in German-speaking communities, I am unable to write even a short letter in German correctly. I can read and converse in German with ease, and my German–English translations – including some of the works of Marx and Engels – have met with the approval of experts. But if I have to write a short note I cannot for the life of me remember whether a table is masculine, feminine or neuter, or what on earth a dative is.

Back to my schooldays. After failing Matric, and wondering miserably what I was going to do now, some mysterious Quaker old-boy network suddenly provided a scholarship which made it possible for my parents to send me off for a further two years to Bootham, the Quaker school in York.

In contrast to Saffron Walden, with its 'daring' coeducational policy and strong flavour of nonconformist moral vegetarianism, Bootham conformed far more closely to the fags, prefects and cold-baths tradition of the British public school. It was the school to which the more prosperous Quakers – the chocolate manufacturers, the lawyers and the doctors – sent their sons. Since it was a Quaker school there was no corporal punishment, and no Officers' Training Corps; but apart from this, every effort was devoted to making it a 'real' public school, with great emphasis on the manly virtues and stiff upper lips.

Despite this, I was remarkably happy at Bootham. For some reason which now evades me, I took only four subjects, all of which interested me, all of which called for a lot of reading and none of which involved much drudgery or learning by rote: English, Economics, History and Geography.

Teaching in the upper forms was modelled more on university than school, with tiny groups of four or five pupils being guided towards learning for themselves. The only really hard work I put in was trying, with only moderate success, to apply half-digested Marxism to the task of baffling the very conventional economics teacher who, typical of the times, had only a very hazy notion of Karl Marx's theories, and believed firmly that they had all been refuted long since.

It was while I was at Bootham that I finally emerged into the open as a public-school Red. Soon after my arrival there in autumn 1932 a mock election was arranged, as part of civics teaching. Several of the senior boys, who had learned that I had Bolshie leanings (they would have been hard to overlook, since my study was decorated with a large photo of Stalin and a poster calling for solidarity with the liberated Soviet areas of China), urged me to stand as a Communist candidate. Predictably I landed right at the bottom of the poll, but I proudly sent the election result to the *Daily Worker*, and had the pleasure of seeing my name in print for the first time.

Sometimes I regret having never kept a diary, but when I happen to dig out something which I actually wrote in those far-off years, I think this might have been a good thing. For I discovered a school essay written probably in 1933 for some essay competition, and at least parts of it make me squirm.

The 22-page essay bears the title 'Socialism in Modern Britain 1880–1920'. Most of it appears to be a reasonably capable précis of the few books available to me, but I recall with pleasure that I did undertake one little bit of original research. Several of the books consulted mentioned an unemployed demonstration in Trafalgar Square in the 1880s when the Foot Guards were called out. In clashes between demonstrators and police a man named Alfred Linnell was killed, and William Morris wrote a stirring song in his memory: 'Not one, not one, nor thousands must they slay, but one and all if they would win the day.'

My difficulty was that some of the history books said this happened in 1886 and others in 1887. So I sent off a polite letter to the left-wing veteran Tom Mann, who was named in one of the books as among those present, and got his friendly reply that the right date was 1886, and he recalled the day vividly.

Some of the jargon in my lamentable essay came from my study of Communist documents: 'reformist-opportunist forces gained the upper hand', for instance, and 'the rank and file lacked ideological clearness'. Yet that was not the worst. The concluding sentences presumably reflected what I was thinking and saying at the time:

> With the formation of the Communist Party in Britain in 1920 there
> appeared to be a really socialist party, with Councils of Action throughout

the country. But it was not to be, and the Communist Party is still nothing but a group of propagandists. How long will it be before the workers exchange slums and unemployment for the bullet and the bomb, and the chance and hope of a better fuller life?

The master correcting the essay added in pencil: 'After a violent death?' I hope it is clear that I quote this sentence without pride.

In the Easter holidays of 1933 I unexpectedly got a chance to take a look at a country where politics had just boiled over – Germany, where Hitler had come to power in January – for my father suddenly suggested a trip there.

Germany as a country of particular interest appears to have swum into my view at about the same time as I became interested in communism, at the beginning of the 1930s. Earlier a girl from a Quaker family in Hamburg had stayed with us in London, and one of my sisters had paid a return visit. This exchange left little mark, except that a favourite German dish for 'afters', called *röte Grütze*, won a place on the Peet family menu; it is a sort of sweet redcurrant jelly.

But it was German politics which won my interest, not German puddings. Lots of things were obviously happening in Germany in 1931–2. The economy was falling to pieces, unemployment reached the six million mark, cabinets were shuffled almost weekly, and out on the streets nazis and Communists, often armed, bashed each other or got bashed by the police. The reports in a large part of the British press were scrappy and confusing, but my *Daily Worker* gave me a simpler picture, prescient in some ways but distorted in others. Hitler's nazism – and fascism in general – represented the last and most extreme stage of decaying but still powerful imperialist monopoly capital. Right-wing forces, both inside and outside Germany, were increasingly backing Hitler, who they hoped would attack and overthrow the young Soviet Union. (Where did the prescience come in? At the presidential elections in 1932 the German Social Democrats gave their votes to the conservative Field Marshal Hindenburg. The Communists campaigned for their own candidate under the slogan: 'A vote for Hindenburg is a vote for Hitler; a vote for Hitler is a vote for war.' Hindenburg won the election, and soon appointed Hitler Chancellor. The Second World War came six years later.)

The *Daily Worker* and other Communist publications never tired of pointing out that the Communist Party of Germany was by far the largest Communist party outside the Soviet Union, and by 1932 was getting six million votes at parliamentary elections (17 per cent of the total). The Social Democrats got rather more votes, and together these two parties in alliance with the powerful trade unions might well have stopped Hitler. But despite the mortal danger – in this case literally mortal – the two workers' parties found it impossible to sink their differences and take joint action. And so, when President Hindenburg named Adolf Hitler Chancellor on 30 January 1933, he was able to take over without any organised resistance.

We all know the rest of the story – I hope. First the Communists were outlawed, thousands arrested, many murdered. Then came other groups: Social Democrats, trade unionists, liberal intellectuals, oppositional churchmen. Parallel to this persecution because of political views or attitudes came the racial persecution: the introduction step by step of a Prussianly thorough form of Apartheid which culminated in mass slaughter of the Jews.

It is perhaps salutary to recall that Hitler's coming to power was taken very calmly in some quarters. *The Times* of London editorialised on 31 January 1933: 'That Herr Hitler should be given the chance of showing that he is something more than an orator and agitator was always desirable.'

I was naturally watching all these developments with great interest, certainly expecting in the early stages that the powerful German working-class movement would do something. Now, out of the blue, my father announced that he had to go to Germany for a week or two on an urgent Quakerly mission, and asked whether I would like to go along.

As far as I can remember, my father's short fact-finding trip had two main purposes: first, to discover whether the small Quaker community in Germany was endangered; and second, to look into the situation of those Jews, mainly converts to Christianity, who were outside the ranks of the ordinary Jewish community organisations.

The trip had been arranged at very short notice, and it may well have been triggered off by a speech on 30 March 1933 by top nazi Joseph Goebbels in which he defined clearly the position of such 'non-Aryan' Christians. 'The test for Jews is racial and not religious,' said Goebbels. 'Persons of Jewish blood who belong to the Catholic or Protestant churches will be treated in the same way as those of the Hebrew faith.'

In addition, the nazis were clearly keeping an eye on Quakers at this time. Corder Catchpool, the British Quaker representative in Berlin, who had been helping to get endangered persons out of Germany, was arrested on 4 April 1933, though he was released a few days later.

So within forty-eight hours I found myself in Germany, for the first but certainly not for the last time. My initial impressions were that everything was as expected. There were incredible numbers of swastikas and in every form, not simply as flags, but on postcards showing the shining nazi symbol rising triumphantly over whatever town you happened to be in, and there were even bakers' shop windows decorates with swastika-shaped loaves and rolls. (The nazis soon banned such 'misuse' of their sacred symbol.)

The streets of Frankfurt am Main and Wiesbaden, the main points we visited, had a good scattering of brown-uniformed Storm-troopers in evidence, many armed and with white armbands announcing that they were auxiliary police. Loudspeakers blaring military marches and marching columns of Hitler Youth trying to look determined and soldierly completed the picture.

In both these cities my father was closeted for long and serious discussions with concerned German Quakers, together with a number of left-wing intellectuals, Evangelical pastors and 'non-Aryan Christians'. I dislike using the nazi term, but it is the most convenient shorthand.

My father told me little about his discussions, but I recall he mentioned that a number of the Germans with whom he had spoken, including Jews, were taking the situation rather lightly. They talked about 'an anachronistic and short-lived return to medieval barbarism' and seemed convinced that the nazis would soon collapse under their own weight, and that then 'decent people' would take over the government. Others took a much darker view, and my father appeared to agree with the latter group.

While my father discussed, and apparently made preparations for, the emigration of a number of particularly endangered persons, I roamed the streets searching for evidence of the anti-nazi resistance which I was sure was blossoming. But apart from a few Communist slogans and hammer-and-sickle symbols painted on walls – and they may well have been left-overs from previous months – I could see nothing.

When I sat down yesterday at my typewriter to describe this first visit, I felt confident that I would not have to rely solely on my memory, for I knew that somewhere amongst my papers there still existed a contemporary account by my own hand. After a search I have now turned it up, a twenty-page illustrated album I made back in 1933 as a present for my father. There are a good number of photographs in the album, but most of the pictures are family snaps of no interest today. To make matters worse, I developed and enlarged the photos myself, and they remain as grey and fuzzy proof of my lack of talent in this field. Even worse, I subtitled the pictures in a flippant schoolboy style supposed to be humorous.

One picture which is not entirely pointless shows a nazi poster proclaiming that the Communists had set fire to the Reichstag, and I comment with a puerile remark that a man peering from a window in the background is a nazi spy. Another photo shows very smudgily a party of Hitler Youth marching through Rudeshaim, and my caption suggest – ha-ha – that they have come to see Hubert Peet off as he boards the Rhine steamer.

After some searching I found one single picture of marginal significance and with a straightforward caption. The picture shows the centre of St Goar on the Rhine, with two flags flying, the swastika and the old German imperial flag. In the caption I confined myself to pointing out that the imperial flag flies considerably higher than the swastika, and that this could be interpreted as a sign of monarchist opposition to Hitler.

Our ten-day trip was soon over. Back at school at Bootham I was a little surprised to find that two Jewish pupils had also spent the Easter holidays with relatives in Germany. They proclaimed to all and sundry that stories of nazi terror were all a Communist invention, and anyway Hitler would soon disappear.

The only direct result of my first look at nazi Germany was a short story entitled 'Sickle and Swastika' which I read to the Bootham Literary Society a few weeks after the end of the holidays. It was all about heroic underground resistance work in nazi Germany, and I am glad to say it appears to have vanished without trace.

4

'Out of Bounds'

ootham School had a twin, a Quaker school for girls called the Mount, on the other side of York. There was practically no direct contact between the pupils at the two institutions, but we knew all the Mount girls by sight, since every Sunday we occupied facing galleries in the big Friends Meeting House in York. In the long silence of a Quaker meeting, eye contact was quickly established with a suitable partner, and since several of our boys had sisters at the Mount it was generally possible to discover the name of the long-distance beloved. I still mourn for a slim volume of John Betjeman's poems about 'long-legged hockey girls' – a first edition which I presented by post to some girl whose name and face I have long forgotten.

One of those anonymous girls unwittingly launched me into one of the most satisfactory episodes in my life. It happened late in 1933, when the world slump and the advent of Hitler to power in Germany had led to the sudden upsurge of left-wing political activity at most British universities. Marxist students, particularly at Oxford and Cambridge, noted that among the new students arriving each year from the public schools there were an increasing number who already considered themselves Reds, and in the best Communist tradition decided that they ought to be organised too.

On 2 February 1934 the London *Daily Mail*, then at the height of its 'Bolshies under the bed' campaign, gave a lurid but substantially correct account of this organisational drive:

The revelations in the *Daily Mail* yesterday of Communist attempts to corrupt the boys at public schools have put headmasters all over the country on their guard . . .

At the universities freshmen from public schools are sought out by avowed Communist groups, and sometimes converted to the Bolshevik creed.

They are then invited to write to friends – sometimes to younger brothers – at the schools they have just left, and thus to become active agents in spreading the Communist poison.

This is by far the most effective method at present at the disposal of the corrupters, and is proving extremely difficult to deal with, since correspondence of this kind can hardly be censored . . .

Often the first that a headmaster hears of this dangerous activity is the news of the formation of a group of boys in the school to study 'social questions' or some other equally innocent-sounding object . . .

Great care has to be taken lest the boys concerned are given any idea of persecution, which might confirm them still more strongly in their perverted opinions.

The *Daily Mail* article ended with the routine statement that 'little doubt is felt by Scotland Yard officials' that all this activity was financed by Red gold.

The girl on the other side of York Friends Meeting House knew a young Cambridge student, who wrote to her asking if there were any Reds at her school. None that she knew of, she replied, but she had heard of one at Bootham. A few days later I received a mysterious letter, which raised my morale, since I was wondering whether I was the only right-thinker in a school world of wrong-thinkers or non-thinkers. Even now, over fifty years later, I think I should omit the name of the writer, to the disappointment of the busy beavers who are still nosing around in left-wing university activities in the 1930s. Here is the letter, dated 11 December 1933, as harmless as you could wish:

MM [a name that meant nothing to me] has told me about you, and I am writing just to ask you:

What are things like at Bootham? Are there any others interested? Are you able to get any papers taken in the reading rooms or library? Such papers as the *New Leader* and *Labour Monthly* are well worth having. I do not think the *Daily Worker* is the right paper for a public school.

Have you tried any form of activity in the school?

NN's son is making a speech at Leighton Park School [another Quaker public school] attacking the League of Nations. I think the best approach both for students and at school is the anti-war line. Write me as soon as convenient.

The letter was signed with his name and a carefully inscribed hammer and sickle, presumably to make it quite clear what he was talking about.

Apparently I replied enthusiastically, and this time the reaction was all that I could have wished for. Liaison within the Federation of Student Societies, the Communist-oriented student group, must have been efficient and swift. For only one week after the original approach I got an official invitation to a preparatory conference of public-school delegates in London in January 1934. This invitation read in part:

> The public schools are the training grounds of the colonial adminstrators and the finance capitalists of the British Empire. An isolated, rigid, educational system is necessary to produce men who are able to maintain in slave conditions millions of black and white workers. Action against such a system of education must be co-ordinated in all the schools. It must also be linked with the work of progressive students in the universities and with the organised working class, who are the most effective, indeed the only, allies in the fight for a live advancing culture.

On 13 January 1934 about fifteen boys and two or three girls from public schools finally met in London at 7 John Street, WC1, which housed several trade union offices and the headquarters of the Federation of Student Societies. Most of us were in our senior years, seventeen or eighteen years of age; most of us would have described ourselves as Communists and had apparently read widely in such Marxist classics as we had been able to lay our hands on; and a majority had almost certainly never met another real live Communist before.

Practically from the start the meeting was dominated by the youngest boy present: chubby and cherubic Esmond Romilly, who was very soon to receive great publicity throughout the British press as 'fifteen-year-old nephew of Winston Churchill', which he in fact happened to be.

The FSS had deputed a student commissar to look after our meeting, and to see that it took the right decisions as previously decided upon by the FSS leadership. Rules had to be drawn up, subscriptions decided upon, a committee elected; and perhaps we would be allowed, after a probationary period, to have a public-school page in *Student Vanguard*, the FSS monthly.

Most of us were so pleased to be set definite tasks, to find out that there were quite a lot of other people like us, and also so thrilled and impressed by the slightly conspiratorial air of the whole undertaking, that we were ready to vote for anything proposed by our student adviser. There were a few mutterings about 'direct action' from a small and rebellious anarchist element, but nobody had anything coherent with which to oppose the official line until Esmond Romilly went into action.

He was not only by far the youngest, but also undoubtedly the scruffiest person at the meeting, wearing a shapeless jacket and baggy trousers, all his pockets heavily laden with newspapers, bits of string and rubber bands. His socks sagged round his ankles, his hair was short but untidy, and he stood out in a group which tended to be spectacled, blazered and neat.

Setting up an organisation would be standing things on their heads, he said. What was needed for a start was a magazine written by public schoolboys for public schoolboys, and if it got enough support then an organisation would follow. With great tactical skill he threw in a quotation from Lenin about the press being the organiser of the revolutionary movement. The magazine he envisaged should relate directly to events in the schools, and would 'champion the forces of progress against the forces of reaction on every front, from compulsory military training to propagandist teaching'. (I made no written note of what he said at the meeting; the words in quotation marks come from a manifesto he issued on his own responsibility just two weeks later.)

As far as I can remember, he did not take over the meeting through any great display of Churchillian personality – though his strong personal magnetism began to emerge shortly afterwards – but simply because his approach seemed to make more sense than the rather dull scoutmasterish one of the official student organiser.

Esmond's speech threw the meeting into some confusion. Our student adviser, horrified to find things getting out of control, began to talk darkly of the need for revolutionary discipline, and a majority, fearing that our small group might break apart before it was even founded, voted rather reluctantly for the officially prepared resolutions.

Most of us, I believe, felt ourselves in a genuine quandary. On the one side stood our revolutionary mentors of the FSS, with their dull but unobjectionable programme – and an important tenet of Marxism-Leninism which we had absorbed in our isolated studies had been the acceptance of rulings passed down from above. On the other hand, Romilly held out the prospect of action, immediate action, on a level we could all understand and in which we could participate, and action which did not appear to conflict particularly with the resolutions prepared by the FSS. So we voted for them.

When the meeting had ended, we shook off the student adviser and a couple of his satellites, and held a rump meeting at a tea shop in Gray's Inn Road at which we urged Esmond to go ahead with his magazine project, and pledged our support. I must have written to Esmond Romilly immediately after returning to school, for I soon received his reply from Wellington College, which he was shortly to leave rather sensationally:

> Dear Comrade,
> I enclose some copies of the 'Out of Bounds' circular. One of the most important features of the paper is going to be news of events (debates, controversies, teaching etc.) in the different schools. This would be unsigned and 'un-written-up' . . .
>
> PS. The paper is not officially or otherwise the FSS organ, though we have their help.

On the same day that Esmond penned his note, the London *Daily Mail* fired the first shot in the barrage of publicity which was to surround Esmond for years to come. This trend-setting article stated:

> *RED PROPAGANDA*
> *Scotland Yard Watches Boy's Circular*
> A circular recently issued announces the publication of a new journal, described as 'a new paper dealing with the public schools in relation to the outside world'.
> Its authors do not intend to be funny. They achieve this effect unconsciously, as the following extract from the circular will show.
> 'Disintegration affects in our period the whole of society. It affects profoundly the public schools. This disintegration shows itself in a deliberate attempt on the part of the public schools to exclude themselves from genuine contact with political and cultural realities, and the positive and blatant use of the public schools as a weapon in the cause of reaction.'
> Then comes the amazing thing – the signature at the end is that of a boy at Wellington College . . .
> Bitter indignation exists there that one of its houses should have been named as the address of the editor in embryo, and the offender is being suitably dealt with . . .
> There is a strong suspicion that the money for it comes from Bolshevik funds, and the whole affair has become of sufficient importance to engage the considerable attention of Scotland Yard, where an attempt is being made to discover the primary source of activity.

Sending a letter of fervent revolutionary solidarity to Esmond while he was being 'suitably dealt with' did not seem a good idea, so there was nothing to do but wait and see what happened. The wait was not very long, because on 10 February newspapers all over Britain published a long

35

dispatch circulated by the Press Association, the first news item to name Esmond, and to identify him as the 'fifteen-year-old nephew of Winston Churchill', a sobriquet which stuck for several years.

> A boy, who is stated to have produced a Communist magazine at Wellington College, disappeared from the college yesterday morning . . . He is Esmond Romilly (15), son of Colonel B. H. Romilly and Mrs Romilly, of Pimlico Road, London, SW, and a nephew of Winston Churchill . . .
> Today Mrs Romilly told a reporter . . . 'I am certain he is under the influence of some Communist or Bolshevik agitators.'

When Esmond ran away from Wellington, he obviously took his address book with him, for within a very few days he had written from his London base – David Archer's bookshop in Parton Street, just off Southampton Row – asking me for school news for the first issue of *Out of Bounds*. His only reference to all the excitement was the casual sentence: 'Things have been rather rushed here lately.'

In the midst of all this hectic activity, the orthodox FSS Public Schools Section was still grinding along in its pedestrian way, sending out duplicated sheets requesting the payment of dues, and suggesting that a 'walking tour for the exchange of views and ideas' might be arranged for the Easter vacation. It all seemed very unexciting compared with Esmond and his clandestine magazine.

Today it is hard to remember whether I was disappointed by the first forty-page issue of *Out of Bounds* which I received at the end of March. Looking through its yellowing pages today, it all seems rather tame. In an editorial, Esmond declared that the magazine would 'fight ruthlessly against the sterile and reactionary influences which permeate the Public Schools', adding the throw-away sentence: 'We shall be deliberately corrupting youth' – a sentence picked up with delight by the *Daily Mail*, which headlined its story on 5 April: *CORRUPTING YOUTH – 15-YEAR-OLD EDITOR'S BOAST*. Apart from the well-written editorial, the magazine carried some uneven 'inside' news items from a scattering of public schools, a debate on the merits of fascism between the 'Leader of the Oundle School Fascist Youth Group' and Esmond Romilly, and an interminable parody of public-school literature from *Tom Brown's Schooldays* to Harry Wharton and Billy Bunter in the boys' paper *Magnet*.

Probably the only items which would be worth reprinting today are two poems by Gavin Ewart – possibly his first appearance in print. Later issues were better, with many generally enlightened articles on flogging and aspects of sex in public schools.

During the Easter holidays, when supporters of the orthodox wing of young rebels were off on a healthy hike – I never enquired whether it really took place – the *Out of Bounds* group met in conference in London. This conference was, of course, held in 'secret', but Esmond, knowing that his best chance of contacting sympathisers was maximum publicity, thoughtfully notified the press, and we got very good coverage indeed, including a front-page picture of our 'secret' conference in the *Sunday Graphic* on 15 April 1934.

One of the decisions we took was to participate in a Communist demonstration scheduled for the next day. We obviously needed a banner, so that evening in the former nursery of the Romilly residence in Pimlico Road (the colonel and his lady must have been away) Esmond, his brother Giles and myself constructed a long red banner.

The *Manchester Guardian* honoured Esmond on 16 April 1934 with a whole leading article, which perhaps bears reprinting, particularly as evidence that not the whole of the press reacted as the *Daily Mail* had:

YOUTH ON THE PROW
That must have been a picturesque descent on Hyde Park yesterday when Master Esmond Romilly with other young public school boys swept down in procession from the heights of Mornington Crescent, bearing a crimson banner which denounced 'The "National" Government of Hunger, Fascism and War'. [The editorial omitted the quotation marks on 'National', here reinserted.]

Master Romilly's creed is Communism, it seems, and among his other distinctions is the fact that Winston Churchill is his uncle. Perhaps that does something to account for yesterday's procession. The opinions of the nephew may not be those of the uncle, but there is a certain family likeness with which those opinions are placed upon the map of the moment and deftly directed into their full share of public attention. In many ways they are rather worthy opinions. Master Romilly is 'chairman of the board' of a publication called 'Out of Bounds' (a provocative title for a schoolboy's magazine), and when that editorial board met yesterday it was decided that the fight would be carried on 'against reaction, political and cultural, Fascism, and war', in the public schools.

Whether a trip to Hyde Park is the best way of carrying on that campaign seems open to doubt; more normal youths would probably be content to spread the light through the medium of school debating societies. But then normal youths would never have had that splendid descent (with red banner) from Mornington Crescent. It reminds one of Gray's image –
'In gallant trim the gilded vessel goes;
Youth on the prow, and Pleasure at the helm.'
Youth is certainly on the prow in the case of Master Esmond Romilly.

And if he should be inclined to protest that it is Duty rather than Pleasure at the helm, he can only be reminded in the old phrase, that 'the pleasure is ours'. London must have enjoyed yesterday's progress even more than he did himself.'

This chapter is threatening to turn into a biography of Master Esmond, but it would be a pity to ignore a send-up of the whole 'public-school Reds' episode that was published in the long-forgotten *Razzle* magazine, which might be described as a rather weak 1930s predecessor of *Private Eye*. The monthly was popular in student circles largely because of its jokes, which were notably off-colour for the period.

Probably in its June 1934 issue (my clipping is unfortunately undated) it ran a full-page story entitled 'Razzle College Goes Bolshevist!' After summarising the *Daily Mail* revelations quoted above, it continued:

We are able to disclose that Razzle College itself, senior of all the great public schools, has already gone Red . . . Stalin himself came over to this country, and got a place in the Fifth Form at Razzle by posing as a son of Winston Churchill. The headmaster thought that the boy's big black moustache was a little unusual, even for a Churchill . . . but the head thought it would be rude to say anything, and anyway, he thought thankfully, it might have been Mr Churchill's Randolph.

Stalin, the story continued, then subverted Harry Wharton, Stalky and Bob Cherry with handfuls of Red gold, and they all went out to draw hammers and sickles on certain blank walls in the building. The upshot was that the whole school went Bolshevist:

Stalin has now gone back to Russia, after admitting quite frankly that he was not Winston Churchill's son and never had been. He explained that since Winston was not his son either, they were quits on that point.

He also said that now that Razzle College was Red, he did not know what to do with it. If all the public schools in Britain were Red he would not know what to do with them. He had only come over here in the first place as revenge on the *Daily Mail*. They kept interfering with his Russia, so he thought he'd interfere with the *Daily Mail*'s public schools.

Back in 1964 Jessica Mitford, Esmond Romilly's widow, asked me to send her copies of any of Esmond's letters I might have, and a few notes on the *Out of Bounds* period. So I sent her the letters and my recollections of a very minor clash in 1934 between our public-school group and some of Mosley's Blackshirts. Fifteen years later, in 1979, a young English writer contemplating a book on Esmond sent me a similar request. I happened to be in hospital, and could not get at my 1964 notes, so I did it out of my head.

Preparing to write these pages, I looked up my files and discovered that my story of the Blackshirt clash had changed in several details. The clash came after five or six of our *Out of Bounds* group had been out canvassing for the Communist candidate in a London by-election. Driving back to Parton Street, we stopped outside the building in which Sir Oswald Mosley had his Blackshirt HQ. Here are my divergent accounts of what happened next:

1964

Esmond decided it was a suitable time to collect some fascist literature, so he and I walked inside and announced our interest in the movement. Several Blackshirts lounging about in the hall did not like our looks, followed us outside, and began to get rough when they saw our red-decorated car. They started to rock it backwards and forwards on its springs, but luckily a policeman came by. Esmond in his upper-crustiest voice appealed for assistance, and we were able to drive on.

1979

Esmond said he would pop inside to pick up some fascist propaganda. He returned promptly at a hurried trot, pursued by four Blackshirts in full fig, shouting 'dirty Red' and 'go back to Russia'. Before Esmond could get the car started, the Blackshirts started to rock it sideways, and we began to have visions of being the first heroic victims of British fascism; anticlimactically we managed to drive the car off without damage. It emerged that Esmond had made the bad tactical mistake of striding into the Blackshirt den wearing a huge red paper carnation, the election favour of the Communist parliamentary candidate.

Basically the same story, but with different details. So much for my memory.

5

The Last Time I Saw Hitler

In the head office of Reuters News Agency in London, where I worked for a couple of months in 1945 as a sub-editor, there was a strict house rule that everybody named in a story, no matter how apparently famous or notorious, had to be properly identified. It was a sensible rule, for names which were household words to Anglo-oriented news editors in London might well be unknown to Reuters subscribers in underdeveloped areas such as the Deep South of the USA.

There were, however, three exceptions to this rule. It was felt to be unnecessary to identify further three persons – Churchill, the Pope and Adolf Hitler. (Checking with a Reuters correspondent recently, I discovered that today only the Pope still figures on the 'instantly recognised' list.) Taking the old Reuters notoriety ruling as a yardstick, the only really world-famous personality I ever encountered within spitting distance was Adolf Hitler.

The story is short and fairly silly. Finally leaving school in July 1934, I set off with a friend from school for a cycling holiday in central Europe. We were both curious to see something of what was going on in nazi Germany. Our trip up the Rhine, across to Munich and then back was uneventful until, on the return trip, we reached the outskirts of Koblenz on the Rhine. The date was 27 August 1934.

As we moved into the town it became obvious that some big event was in the offing, for there were unusually large crowds on the pavements and clusters both of ordinary policemen and of SA men, Hitler's brown-uniformed Storm-troops.

40

Soon a Storm-trooper stopped us. He was rather baffled when we held out British passports and failed to understand him, but we finally grasped that we should get off and walk. On the next block another SA man ordered us to get back on our bikes and ride, and this confusing on-again off-again continued for quite a distance.

By this time the pavements on both sides were jammed with citizens, many in variegated nazi uniforms and all, from grannies down to the kids, equipped with paper swastika flags. In front of them stood a solid rank of SA men with their arms linked; and there in the middle was the road, totally empty except for two slightly bewildered young men on bikes. We had, by chance, entered Koblenz precisely at the moment when the cordons had been closed, we were inside the cordon, and nobody knew quite what to do about us, particularly since we were foreigners.

Before some more competent official could decide to push us and our bikes back into the packed crowds behind the cordon, there was an enormous roll of cheering behind us, and yet another SA man ordered us to dismount and stand still at the side of the road.

Behind an escort of motor-cyclists a massive open Mercedes, driven very slowly, appeared. It was, of course, Adolf Hitler, on his way to a mass meeting calling for the return to Germany of the Saar Territory, then administered by France.

By chance we had been stopped at precisely one of the spots where the programme laid down that Hitler should go through his routine of being welcomed by his devoted youth cohorts. The Mercedes slid to a stop, the cordon beside us suddenly opened, and a small group of boys and girls, all in the uniform of the junior Hitler Youth (the official name for the members was 'Pimpf', which does not mean what it sounds like, but simply 'imp'), surrounded the Mercedes and handed bunches of flowers to the Führer. Hitler smiled and mussed their hair in accordance with the script; the kids then dutifully returned to the ranks.

The whole apparition lasted scarcely a minute, and it was only when Hitler had driven on again that I realised I had fluffed probably my only real chance of herological fame. For in my saddle bag, right to hand, I had a small Belgian automatic, which I had acquired with the idea that, since bloody revolution was obviously just around the corner all over the world, it would be well to be armed. I would probably have missed, though Hitler was only about five yards away.

Recently I laid my hands for the first time on Jessica Mitford's autobiography, *Hons and Rebels*, and noted that she too had had murderous thoughts. It would have been easy for her to get close to Hitler through her sister Unity. So I shipped her a copy of the preceding pages, and she replied: '*Re* our common fantasy of bumping off Hitler – I wonder how many others shared the same thought? Well, loads of Germans, no doubt. I mean, foreigners like us.'

6

Cub Reporter

Now that I had left school I had to decide what to do next; earlier I had never devoted much thought to the subject. For somebody with a moderately ready pen and no particular qualifications, journalism seemed to be the answer, particularly since it ran in the family.

The local paper in Beckenham, where we were by then living, did not need any beginners. But I finally managed to get taken on as a cub reporter, at the magnificent wage of 10 shillings a week, by the nearby *Bromley and West Kent Mercury*.

As the lowliest figure on the staff, I naturally got all the low-grade jobs nobody else wanted, such as working-class weddings and funerals. At that time – and the situation may well be the same today – local weeklies like the *Mercury* worked on the assumption that one vital way to boost circulation was to cram as many local names into the paper as possible. (During slack periods in the reporters' room we sometimes meditated on the dullest story we could submit which would have a chance of publication: 'Bromley Man Cuts Self While Shaving' was voted the best suggestion.)

Weddings and funerals provided a fine opportunity for a flood of names: bridesmaids, of course, together with the name of the proud aunt who had made their dresses; the best man; prominent guests; and at funerals the mourners and the full text of the messages on the floral tributes.

The theory was that everybody who thought they might be named was going to buy a copy, and probably a spare copy as well to send to their aunt in Scunthorpe. A good long list of names brought a happy gleam into the

43

editor's eye; but one misspelled name moved him to threats of instant dismissal.

Once a week I got some relief from the dreary round of hatches, matches and dispatches in Bromley, and took off for the outlying district of Chislehurst to gather the local news from there – the British Legion, the Boy Scouts, the small-bore rifle club and so on. A major portion of the news came from the churches, with their mothers' meetings, lantern lectures on far-flung mission stations and jumble sales in aid of the steeple restoration fund.

It was during my Tuesday trips to Chislehurst that I formulated Peet's Law of amiability: 'The lower the church, the surlier the priest.' Never having had the chance of testing this law elsewhere, I cannot testify to its universality, but in Chislehurst it was right on target. The Roman Catholic priest was a darling: 'Come in, lad. I'm just having a glass of sherry. Will you join me?' The very high church Anglican, a severe but benevolent character, was always good for a cup of tea or a biscuit, and had taken the trouble to write out in his prim neat hand all his items of church news – with plenty of names.

After that, things began to deteriorate. The Congregationalist and Baptist ministers were correct but never hospitable, and by the time I got down to the preacher of the minor sect with the corrugated-iron chapel, I knew I would be kept standing on the doorstep in the pouring rain while he grudgingly gave his news round the edge of the front door, which he kept on the chain.

Real life, for me, only began after working hours, and we often worked late, covering evening functions. I got the lantern lectures on beetles; the more senior reporters naturally reserved for themselves dinners at the Conservative Club.

Sitting around the office between assignments, I had soon discovered that one of the other reporters had leftist views. Feeling each other out moderately cautiously, we soon realised that we saw eye to eye on many questions, and one day when we happened to be alone he suddenly said, 'Actually, we really ought to join the Communist Party.' It was clear to us that there would be no future for us on the *Mercury* if we became known in Bromley as Communists – and I believe there was no Bromley branch of the Communist Party at that time. So we decided to join the party in Deptford, not many miles away, where we were not likely to be recognised.

We were received rather sceptically by Kath Duncan, the local party secretary, a tough and militant teacher. To test our staying power, she offered us an assignment which nobody else wanted: selling the *Daily Worker* every night outside Deptford Tram Depot.

At that time the *Daily Worker* was boycotted by the newspaper wholesalers, and therefore not bound by the general press agreement not to put the morning papers on sale before the morning hours. As a result, in many parts of London volunteer sellers took up their posts at busy corners from about 10 p.m. and intoned, rather mournfully in my memory, 'Buy tomorrow's *Daily Worker*, one penny.'

So for several months my colleague Reg and I stood manfully outside the tram depot and sold our papers to the drivers and conductors coming off duty. It was a good pitch, and we sold up to fifty copies every night. This was not, perhaps, because the tram men were particularly keen on communism, but because the *Daily Worker* had a very good racing tipster. The tipster angle worried many of the more earnest supporters of the revolution, who regarded it as a bread-and-circuses deviation; but it certainly helped to sell the paper.

7

Some Talk of Alexander

Somehow flogging racing tips at the tram depot at midnight did not seem to be helping the revolutionary cause to any perceptible extent, and I began to search for more active fields. Somewhere I came across a copy of the once-famous 'Twenty-one Conditions for Joining the Communist International', approved by the Second Comintern Congress in Moscow in 1920. (This list of conditions is generally attributed to Zinoviev, the leading old Bolshevik executed by Stalin in 1936, but the draft was actually prepared by Lenin.)

It was condition 4 which struck me:

> The obligation to spread Communist ideas includes the special obligation to carry out systematic and energetic propaganda in the army. Where such propaganda is prevented by emergency laws, it must be carried on illegally. Refusal to undertake such work would be tantamount to dereliction of revolutionary duty, and is incompatible with membership of the Communist International.

(Here I must interrupt myself once again to insert an anecdote arising from these twenty-one conditions which I believe to be substantially true and which deserves to be rescued from oblivion. One of the conditions for Comintern membership stated: 'All leading Party press organs in all countries are obliged to publish all important official documents of the Executive Committee of the Communist International.' This was later interpreted to mean that party newspapers had to publish these official documents in the often cumbersome wording of the authorised translation provided by Moscow. Some time in the late 1920s such an authorised English translation of a Comintern resolution 'On the Woman Question' landed on the desk of the editor of the New York *Daily Worker*. He read it and blanched. Guardedly worded telegrams were sent to the Comintern asking for permission to reword parts of the English text. Peremptory replies came in from Moscow saying 'Publish or else'. Finally a special emissary was sent off from New York to Moscow and he managed to obtain permission to do a rewrite job. The original text had stated: 'It is mandatory for the outstanding organs of the party membership to penetrate the lower sections of the female proletariat.)

Now back to the responsibility for subverting the army. It seemed obvious to me that the Communist Party in Britain was falling down on the job. Perhaps I should have a try. Later I learned that an illicit revolutionary newspaper for the British troops called *Soldiers' Voice* was in fact appearing irregularly, but I have never found anybody who saw a copy. Possibly it was produced only so that a file copy could be sent to the Comintern archives.

It all sounds fairly ridiculous, and looking back from today it seems clear that I was fed up with reporting the affairs of the Chislehurst Women's Union for the princely sum of 10 shillings weekly, which meant I was forced to live at home at the expense of my father. The argument about revolutionary responsibility was simply a rationalisation.

Whatever the true motivation, I decided to join the British Army. If I could not subvert it, I told myself, I could always purchase my discharge (this then cost £20 during the first three months of service) and then sell a 'revelation' story about the life of the private soldier to some progressive periodical. So 1 April 1935 – a nice date to choose – found me walking into the Central Recruiting Office in New Scotland Yard, just off Whitehall.

You could sign up for seven years' service in a run-of-the-mill regiment or, if you were over six foot, for four years in the Brigade of Guards. Four years sounded better than seven, so I said, 'Guards, please.' Apart from the shorter service, this meant a bright red jacket and a bearskin cap. The recruiting sergeant put on the brakes. 'It's not whether you pick the Guards. It's whether the Guards pick you. The King doesn't want a shower of lanky louts with a squint guarding his palace. He wants smart soldiers.'

A few minutes later a small body of potential Guardsmen was herded across to Wellington Barracks. Here we were regarded with some distaste by an extremely languid officer who muttered a few words about what a great honour was being conferred upon us, and the whole thing was tied up.

Back at the recruiting office the sergeant took down our details, including the address of next of kin. 'That's for when you get run through by a fuzzy-wuzzy,' he said. A minor hitch occurred when he enquired about my religion.

'Atheist' or 'Quaker' might well be unacceptable, so after a short pause I murmured, 'Agnostic.'

The sergeant looked a bit bewildered. 'Never heard of that before,' he muttered. 'Is that one of those weirdie churches?'

Stumbling I started to try to explain, but he soon cut me short. 'Now, son,' he said benevolently (he was very benevolent until he had caught his bird), 'take a fatherly hint from me. In the army you are either C of E or RC. You can be NC if you insist, but I wouldn't really advise it.' So I became an instant convert to the Church of England, which seemed less complicated than being a Catholic or a Nonconformist.

Then we placed our right hands on a pile of bibles, or the King's Regulations, or whatever, were duly sworn in and received the King's Shilling, which inflation had raised by that time to the King's Florin.

Now we were in the army, and the benevolent sergeant instantly transformed.

'Now get this!' he suddenly roared. 'You are soldiers of the King now, and will obey, instantly and without question, all orders given you by officers and non-commissioned officers. You two get brooms and swabs and clean out the office, and you two get down to the latrines and polish them inside and out until you could eat your dinner out of them, and I'll bloody well see to it that you do eat your dinner out of them if they are still filthy.'

A few hours later, with a few other lanky louts, I was at Caterham Barracks being issued with my first uniform. To our disappointment it turned out that we got rather scruffy khaki, First World War style, complete with puttees, instead of splendid scarlet. Guards recruits, we were informed curtly, only got dress uniform when they had learned to move like soldiers, not like a shower from civvy street.

I never got round to writing those revelations about army life when I left the army three months later, but I did start to write about my impressions. A couple of pages of an unfinished article dated July 1935 have inexplicably survived in an old shoe carton stuffed with school reports, certificates from the Royal Life Saving Society and tattered copies of *Out of Bounds*. They may bear quotation as evidence of what I felt at the time:

> 'We want you to be intelligent, of course,' said the company officer, 'but we don't want you to think.' Since he was reading the lecture, which he was

delivering to a squad of recruits, from a booklet issued by the War Office, entitled 'Notes for Lectures to the Recruits of the Brigade of Guards', one can only assume that he was expressing the official sentiments.

Even the intelligence which they expect you to have does not seem to be of a very high order. When one is going through the course of weapon training, for instance, as long as one is able to repeat in parrot fashion phrases such as 'The object of all firing instruction is to teach a man to handle his rifle correctly, both in the open and under cover, so that in wartime correct action becomes instinctive' the instructor is quite satisfied even if you have not got the faintest idea of what it means.

The way in which an ordinary day is spent by a recruit to any of the regiments of the Guards is rather interesting. Two hours are spent on the parade ground, doing the exacting drill which has made the Guards the smartest, if not the most efficient, troops in the world. One hour is spent at school learning about the battle honours of the regiment and the way the Duke of Marlborough disposed his troops at the battle of Blenheim. Then, at weapon training, the instructor tells you that your rifle must always be cleaned with an oily rag.

As soon as you return to the barrack room you will clean it with a brush and some blacking, and the instructor knows that you will do so, but for some obscure reason he continues to teach you to do it the way you never will.

One hour of physical training will complete the day's work – except for the fact that you will spend another seven or eight hours cleaning your kit for the following day. During the six-month training course it would be remarkable if a recruit had as much as half an hour a day as spare time.

Reading through these lines today, all these years later, I feel slightly astonished by the mildness of tone. In retrospect this mildness may be due to the psychological impact of something which happened on my last day as a trainee Guardsman. My discharge papers had gone through, and I was marched in before some senior officer. The short conversation went like this:

'Do you wish to withdraw your application for discharge?'

'No, sir.'

'I see here in your papers that you claim to have been a journalist. I must warn you most forcibly that you are forbidden to put anything in the papers about what you have seen or done here. Official secrets. That's an order.'

'Sir.'

'Take him away, sergeant.'

And that was that.

As the surviving pages of this old manuscript may suggest, my deepest impression in Caterham Barracks was of the odd mixture of fierce and often senseless discipline, and simultaneously the almost overt encouragement of methods of evading some of the more insane rules. A couple more examples will show what I mean.

Recruits were quartered in groups of twenty in cavernous old barrack rooms, each group under a 'trained soldier' – a long-service Guardsman too dim ever to have reached even the lowest non-commissioned rank. Our trained soldier was, incidentally, the only senior whom we were permitted to address directly. If you wished to speak to some godlike figure – a sergeant, for instance – you had to do it through the trained soldier. He was responsible for showing us the ropes and teaching us the rules; but since it was impossible to comply with many of the rules he also had to show us how to break them.

Take, for instance, kit inspection. Every day of the week at crack of dawn we tumbled out of bed, washed sketchily in the pre-Victorian washroom, hurried to breakfast and rushed back to 'build beds'. The mattresses, consisting of three square 'biscuits', had to be enfolded neatly in the blankets and erected on the metal-slat beds in armchair shape. The sheets had to be precisely folded, with knife-edge creases, and placed very exactly between the blanket segments. 'Small kit', consisting of knife, spoon and fork, boot brushes, brass buttonstick, bayonet burnisher, spare boots and other oddments including a housewife (pronounced 'husif') and, I believe, a balaclava helmet, had to be laid in their prescribed place on the seat of the armchair.

The whole fairly complicated procedure could just be accomplished, when you had got the hang of it, in the ten-minute gap between breakfast and inspection. But there was a snag: all the articles of kit on display had to be not merely clean but polished to a high sheen. Some you could polish up the night before, when you could also sandpaper your boot brushes; but your cutlery was another matter. Since breakfast generally consisted of fatty bacon, your knife and fork were thick with goo, not easily removed by a quick dip in the bucket of lukewarm water at the exit from the mess hall. It was practically an impossibility to get them shining bright before the inspection.

For the first few days of training, inspection was relatively lenient. A few of the untidy beds were overturned, the inspecting officer muttered about pigsties, and the sergeant who tailed him returned a few minutes later to promise eternal damnation if we could not learn to be clean.

One evening as we sat on our beds blancoing our leather equipment (this was a particularly evil piece of Guard's bull, for after the blancoing you had to polish each and every one of the little brass studs which held the braces and pouches together, a total of 124 finnicky Brasso jobs, with the end of your pull-through) our trained soldier started to soliloquise. Looking into the air, and addressing nobody in particular, he said: 'Cutlery is always a bit of a problem; takes a lot of time to bring your spoon up mirror-like. I heard once of a bright recruit who went down to the camp shop and spent his last shilling on a spare knife, spoon and fork. Saved himself a lot of trouble. Course, you don't want to get caught . . . '

Soon most of us had not only double sets of cutlery – one resplendent for show, and one often filthy for use – but also special display boot brushes, buttonsticks and all the rest.

There was similar bull and anti-bull in all fields, but I was particularly tickled by the spit-and-polish fantasy of the heating system. The cavernous barrack rooms were rather inadequately heated by an open fire, and the coal for the fire was theoretically kept in a vast black cast-iron bathtub next to the fireplace. Since the military mind apparently works that way, it had become a fine old tradition that the inside of the tub should be whitewashed. A dirty sack of coal emptied into the tub would spoil the effect, so we spent long hours actually polishing the more presentable lumps of coal before they were artistically arranged in the tub. Naturally the polished coal was never thrown on the fire; the coal for use was kept in a box under the trained soldier's bed.

For the most part the life of a Grenadier Guard in the 1930s was a deadly round of drill, more drill, parades, inspections and the numbing hours spent each day in cleaning and polishing. Finding no time or energy to 'bore from within', and realising that I had not the slightest idea of how to go about it, I managed to borrow the £20 needed, and happily purchased my discharge.

At the time I would have written off my three months as a dead loss. Later I found my solid grounding in the mechanics of the rifle and machine gun of considerable value. And one odd relic of the drill-square at Caterham remains with me today. When my wife notices me slouching more than usual, and bids me to stand up straight, I automatically go into that state of vertical rigor mortis known as standing to attention.

8

Up the Negus!

Today it seems impossible to remember whether the next abrupt decision in my life was based on pure fantasy, or whether I really meant it.

In the summer of 1935 the forces of darkness were on the offensive once again. The Italian dictator Mussolini had invaded Ethiopia, and the forces of light, personified by Emperor Haile Selassie, the Negus, direct descendant of the Queen of Sheba, obviously deserved the help of all progressives. There was I in Britain, a trained military man – at least I knew how to present arms and form fours with great precision – and over there in Ethiopia were the anti-fascist masses waiting to be taught how.

Since I had no money to pay the fare, the next-best way to get to Africa seemed to be to hitch-hike. This had the advantage that it would take some time, and it would give me an opportunity to see a good slice of the world. A quick study of the map showed that the land route to Addis Ababa inevitably led through Istanbul; and the route to Istanbul led through Vienna. Impatient to get to the war, I shot off a letter to the Ethiopian Legation in London offering my services, and asked for the reply to be sent to Poste Restante, Vienna. My father, disapproving of my plan to see the world – the war was not mentioned – declined to part with even a small sum to get me on my way. So I sold for £7 my clapped-out motor-bike, and set off.

The cheapest boat to the Continent landed me in Antwerp, and there came my introduction to the problems of hitch-hiking, which had always looked so simple in Hollywood films, my only source of knowledge. These films had shown me that to get a lift you simply stood at the side of the road facing oncoming traffic, raised your bent right arm and pointed with your thumb over your shoulder in the direction you wanted to go. If I had studied the films of the time more closely, I would have noticed that the most successful hitch-hikers were those accompanied by a young female, often Claudette Colbert, and they hid behind a small bush until the girl had stopped the car. Even if I had noticed this gambit, I certainly did not know any girls who wanted to go to Ethiopia.

But what Hollywood had not shown me was how you got to a stretch of open road outside a large city like Antwerp, or how you selected a pick-up point where the car driver was still going slowly enough to be relatively willing to stop. During the following weeks and months, as I wandered across Europe, I gradually learned the tricks of the trade. Some I worked out for myself; others came from fellow voluntary vagrants, many of whom delighted in demonstrating their ability to get maximum transport, often with side-benefits like a meal or even a bed for the night, at the cost of minimum exertion.

Before leaving London I had collected various hints on marginal living from an aged Australian, who claimed to have criss-crossed that continent the hard way as a boy. Some of his tips were irrelevant to central Europe – how to deal with dingoes, for instance – but others were helpful. 'Always have some sort of cooking pot,' he said. 'If you have to scrabble roots from the ground, they taste pretty foul raw.' His main piece of advice would have been better ignored: 'Never carry a proper pack; it makes you look like a new chum.' A blanket roll was the thing. A blanket or old coat, rolled up and tied at the ends with a bit of rope and slung across your shoulders, was the proper way to carry your gear.

I have always been a sucker for good advice from experts, so I obediently rolled a spare shirt, a towel, a small saucepan and a few odds and ends into an old raincoat. The disastrous thing was that my old swagman had not told me what you did if it rained or got cold; and, in my memory at least, the summer of 1935 was cold and rainy clear across Europe. If you unrolled the pack, you were left with a horrid little heap of intractable objects, for it is difficult to stuff even a small saucepan into your pocket. I finally solved the problem when I found a small sack at the wayside.

The problem of how to get out of the centre of Antwerp to the open road had to be solved by taking a tram to the end of the line. I could do this without breaking into the five £1 notes which constituted almost my total capital, because before I was leaving I had collected from friends and relations a small bagful of Belgian centimes, German pfennigs and other assorted small change – the useless odds and ends of currency which many people accumulate in an old teapot or a vase on the mantelpiece when they return from foreign parts. Since some of my relations had last been in foreign parts around the turn of the century, quite a lot of the coins turned to be totally out of date; but several times when I went into a small bakery to buy a couple of stale rolls, the shopkeeper would inspect the coins with interest, say he hadn't seen any of those for nigh on thirty years and give me my rolls anyway.

Coming from the placid security of a Britain on whose flag the sun never set, and which had apparently never had a currency reform, it had simply not occurred to me that in most European countries the situation was different. Older readers will recall that in the 1920s and 1930s – and later still for all I know – pennies and florins bearing the portrait of Queen Victoria were not only still legal tender, but turned up quite regularly in your change, and pennies from the reign of King William IV, who had died one hundred years earlier, still appeared from time to time.

Soon I settled down to the routine of life on the road: the search in the evening for a dry spot to sleep, often fairly comfortably in an isolated barn; the sometimes frustrating roadside wait for a vehicle to give you a lift; the often very friendly lorry drivers who shared their sandwiches; and the luxurious meals of pea soup out of a packet costing a couple of pence which I brewed up over a small fire.

Getting a lift was helped by the fact that I had no particular destination, except that I favoured anything going in a generally south-east direction, vaguely towards Vienna. Sometimes there was a break from the short rides in lorries on local runs (long-distance lorry traffic does not seem to have been widespread in those days). Sitting on a bridge over the Moselle River near the frontier between Luxembourg and Germany, I got into halting conversation with a young German who had tied up his two-man canoe under the bridge. When he offered me a lift I gladly accepted, but it turned out that he expected me to help paddle. For the past fifty years I have been convinced that we paddled firmly and strenuously upstream against the current mile after mile. Consulting a map while writing this paragraph, I discover that we must have been going downstream.

This young canoeist was the first fellow traveller I encountered to show me that life on the road need not necessarily be limited to uneasy nights in a dry ditch, and meals of burnt pea soup. After hours of toil, we saw ahead of us a village decked out with bunting, and as we got nearer we could hear the village band thumping away.

My new friend soon insinuated himself into the centre of the village festival, introducing me all round as a rarity – a real live Englishman on the tramp – and I found glasses of wine being pressed upon me. It was pleasant cold acid stuff, rather like sour lemonade. Coming from teetotal surroundings, I was well up theoretically in the dangers of the demon alcohol, but this did not seem like alcohol, and anyway everybody else appeared to be knocking it back like water. (The teetotalism of the Peet family seems to have been very total. In the family larder stood a quarter bottle of brandy marked 'for emergencies'; the emergencies must have been rare, for the bottle was still there, and still firmly corked, some twenty years later.)

I have vague memories of singing, at popular request, an English folksong – probably 'Knocked 'em in the Old Kent Road' – and remember no more until I came to in the grey of morning, lying in an outhouse, vowing never to touch the stuff again.

Gradually I found my feet as an amateur tramp. At Titisee in the Black Forest I joined forces with a German student drop-out, and in the following days he showed me some of the ropes. 'Hungry,' he said soon after we met, 'you never need be hungry if you have enough cheek.'

It was about two in the afternoon, a time when all right-thinking Germans have finished their midday meal. My experienced guide took me firmly by the arm and marched me into the kitchen entrance of the largest hotel in the spa where we happened to be. With calm authority he explained to the chef that we were foreign students extending our education; if there was any washing-up to be done, we might consider it, but in any case we had not eaten for twenty-four hours.

It worked like a charm. The chef passed us on to a fatherly head waiter, who said we should wait outside for a minute and then soon emerged with huge platefuls of potatoes and gravy, and odds and ends of meat. In the weeks that followed, I found that the gambit rarely failed. You had to work it at a big hotel, preferably a luxury one, and you had to appear at just the right moment, when the lunch or dinner rush was over, but before the excess food had been scraped into the dustbin.

My friend Kurt showed me how to get food at the other end of the social scale too. Here small villages were better territory than towns. You simply knocked at random on a door and asked politely for a piece of bread. Sometimes you actually got a chunk of stale bread, but this was not the aim of the operation. Generally the bread was thick-spread with dripping. Sometimes the lady of the house pressed a short length of sausage on you, now and then with a cup of cold tea or even a small glass of wine.

After some six weeks on the road, I finally reached Vienna. My first call was at the Central Post Office to see whether the Negus wanted to help. All I got was a neat and polite postcard which stated:

'The Minister of the Empire of Ethiopia presents his compliments. He is grateful for your offer of aid, but at the present moment there would not appear to be any way in which your services could be utilised.'

9

English Tutor

Vienna was enchanting, but I had practically no money, no job (like a large proportion of the Viennese) and not the faintest idea of how I could maintain myself.

So off to the British Legation. The public-school accent worked like a charm, and within a few minutes I found myself taking tea with the British Minister; full-blown ambassadors were rare in those days. After small talk about the weather, and school – it emerged that my school had played cricket against his school, which helped – I explained that I was looking for some way to maintain myself.

'We are really not an employment agency here,' the Minister said cheerfully, 'but perhaps we can do something for you. One of the fellows from the Austrian Foreign Ministry was on the blower to me this morning, very decent chap for a foreigner, and he said his brother was looking for a student, some respectable type, who could tutor his son in English. Got some sort of exam coming up. So if you toddle around to see this fellow's brother, he may be glad to see you. Drop in some time and let me know how you get on.'

(Consulting contemporary documentation while writing this, I discovered that Sir Walter Selby, the British Minister, must have been less of a caricature than I have made him in reconstructing that ancient conversation. One year earlier he had been the only member of the diplomatic corps in Vienna who had protested to the Austrian Government at the mass executions of Austrian socialists involved in the short civil war of February 1934. Protests from British Ministers still carried weight then, and his intervention saved a number of lives.)

The brother lived not far away. He had just got home for lunch from his work in some obscure ministry – pensions and crown lands, or something of that sort – and I was mildly astonished to find that he was all dressed up in uniform, with a pill-box hat. Mid-ranking officials in Austria all wore uniforms at that time, even for desk work on pensions. He looked for all the world like one of the Austrian officers caricatured by Josef Lada in his famous illustration for Jaroslav Hašek's *Good Soldier Schwejk*.

Luckily he spoke reasonable English, for my German was still minimal. My optimistic dreams of earning some money were soon dashed when he explained that he wanted an English student who could spend the next few weeks at their holiday cottage in the Semmering Mountains some fifty miles south of Vienna. He could offer only hospitality, no money, he explained rather hesitantly. Even a senior official found it hard to make ends meet, and fees were very high at the exclusive grammar school where his sons were pupils.

But he sure I would enjoy the good plain food and get on well with his son, who was a nice boy, but very lazy. The prospect of regular meals after rather lean months was attractive, and finding a place to sleep was urgent, because the youth hostel where I was staying had pointed out that they only catered for transients.

So I assured the uniformed pensions official that I would be delighted, could start immediately, and could I have the train fare, please? He seemed a little surprised, because in his experience the English were always at least well to do, but he carefully counted out, coin by coin, the exact train fare, warning me that I would have to walk about five miles from the station to their cottage. Then he penned a short note to his wife explaining my arrival, and sent me on my way. So for the first time since leaving London I became a fare-paying passenger, except for that tram ride in Antwerp.

My main memory of the three or four weeks in the mountains is of food. It may have been plain food by Austrian standards, but since it was all unusual it was a luxury: thick slices of crusty dark bread from the village bakery, huge round open tarts piled with blueberries we had gathered, roast pork seasoned with caraway seeds.

The lessons went quite well, in both directions. Fritz was a friendly intelligent lad a few months younger than I, but even lazier. We talked together in an odd mixture of school English and primitive German, moving to baby-talk English at meals, when his mother decreed that English should be the sole language. Luckily she understood not a word, so we could display amazing progress. Fritz offered English sentences at random, and I answered at random. At first our chat bore a strong resemblance to the 'rhubarb' in a stage crowd scene, but gradually we shifted into real conversation as Fritz realised he had unknowingly absorbed quite a lot of English at school.

It was in the Semmering Mountains that I was first confronted with the fact that language textbooks often inflict upon pupils not only masses of unnecessarily complicated grammar, but also many words which appear to be of only marginal utility. Struggling through an English-German translation in his school textbook, Fritz encountered a word which was not in his dictionary. The word was 'tilth', and I had to confess it meant nothing to me. Later reference to the *Concise Oxford* informed me that tilth is 'Tillage, cultivation, depth of soil affected by this.' I doubt whether Fritz or any of his grammar-school colleagues ever encountered the word again; just as I was writing these lines I stumbled upon it in one of Doris Lessing's short stories, but this must have been the first time in nearly fifty years.

And it still happens today. Quite a sensible adult 'brush up your English' volume published recently in the German Democratic Republic introduced the word 'cruet' in the very first lesson. Not so obscure as 'tilth', perhaps, but not one of the one thousand most useful words I would have chosen myself.

At school, one of the few things which awakened our interest in Latin was the discovery that some Latin poets wrote very freely about some unmentionable subjects. Ovid's *Ars Amatoria* was apparently packed with what I am sure we described as 'hot stuff'. The only problem was how to locate such passages without plodding through the whole book. Then some genius hit on the answer. In those days a London publisher named Loeb produced cribs, literal translations of the main Latin classics, which gave a helping hand to many young people. Mr Loeb may have ignored the ethics of education (his invaluable volumes were printed especially small, so they could easily be concealed in the sleeve or under the desk), but he apparently could not afford to ignore the taboos of still-Victorian Britain. His little books gave a full English translation, except for any portions regarded as smut; these were left in the original Latin. All we had to do was to club together to buy Mr Loeb's translation of *Ars Amatoria*, and skim through it to see which lines were left in Latin and concentrate our joint efforts upon these.

I decided that a variant of the Loeb method was just the thing to get Fritz interested in English. Since I had no copy of *Lady Chatterley*, the only dirty book in English of which I was aware, I had to fall back on my memory. My stock of dirty jokes was strictly limited and very juvenile, but Fritz loved them. So he made considerable progress, learning at the same time a number of words which were not then in the dictionaries. Filth instead of tilth.

10

Food for Talk

The summer holidays were over, and I was back in Vienna, bronzed, plump and broke. Not entirely broke, for during my jaunt across Europe I had kept my father supplied with a steady stream of articles, ranging from 'The Saar Six Months after the Plebiscite' to 'Hitch-hiking in the Black Forest with a Lorryload of Pigs', most of which he had been able to market. I now had enough money to keep me afloat for a few weeks if I lived on bread and horse sausage.

A chance encounter in a very cheap restaurant proved fruitful. The man I met was Al, a middle-aged American expatriate (middle-aged to me; he was probably all of thirty) who turned out to be extraordinarily vague about his antecedents, changing the subject abruptly if asked where he came from, what his profession was, if any, and why he was living in Europe. When I got to know him better I discovered he received a small remittance via American Express once a month, and I concluded that he had left the States under some sort of cloud, and was being paid to stay a long way away and in deepest obscurity.

Al may have been vague, but he turned out to be a remarkable fixer. When I admitted I was down to my last few shillings, he asked me what I could do. I was really a journalist, I claimed proudly, but perhaps I had more chances as an English teacher. What I needed urgently was a place to sleep, for the youth hostel to which I had returned had just thrown me out for the second time.

'Let's see if we can fix that right away,' said Al, and he led me across central Vienna to the Café Louvre, a rather ornate coffee-house which turned out to be the unofficial headquarters of the foreign press corps in

60

Vienna. There he introduced me to a massive elderly (all of perhaps forty-five) American journalist in a rumpled blue suit covered in cigar ash. 'No,' said the journalist, 'I can't use a leg-man at the moment, but maybe we can get you a bed. I'll call my wife.'

The journalist rumbled away, halting at every second table to exchange a few words with colleagues. In a few minutes he was back.

'You Irish or something?' he asked. 'You've certainly got Irish luck.' And he handed me an address scribbled on the back of an envelope. 'I don't know her, but she's a widow lady, a friend of my wife, and she's been badgering her for weeks to turn up an American or English student to tutor her dumb cluck of a son – those are my wife's words. She can't pay you anything, but she's got a spare room which she'll let you have for one hour's English a day.'

It turned out to be an astonishing stroke of luck. The son was slightly dim, but willing, and the spare room was far better than anything I could have expected. The widow lady was terribly refined but of reduced means – the lovely archaic term 'indigent gentlewoman' fitted well – and when her son's marks in English began to improve she threw in a free breakfast every day as a bonus.

In the following months I met the bulky American journalist several times, mainly in the Café Louvre, but began to avoid him after he had pinned me down several times with long and rambling monologues blaming the state of the world on President Roosevelt, the Freemasons, the Pope, King George V and, of course, the Jews. The Negroes and the Commies came into it somewhere, but not prominently. He called Roosevelt 'Rosenfeldt', a term which nazi propagandists were tossing about in an effort to suggest that he was Jewish.

His name was Robert Best and he was the Vienna correspondent of the United Press. During the Second World War, listening to the nazi overseas radio service from Berlin, I suddenly heard his well-know rasping voice once again. 'B-B-B – Bob Best's Bulletin,' he boomed, and proceeded to deliver much the same confused monologue as that to which the Café Louvre's customers had been exposed. I believe that for diplomatic reasons the Pope had by that time been phased out.

Robert Best, the American Haw-Haw, was arrested at the end of the war and flown back to the United States, where he was indicted for treason. Like Ezra Pound the poet, also an Axis broadcaster, he was found insane and never brought to trial.

My friend Al was delighted that his first bit of fixing had gone so well. 'We've got you a bed; now we have to fix you up with victuals,' he said. Almost immediately he came up with a plan. Vienna was full of relatively impoverished aristocrats who would be delighted to brush up their English, but felt they could not afford it. Offer them a couple of hours' cultured English conversation in exchange for a square meal, and they would jump at it. 'And I've got a real live count lined up right now. He wants to look at you to see if you're respectable and a genuine Britisher.'

The interview went smoothly, and I was promptly engaged to make polite English conversation with him and the countess at lunch every Monday. This was the breakthrough to fairly regular, though often tiring, meals. Word spread rapidly that a hungry young Englishman was at large in Vienna. 'And he speaks such beautifully clear English, darling, I can understand every word!'

My engagement book soon filled: lunch here, afternoon tea there and, more rarely, dinner. Luckily for my sanity, a few of my new acquaintances could speak quite good, if rusty, English, and table talk could move away from the ghastly grind of 'Do you like to go to the opera?' – 'Yes, I like much going to the opera.' In addition to the flow of food, one or two pupils rather hesitantly slipped an envelope containing a small sum into my hand as I said goodbye.

Other and even odder channels opened up for life on the barter system. The owner of an international newspaper stall at the corner of Kärtnerstrasse and the Graben – Vienna's Piccadilly Circus – eyed me disapprovingly for a few days while I scanned the headlines of the *Continental Daily Mail* without buying the paper, and then struck up a conversation. I seemed to have no money to buy a newspaper, and he had a suggestion. Quite a lot of his customers were English-speaking tourists, and if I would like to teach him how to count in English, and a few simple phrases, he would lend me English-language newspapers and magazines for an hour or two if I promised to bring them back clean and neatly folded, fit to be sold.

So for a couple of months I stood for a few minutes at the windy corner every day practising easy newsvendor's English, and then dodging back to my room not far away for a good read. Sometimes I took over the stall for a few minutes while he went off for a quick glass of wine or a leak.

Once we landed a minor coup. After our lesson, he loaned me the latest issue of *Esquire*, the American magazine, which had just come in. I skimmed through it quickly in my room. When I returned, I saw he was making urgent gestures that I should hide it under my coat. 'Go round the corner and wrap it up in this,' he said, handing me an old newspaper, 'and then give it to me when nobody is looking.' I complied, and he whispered, 'Tell you all about it tomorrow.'

When I returned the next day, he handed me a 10-schilling note – nearly 10 shillings in sterling, quite a large sum for me – and explained.

'Just five minutes after I lent you that magazine, the police came rushing round and confiscated all my copies of *Esquire*. They said it contained a libellous article about Prince Starhemberg, the boss of the Heimwehr. Word soon got around, and regular customers offered handfuls of money for the banned issue. That's your share.'

My only regret was that in my quick flip through *Esquire* I had missed the libellous article about the Prince, who headed the Heimwehr, a 40,000-man fascist militia, one of the major props of the clerico-fascist clique running Austria at the time. But it was easy to guess what the article had been about, for the Prince was notorious throughout Austria for his enormous and conspicuous consumption of young ladies, the flashier the better.

Another sideline which slowly emerged provided me with entertainment and drinks in the evening. Once a month my friend Al was mildly in funds when his regular remittance had come in, and he would invite me to share a litre of wine in one of the cheaper bars. Every bar had a young lady who sang the latest hits, and at that time American songs were in great demand. Since most of the singers knew no English, and had picked up the songs from the radio or from records, the words bore only a faint relationship to the original lyrics.

After finishing a couple of numbers, the singer would flit from table to table encouraging the customers to drink, and in one bar the young lady, hearing us talk English, suggested that we might like to give her a friendly hand with song texts. Al, always quick to spot a chance, asked what would be in it for us. So she went across to consult the owner, apparently a very good friend. Soon he came over.

'There'll be a litre of wine for you, on the house, any evening you can spare a bit of time to help her with the words.'

Which explains why, after all these years, I still know most of the verses of many of the top songs of the mid-1930s, such as Fred Astaire's 'Putting on My Top Hat', or the cowboy dirge 'Roll Along, Covered Waggon'. I must confess that we sometimes fudged things a bit. There were half-sentences we could not catch, even after ten replays on the gramophone in the back room of the bar, and a few words the poor girl simply could not pronounce; in such cases we happily rewrote a line or two of the lyric, and apparently nobody ever noticed.

In the first few weeks of living it up, or down, in Vienna, politics seemed to recede somewhat into the background. The mere fact of 'abroad' was strange and exciting enough. I had been away from Britain before, but only for short periods, in company, and with a certain amount of cash in reserve to fall back on. Now the situation was quite different; I was on my own in a very foreign environment, with no money, but a stubborn determination to make my own way rather than write home for my return fare and return to an uncertain future as an apprentice small-town journalist – if I could get a job.

Austria had limped through the 1920s with great friction between the largely socialist electorate of Vienna and the industrial centres and the very conservative and often monarchist countryside. The conflict had come to a head in February 1934 when the right had established a clerico-fascist dictatorship and smashed the socialist movement in a bloody three-day civil war. Compared to Hitler's dictatorship over the border in Germany, the Austrian dictatorship appeared mild, and its rule was moderated to some extent by traditional Austrian sloppiness. The position was complicated further by the existence of a very considerable nazi movement, which agitated potently for the absorption of Austria by its more powerful and dynamic northern neighbour. The nazis had been driven underground in July 1934, after they had assassinated Dollfuss, the first clerico-fascist dictator; but it was an open secret that they had many supporters in high places.

Naturally the socialists, though totally banned as a party, were also active underground, and after a couple of months in Vienna I managed to establish contact. Actually it would be more correct to say that the underground contacted me.

Somewhere along the line I had struck up an acquaintance with an elderly Austrian teacher of English who was obviously progressive. He suggested I might like to earn a schilling or two by coming along and talking, in English, to his English-language class at an adult education centre in a workers' suburb. 'Just a talk about English life today: what people wear, and English cooking, and pubs, and things like that. Nothing political, of course.'

So I went along, and told the class about English schools, and houses, and my work as a reporter on a local newspaper, and as many other sanitised themes as I could think of. When I ran out of steam, we had a question period. It started harmlessly enough with questions on the royal family – later experience in several countries has shown me that the British royals have an undying appeal even for Communist audiences. But the questions quickly moved on the the various political parties, and why, for example, the British Labour Party had so many voters but so few newspapers.

In my replies I tried to be as non-committal as possible, for I had no wish to get my Austrian friend into trouble. Even so, the way I phrased some of my replies apparently struck a note with one or two of the pupils.

When the evening class ended, two of the more persistent questioners suggested rather hesitantly that I might like to join them for a cup of coffee. We chatted for several hours, and it soon became clear to me that they were not just interested in getting some English conversation on the cheap. Very discreetly they sounded me out. I was perhaps over-careful in my replies, remembering all the stories about stool-pigeons.

We agreed to meet again in a few days. This time the senior of the pair, to establish his credentials, told me we would not be seeing each other again for quite a while, because next day he had to go off to serve a six-month prison sentence. He had been arrested immediately after the fighting in February 1934 as an active member of the Schutzbund, the socialist militia, sentenced summarily to six months and then set free provisionally because all the gaols were crammed. This was part of the half-hearted fascism of the Austrian fascists: hundreds or even thousands of their opponents went on a waiting list until cell room was free. 'Of course, I could run away to Czechoslovakia, but they'd be glad to get rid of me. This way I can go on opposing them here when I get out. But now I've got a straight question for you. You were obviously connected with the left in England: what is your position?'

By this time I had convinced myself that they were not police narks trying to trap me, and I told him I considered myself to be a Communist. 'Aha,' he said. 'I thought it might be like that.' And he proceeded to give me a short briefing on the situation of the anti-fascist underground. Some of the Schutzbund men in Vienna, disappointed at the way the powerful Socialist Party had collapsed, had joined the ranks of the underground Communist Party, which had always been small in Austria. Very many, he thought a majority, also rejected the leadership of the old Socialist Party, and had formed a new left-wing group, the Revolutionary Socialists. This new party was working out a people's front agreement with the Communists, but there was a lot of old rivalry to be overcome.

At a later date, he said, they might try to put me in touch with the Communists if I liked, but in the meantime would I mind giving a little help to their group? For a start, could I make a quick trip to Bratislava in Czechoslovakia in the next few days to bring back a batch of the latest left-wing literature?

Thrilled at the opportunity to do something active in the revolutionary underground, I jumped at the chance. From then on, for several months, I made a weekly trip to Bratislava, only about one hour away by overland tram, returning with increasingly large bundles of socialist and Communist literature in German which was being published in Czechoslovakia by refugee groups. After a few successful trial runs, I was entrusted with letters in both directions. Many years later I discovered that Kim Philby, the famous 'Third Man', had been travelling the same route and doing the same things – but some months earlier.

Some time in the autumn of 1935 my underground friends told me that most sections of the left resistance had decided to stage a public demonstration to show everybody they were still very much there. The place and date had been carefully chosen to attract maximum public attention, and to expose the demonstrators to the minimum chance of reprisal.

On All Saints' Day in November it is the custom in Austria, and in other Catholic countries, to visit the graves of the near and dear and deposit flowers. Since many hundreds of worker victims of the February 1934 fighting were buried at the huge municipal cemetery, the Centralfriedhof, the underground busily spread the word: all the left should go to the cemetery; All Saints' Day was to be All Reds' Day.

Everybody willing was given leaflets to spread, and I too received a large packet. The leaflets I had to pass on were worded in an extremely neutral fashion: 'On All Saints' Day our dead heroes will be honoured at the Centralfriedhof at 11 a.m. The struggle continues.' They bore no signature or identification.

For several hours that evening I worked my way through the more proletarian areas of central Vienna. With no experience of distributing clandestine leaflets, I recalled a trick I had read about in a pamphlet describing Communist underground activity in nazi Germany. At that time toilet-paper, particular in the lavatories of public loos, was dispensed not from rolls but from a patent appliance which provides paper one sheet at a time: when you take one sheet, the next automatically pops out. With a little practice it is easy to extract the unused paper by inserting your fingers into the porcelain holder and pressing the catch. Then all you have to do is to interleave your leaflets with the toilet paper, and you have an automatic propaganda dispenser. Obviously you insert your seditious bumf well back in the box so that it does not start to emerge until you are well clear.

So, for the expenditure of a few small coins and at very little risk, I helped spread the word in some fifteen pubs and cafés, and several public lavatories.

All Saints' Day turned out to be cool but sunny, and as usual the trams out to the municipal cemetery were crammed. Many of the passengers were genuine personal mourners of all classes, bearing large wreaths with personal dedications to their dead aunts. Others were fairly obviously something else, for they were grasping small bunches of flowers, preferably red, and many of them exchanged quiet signs of recognition when they spotted an old comrade from another district.

Outside the cemetery gates the police were massed, seated in a whole row of those old-fashioned charabancs without doors, a special construction which enabled the cops to leap out with minimum delay. They were very much in evidence, but just sitting there morosely, quietly watching the stream of mourners. The crowd was so dense, and so mixed, that it would have been almost impossible for them to cut out the demonstrators, who moved in twos or threes, without trampling underfoot the thousands who had come, as every year, to visit the family graves.

Not knowing where to look for the graves of the socialist militia, I simply followed a small group of mourners each of whom was clutching one single red carnation. We soon found ourselves jammed in a slowly moving stream which shuffled past the mass graves, already covered in mounds of flowers.

Word had been passed days before that, to rob the police of any excuse to intervene, there should be no overt manifestations: no flags, no banners, no slogans, no songs. We were simply mourners, behaving with the decorum suitable to a cemetery. But as we edged slowly past the graves, where a number of square men with the unmistakable look of the plain-clothes cop were noting faces, a curious muted buzzing began. The buzz rapidly spread, and everybody grasped what was happening; some small group, with mouths firmly closed, had begun to hum a revolutionary tune, and the humming rapidly spread until first hundreds and then thousands joined in. The tunes followed one another: 'The Internationale', anthem of the Austrian socialists as well as the Communists; 'Undying Heroes', a revolutionary funeral march; and the catchy melody of 'We Are the Workers of Vienna', which one year later formed the basis for a popular marching song of the British Battalion of the International Brigades in Spain.

It is impossible to estimate how many people took part in this last public demonstration of the left in Vienna for ten long years, but there must have been tens of thousands. After showing that they were bloodied but unbowed, these anonymous revolutionaries mingled once again with the family mourners and dispersed, without a clash with the police, but with the very definite feeling that they were a force to be reckoned with.

Three years later, in March 1938, Hitler took over Austria, and here, as in the rest of what had become 'Greater Germany', the resistance was driven deep underground.

11

Goodbye to Prague

Living on the barter system was fun for a while, but it became wearing, particularly at weekends when nobody seemed to want the man who came to dinner. A more normal way of earning a living appeared to be indicated. Every day I passed the big sign of a well-known international language school right in the centre of Vienna, but I assumed that such an institution would be fully staffed with properly trained teachers. Finally I summoned up my courage and went in to ask for a job. The director asked to see my passport, and established that I could speak clearly and distinctly in standard English. 'When can you start?' he asked.

So there and then I became a wage earner. It turned out that I was only marginally better off, because the work was hard, the pay poor and the hours exorbitant. On a busy day we might well take classes from nine in the morning until ten in the evening, sometimes with only one hour off.

The work was not only mentally but physically exhausting, for this school worked on a special patented system of instruction. The theory was that the best way to learn a language was as a baby does; and certainly in the first stages the system worked well. The very first lesson started with the teacher holding up some simple object and saying very loudly and clearly, 'Book', or 'Pencil.' Then he or she gestured to pupil after pupil to repeat the word. Soon things got more complicated: 'I open the door', 'You sit at the table' and so on. All this meant that the teacher was forced to act out the whole lesson, darting about, opening windows, running and pantomiming madly.

In an effort to encourage the flagging interest of my classes I soon introduced a few variants always good for a laugh, such as sitting on the table or under it, or eating a book. But the director of the institute made a practice of listening quietly outside the classroom doors to see that instruction followed the printed book word for word, and to ensure that not a single word of German was spoken in explanation. He soon put a stop to my clowning.

Sitting one day in a café, reading the local newspapers – I could now afford both cafés and newspapers – my eye was caught by an advertisement in English printed in bold type in the 'Jobs Vacant' column:

'Wanted urgently for English language school in Prague, fully-qualified teacher, English mother-tongue essential. Good pay and conditions.'

I had never been to Prague, which by all accounts was a lively city, and 'good pay' sounded attractive. I promptly sent off a special-delivery letter slightly overstating my qualifications, and got the job sight unseen.

Prague was a great improvement on Vienna. In 1936 Prague was a very lively democratic island in the increasingly totalitarian sea of central Europe. Berlin had fallen to fascism in 1933; Vienna had been in the grip of an inefficient and half-hearted variant since 1934; and Budapest had been under Admiral Horthy's version of extreme right-wing rule since the early 1920s.

So Prague was crammed with life: not only the busy intellectual life of the Czechs, but that of those who had recently fled from Germany and Austria. An earlier and reactionary element of emigration was provided by the White Russians who ran innumerable bars and small restaurants. Rather unexpectedly, too, there was a small group of British emigrants in Prague, concentrated to a high degree in the English language school where I had now become a teacher.

Even though I must have been unbearably naïve in those days, it was not long before I realised that a high proportion of my fellow teachers were indefinably different – in fact, gay. I never pressed the question as to how this concentration had come about, but it appeared that some years earlier some homosexual teacher, fleeing the fearsome penalties then meted out in Britain, had found his way to Prague, where attitudes and law were much more enlightened. He found a niche, a moderately comfortable one, as a teacher of English. Word had spread on the network, and others followed. They were all good teachers, with a pleasant manner, and I cannot remember ever working with a more congenial group.

Prague proved to be a stimulating experience after slowly withering Vienna. Since I was already fluent in German I naturally gravitated to the German-speaking section of the community. There was excellent German theatre and cabaret, staffed in part by the cream of talent which had been forced to leave nazi Germany.

Almost everybody I met claimed to be writing a book, and some of them even were, and this gave me the idea of writing my book. It appeared to me that a book dealing with the ups and downs of a young Englishman trying to keep afloat in central Europe by teaching English might be interesting, and I had all the raw material to hand – odd pupils, curious encounters, a naïve English narrator. Four or five chapters were already completed when I happened to buy at a big Prague bookshop one of the first issues of *Penguin New Writing*, a literary magazine published in book form. And there was a pre-publication chapter of Christopher Isherwood's *Goodbye to Berlin*. It was set of course in Berlin, and mine was set in Vienna and Prague; but he had got in first with much the same cast of odd pupils, curious encounters, a naïve English narrator and even, in the background, political commitment on the left. My unfinished book would look like a cheap imitation.

This may be the reason why Lisa Minelli never starred in a film based on *Goodbye to Prague* by John Peet. Probably luckily, the unfinished manuscript did not survive my subsequent wanderings.

Our language school was doing a roaring business. For speakers of minor languages like Czech, knowledge of a more widely known language is imperative if one wishes to travel. The older generation mostly had some knowledge of German from the times before 1918 when Czechoslovakia formed part of the Austro-Hungarian Empire; but many of the younger generation rejected German as the old 'imperial' tongue, and learned English instead. Apart from this, by 1936 many people in Prague were watching very apprehensively what was happening in neighbouring countries. The situation was summed up in a very bitter little saying which was making the rounds: 'Are you learning English, or are you Aryan?'

It was not only members of the large Jewish community in Prague who jammed our classes. Many others expected the worst to come to the worst and wanted to be prepared for possible emigration. So from morning to night we taught the people of Prague English. Most of the teaching was done on the premises, but for special pupils paying a higher fee a teacher was provided on your own doorstep.

The oddest of these outside jobs was a wealthy businessman who had decided to leave central Europe while the going was good. He wanted to brush up his English, but decided he had no time to attend lessons. Instead he hired a teacher for a whole day once a week. The theory was that in the intervals of his busy round he could practise the language. I got this job several times, and it was rather nerve-racking.

Reporting to his office bright and early – say, at seven o'clock – you found him waiting on the doorstep. 'Hurry up,' he said, stepping into his car, 'now we have the lesson on the way to factory. First I take look at newspapers.' Since he was a fast reader, there was time before we arrived for at least two minutes of conversation about the commercial news he had just read.

And so the day passed: factories, offices, banks, even once relieved by a lightning visit to his uncle's funeral, where he managed quickly to accumulate some useful English words like 'coffin', 'hearse' and 'mourners'. The method may have had some merit, because he always insisted in talking in English about what he had just done, or was going to do next, and thus he acquired quite a lot of the businessman's vocabulary, instead of droning through the rather dreary school textbook tales about milkmaids off to market with a basket of eggs.

Less hectic, but more gruesome – for me at least – was another outside duty. Every day one of our teachers (there were thirteen or fourteen of us) was detailed to give lessons at a finishing school for young ladies on the outskirts of Prague.

The young ladies, in their late teens, were cooped up in an exclusive and expensive boarding school where they were supposed to learn English and French, needlework and riding, and other genteel pursuits. When I put in my first appearance, the young ladies appeared pleased. I was roughly in their own age group, and they hoped for first-hand information about the customs, dances and fashions of their contemporaries in Britain.

They were even more pleased when they discovered that I was rather shy, and they could make me blush very easily. They promptly put their heads together and worked out new and increasingly brutal methods of reducing me to flush-faced confusion.

It started quite harmlessly, and possibly by chance. We had struggled through a textbook lesson about telling the time. 'What time do you have breakfast?' and 'When does the train leave for Birmingham?' and so on. I then encouraged them to frame their own questions. A smouldering beauty in the front row raised her hand, giggled and said, 'What time you go to bed, and you go to bed alone?'

Dark red confusion right down to the fingertips. I had a few moments to rally while the brighter girls tittered and nudged each other, and the duller girls had the question translated for them. I decided to ignore the content of the question and concentrate on the form. 'I'm afraid the grammar was not quite right. Can somebody else ask the question in the right way?'

Another pupil raised her hand, and I did not like her smirk. 'What time are you going to bed, and are you going to bed alone?'

It did not really seem to be a good opportunity to explain once again in great detail the complications of English tenses. So I said sharply, 'No, the right form is: What time *do you go* to bed? With regard to the second part of the question, in polite conversation in English you do not ask such personal things.'

The bell saved me from further questioning, but of course I was sunk.

Two weeks later my next day at the finishing school rolled round. I had not dared to tell my colleagues of my ordeal for fear they might laugh at me. The girls were all seated at their desks, as prim and proper as might be, but there was an air of suppressed excitement. Something must be coming, but what?

All went quietly for a while as we finished up one chapter in the textbook, and turned the page. Then I saw the terrifying beauty in the front row had raised her hand again.

'Please, sir, I read an English book and I find words not in dictionary. Can you tell me meaning?' It sounded harmless enough: more obscure words like 'tilth' perhaps.

'Yes, tell me the words.'

'I have list,' said the angel. 'First word is "fuck".'

Scarlet in face, gasping for breath, I quickly considered falling unconscious, but felt it would be un-British. The whole form, obviously in the picture, stared at me with sparkling eyes. England might be far, and honour a name, but I must have absorbed a bit of stiff-upper-lipping at some stage, and I wasn't going to be made a fool of by a bunch of bloody foreigners, and silly girls at that.

'That is a very unusual word to find in a book,' I said, my voice about an octave too high. 'Can you tell me the title?'

'Oh, yes,' said the radiant whited sepulchre modestly. 'Very nice love story: *Lady Chatterley*. Can I read you other words?' And she produced from under her desk a copy of the Paris edition of the book, freely available in continental Europe but thoroughly banned in Britain.

'No, you cannot read me the other words,' I said as severely as I could. 'I am sure they are rude words a young lady should not know.' The stiff upper lip was wilting, and I took the coward's way out. 'I am not feeling well. I must go home and go to bed.' I started to leave the room.

But the last word was with the modest beauty. 'You go to bed alone?' she fluted as I passed her desk.

Back at our language school I explained to the director, without all the terrible details, that I did not get on too well with the young ladies, and could I be taken off the finishing-school roster please? He was a little surprised, he said, because they had always seemed a very pleasant and well-behaved group, but he took me off the roster, which is one of the reasons I am alive and well and living in East Germany today.

12

No Bastard Ran

Many novelists whose stories encompass the 1930s have discovered a useful dustbin: a redundant character rushes off to the Spanish Civil War to fight against Franco in the International Brigades, and gets killed. If all these fictional characters had actually existed, our British Battalion of some 2,000 volunteers would have been considerably larger.

I have to admit I was one of the late-goers. As a young, fit, footloose semi-Communist with a certain minimum of military training – but much more than that of most British volunteers – I should have been among the first to go.

The reason for my tardiness was simple. I had fallen in love, for the first time, with a plump and bouncing Czech girl in Prague. Despite this rival attraction, I made a rather half-hearted attempt to contact those responsible in Prague for dispatching volunteers to Spain, and received a cryptic reply that they were not interested in an unknown English applicant, and that I should take the matter up with the proper circles in London. So I let the matter slide.

But my conscience nagged, and the picture cleared when it became evident that the bouncy girl was bouncing in other directions. So when I returned to Britain for a holiday in summer 1937 I tried to enlist there.

By this time, enlistment in the International Brigades had become difficult, because early in 1937 the British Government, acting in the name on non-intervention, had invoked an ancient law – the Foreign Enlistment Act of 1870 – threatening recruited and recruiters with a long term of imprisonment. So the recruiting office had gone underground, and had become hard to find. I have always wondered how those fictional volunteers managed to overcome this obstacle.

I had almost despaired of making contact when, at an 'Aid Spain' rally in Friends House, Euston Road, I met again my old friend Esmond Romilly, who had been one of the earliest British volunteers in Spain, and one of the very few of that small band of pioneers who had survived.

'Nothing easier,' he said briskly when I told him of my difficulties; and a couple of days later I found myself being interviewed in a poky attic office just off Charing Cross Road. The recruiting officer, a gaunt Scots Communist, gave me what was obviously his standard talk.

'I'd be sending you to your grave,' he said. 'In addition, the pay is lousy, the food is terrible, and you'd be fighting with a rusty shotgun against those nazi tanks.' I knew, I told him. Grudgingly he admitted that my minimal service with the Grenadiers might be of some use: 'Most of our lads don't know which end of a rifle the bullet comes out of.' He would accept Romilly's assurance that I wasn't a copper's nark, and when could I leave? The same evening? Then he slid open his desk drawer, presented me with a third-class return ticket to Paris and instructed me to be on No. 1 Platform at Victoria Station at 7.30 sharp.

Could I speak French? I admitted I could get along in the language, and on the spot he appointed me conducting officer to the group of five volunteers who would be leaving that evening. All I had to do, he said, was to keep them together, see that nobody got drunk and deliver the group to a Paris address I had to memorise.

The drill was simple. Almost none of the British volunteers, overwhelmingly working-class, possessed passports. By a happy coincidence, no-passport trips were available to the 1936–7 World Exhibition in Paris, and all you needed to show was a return ticket. When the recruiting officer heard that I had a passport, he promptly gave me a single ticket instead of the return.

Everything went smoothly, though there was some grumbling from one member of the group in my charge, who thought, with some reason, that he should have been made responsible, since he was already a veteran of the Spanish War. Captured by Franco troops at Jarama in February 1937, he had spent a terrible year in fascist prisons before being repatriated under a prisoner exchange agreement negotiated by the British Government. Now he was hurrying back 'to have another bash at Franco', though he was certain to be shot if captured a second time.

In Paris, where volunteers from all parts of the world were assembled for onward transport, we were given a medical examination, and subjected to several more anti-pep-talks or dissuasive lectures, with the general tenor that service in Spain was rough and tough, and if we wanted to back out we still could. The aim of the dissuasion technique, and accompanying individual interviews, was obviously to screen out the adventurers, the immature, the unstable and, if possible, spies of various sorts. In fact, remarkably few people in these categories reached Spain, though, according to what should perhaps be classified as 'reliable rumour', the Czech authorities managed to infiltrate several officers as informers. In at least two cases, so the rumours go, these 'spies' espoused the Republican cause with enthusiasm when they got to Spain, and gave valuable aid.

The French stage of the underground network functioned smoothly. Night train to Béziers, a little town in south-western France, with volunteers reporting in very small groups to memorised addresses, mainly small cafés and hotels. Then a night ride by lorry to an isolated farmhouse high in the Pyrenees, followed one night later by a gruelling eight hour march over smugglers' paths, some of it above the snow-line – though it was September. Then a train ride halfway across Republican Spain to the base of the International Brigades at Albacete, where our batch of two hundred volunteers from all parts of the world was sorted into language groups, and sent off for training to small villages scattered round Albacete.

By late summer 1937 when I arrived the main body of the foreign volunteers was organised in five brigades. Since even some of the standard histories of the International Brigades make a hash of this detail, it may be worth noting the line-up. The brigades were arranged on the basis of language as far as possible, though it was obviously difficult to fit in small groups such as the thirty Albanians. These groupings were:

11th Brigade: German-speaking.
12th Brigade: Italian-speaking.
13th Brigade: Slav languages (Czech, Polish, Bulgarian and the Yugoslav languages).
14th Brigade: French-speaking.
15th Brigade: English-speaking.

In September 1937 the training base of the 15th Brigade, consisting of the British Battalion, the Lincoln-Washington Battalion (US) and the Mackenzie-Papineau Battalion (Canadian), was situated at Tarazona, some twenty miles from Albacete. I arrived there with about fifteen other new British recruits, and we were immediately put through a crash course, for reinforcements were urgently needed for the battalions at the front. I was appointed acting unpaid corporal for the new British group, on the flimsy grounds of my military experience.

'March your squad down to the armoury, draw as many rifles as they'll give you and teach them anything you know,' said a very smartly turned-out soldier with a silver bar on his shoulder – a lieutenant. 'The rifles here at base are a load of junk; anything that fires is up at the front. But maybe you can show your boys how to point them roughly in the direction of the enemy. Just teach them anything you can, man.'

The smart lieutenant was a young American Negro, and my impression was confirmed that I had come to the right place. Back in Albacete I had seen that units of the International Brigades marched to the music of revolutionary songs, and saluted with the clenched fist. But a black officer giving orders to white soldiers – a mixed bag of Scots, English and Welsh workers, plus one Yeshiva student from Whitechapel and a middle-class semi-journalist – that was solid proof that this really was a new-style army in which all men really were brothers. The incident may seem trivial in the 1980s: in the 1930s it was sensational.

This book is not intended to be an account of the Spanish War. There are already hundreds, if not thousands, of volumes on the subject. I shall confine myself to a few odd sidelights, which other authors appear to have overlooked, throwing in a couple of episodes which I recalled in fictionalised form at later dates.

The British Battalion of the International Brigades was undoubtedly composed of English, Scots and Welsh volunteer soldiers, with a very useful addition of Irish, often men with IRA weapons training or experience, though some intransigent Irish patriots could not stomach belonging to anything 'British' and joined the American Battalion. However, it had notable differences to any other body of British troops in recent times. Most of the members were markedly literate, though the proportion of 'intellectuals' was far lower than legend has it. The legend arose, of course, because the intellectuals tended to go home and write about it.

And the average Brigadier was far more highly motivated than the average soldier in a 'normal' army. In extreme situations, and the Spanish War provided such situations practically every hour on the hour, he really was ready to lay down his life, because he sincerely felt he was fighting – and quite probably dying – for a better world, or at the very least to prevent the world from becoming even more beastly.

Yet despite the differences, certain British military traditions – or perhaps just British traditions – persisted in the Battalion. One of these traditions caused excessive concern to the more seriously minded volunteers from other countries. This was the curious British habit of taking the piss, in a friendly way, out of hallowed symbols and slogans, patriotic or political.

It is, of course, something which the British have been doing for a very long time. It is my guess that even Cromwell's highly motivated Ironsides sang songs about Cromwell's wart and parodied their uplifting hymns; and certainly in the two world wars some of the most popular soldiers' songs were, to the ears of those of other nations, surprisingly defeatist. 'Oh, my, I don't want to die, I want to go home' is a marked example, and we sang this in Spain too. When we marched (or more often shambled, for most of us wore rope-soled sneakers for lack of better footwear) along the dusty cart-tracks of Spain, we as often as not intoned a dirge about being Fred Karno's army, or proclaiming we would rather hang around Piccadilly Underground.

Serious German political commissars and Soviet advisers inevitably assumed that the Battalion was in a state of semi-mutiny, and would make urgent representations to our political commissars. The political commissars ('comic stars' was the usual Brigade term) often did not fully grasp what the complaints were about – they often led the singing themselves. But as disciplined anti-fascists they felt that these steeled revolutionaries from other lands probably knew what they were talking about, and word was passed round that we should lay off.

The matter came to a head when some poet in the ranks deliberately mangled the chorus of a very popular topical march, based on an old revolutionary song from central Europe. The original English text went like this:

> For we shall Franco's ranks demolish,
> The great Miaja leads us on;
> For on our rifles depends our freedom,
> *No pasarán, no pasarán!*

In the amended version from the ranks the two last lines were changed to:

> For on our rifles we hang our washing,
> No bastard ran, no bastard ran.

Once again the protests poured in. The new text was unpolitical, anarchist, stupid and a direct insult to the Spanish Republican leaders who had coined the slogan 'No pasarán!' – 'They shall not pass!'

So again word was passed down that only the authorised version was authorised. For a few days discipline prevailed over inclination, and on the march our rifles upheld our freedom. But anarchic tendencies soon raised their ugly heads again, and singing commissars clinging to the official text were hopeless outsung by soldiers who were prepared to die for the Republic, but liked 'no bastard ran' better.

This may be the right place to recall what could well be the daftest revolutionary song of the present or any other century. Inexplicably popular on left-wing demonstrations in Britain in the 1930s was a Soviet chant, 'The Song of the Red Air Fleet', with the following chorus:

> Fly higher, and higher, and higher,
> Our emblem the Soviet star;
> And every propeller is roaring 'Red Front'
> Defending the USSR.

Though this song had been rather out of place in a demonstration against the Means Test in Deptford, it did seem to fit better at the front in Spain, where at some periods Soviets fighters swept the skies clear of German and Italian planes flying for Franco. However, it was probably only in Spain that most of us became acutely aware of the inanity or even insanity of the second verse, which deserves quotation in full:

> But for the wage slaves,
> And toiling masses,
> A song of hope in our propellers whirled;
> We drop them leaflets
> While we bomb their bosses,
> We are the first Red Air Fleet in the world.

I have been unable to ascertain whether the Russian original is quite as silly.

None of the many books on the war I have read throws any light on a very minor mystery: why the British Battalion never had a special name. Every other battalion, and even some individual companies, had a resounding revolutionary name: Commune de Paris, Garibaldi, Dimitrov and so on. In the 15th Brigade the Canadians had their Mackenzie-Papineau Battalion, named after two historic Canadian rebels, and the US volunteers for a short time had two battalions, named after Washington and Lincoln, and later consolidated as the Lincoln-Washington Battalion.

Even quite serious books on the Spanish War insist on a curious legend that the whole 15th Brigade was called the Abraham Lincoln Brigade, but such a unit never existed except in the writings of busy fund-raisers back in the States. I have a private theory that this phantom came into existence because the copywriter could not remember how many 't's there are in 'battalion'. There is a little-known historical precedent for this. Karl Marx's handwritten English-language manuscript of *The Civil War in France* shows that he had just the same trouble. He first wrote 'bataillon' (the French and German spelling), scratched it out and tried again, and then very sensibly gave up and wrote 'regiment'.

For some unexplained reason, then, the British Battalion had no 'name of honour'. No. 1 Company, in which I did most of my service, was called the 'Major Attlee Company' after the Labour Party leader, but the Battalion itself was simply 'British'. For a very short period after its formation in early 1937, it bore the name 'Saklatvala', after the Indian revolutionary who was rather remarkably Britain's first Communist MP in 1923; but this was soon quietly dropped, possibly because it was regarded as too obscure or too sectarian.

I recall raising the subject of a battalion name, together with several other soldiers, in a quiet period out of the line in July 1938, just before the great Ebro offensive. We bandied around suggestions for a while. 'Oliver Cromwell' seemed a good solid name to many of us, but our company commander, an old IRA man, turned it down flat with a heated speech about what Cromwell had done to Ireland. Other names surfaced: 'Winstanley', the famous Leveller leader under Cromwell; 'Tom Paine'; or 'Harry Pollitt', then head of the British Communist Party – but no consensus was reached. When a humorist suggested 'Fred Karno' the meeting under the hazelnut trees broke up in disorder, and a few days later we had no time to worry about names.

13

Factual Fiction

There may be some literary convention which lays down that auto-biographies which try to stake some sort of claim to historical accuracy should not be cluttered up with works of fiction. Even so, I cannot hope to offer any better account of what things were like as a front-line soldier in the closing months of the Spanish War than two short stories I wrote on the subject, one in 1942, when things were still fresh in my mind, and the other nearly forty years later. Both are autobiographical, and stick close to actual events.

Almond Blossoms

When death and horror are a daily accompaniment of life, they grow much too big to be comprehended. It is then that you begin to revolt against the little horrors which you can grasp, for the huge things which surround you are too large to hate. That was why the rape of the almond trees had hurt Slim so.

The battalion was lying in support positions, just north of the river, slowly growing together again after the long retreat. Ten days earlier they had streamed back over the mountains and down to the river. Now they were across, and somehow, miraculously, the enemy had been halted. Fresh troops were coming up, but as always they were woefully inadequate, and their arrival had only meant that the battalion was in reserve positions just behind the front, and not actually on it.

Each night they stumbled out of the creek which through the long hot days gave some shade, and some protection from the enemy flyers, and dug trenches to repel the enemy attack which was sure to come. They were digging through groves of almond trees, covered with blossom, and even in the night they could see the luminous pale blossom above their heads. But as the trench extended to a place where it was in full view of the enemy, lurking across the river, it was plain that the fresh coffee-like earth would be only too visible to them. There was only one camouflage: branches from the trees. As they worked they tore the branches from the living wood, and flung them, jaunty in their fresh pink and green, on to the parapet. Trees which had been growing and producing for generations, torn down to give protection for a few days, until they faded.

Even as he tore and twisted the branches, Slim could feel a pain, a physical ache, at the wanton senseless destruction. He wanted to stop, but he went on hacking and pulling, for that is war.

One morning, as they were lying in the dry creek, trying to ease their aching muscles on the shingle of the river bed, a soldier from the front line walked in, half leading, half carrying a figure more scarecrow than man. One of their own men, cut off from his comrades in the retreat, he had wandered through the hills in enemy territory with one companion, made his way to the river, swum across in the night, and been picked up just before dawn, lying insensible on the bank. As Slim tried to make him drink some coffee, he began to talk. Not deliriously, but quickly and intently, as a man speaks when he is using all his little remaining strength to say something which must be said. He spoke of his journey – fifteen days of hiding, like hunted beasts, as soldiers scoured the hills, looking for fugitives like them. Fifteen days of privation, as they lived on the green olives they could pick from the trees, and the odd scraps which litter the path of a retreating army. Finally they had reached the bank of the river, with only the strength to crawl. Then, with freedom in sight, his friend had been too weak to cross the river. The scarecrow turned his deep burning eyes on Slim, and said, 'I hid Adam in a bed of rushes, fifty metres upstream from the green boat which is standing by the river. I promised I would go back for him tonight.' Then his head fell sideways on his shoulder, and he was still. Early that night before the moon rose, Slim made his way to the front line and went with three men, from the company who were holding positions there, down to the spot on the river bank where they had found the scarecrow. Quickly he undressed, and slid quietly into the icy hurrying water. Striking against the current he began to cross. Before he had gone far, his knees touched bottom, and he found he was on a sand bar in mid-stream with too little water to swim. He waded forward, bent double, and feeling that his white gleaming body must be visible for miles. Then into deep water again, swimming softly now, for he was near the enemy bank.

Crawling on to the bank, he lay for a moment panting, then crept to the black bulk which was his landmark, the boat. As he reached the edge of the clump of reeds, he saw that the moon was rising, casting weird shadows on the cold white sand. Into the reeds he went, calling in a whispered shout,

'Adam! Adam! Your friend sent me. Adam, where are you?' but there was no answer.

A sudden scurry of rifle shots down stream. Who were they shooting at? He lay pressed close to the sand and could hear his own breath as it whistled in gasps. Then he heard a clinking of bridles, and soft hoof beats on the sand. An enemy patrol. The moon was shining brighter than it had before, and the rushes among which he lay grew thinner and thinner, and less and less of a hiding place. The cavalry patrol rode nearer, Slim was filled with coldness. A frigid clamminess spread inside him, his naked limbs were burnt by the icy sand on which he lay, and the moon touched his wet glistening body with fingers of frost. Incongruously enough, a large part of his terror was the fear at the idea of being made a prisoner while he was naked. The idea seemed so ridiculous. Seconds lasted for hours as the patrol rode nearer, till they were on top of him, and peering through the rushes he could see the hooves of four horses.

They passed. For another century Slim lay still, as the cold, physical only now, bit deeper and deeper. He tried to move, and for one terrible moment he felt that he was frozen in position, spreadeagled face downwards on the sand. Then the blood began to run again, and he could move. He would never be able to find Adam now. Probably he was dead already, and even if he found him still alive, he would never be able to carry him across the river. He wondered if he would even be able to bring himself across, paralysed as he was with cold and fear. He slipped again into the water, and found its touch almost warm.

Swimming slowly to conserve his strength, he struck out. As he reached the sand bar, he heard the whoosh of a bullet hitting the water beside him and fell on his face in the shallow water., Other rifles crackled as enemy riflemen spotted his white body while he stumbled drunkenly through the shallows and into deep water again.

Once before he reached the bank he thought that the current would sweep him away, but he made it and friendly hands were waiting to drag him from the water and under cover.

He had failed. He had come back alone. But somehow, Slim always feels that he has made amends for the rape of the almond trees.

Mirror Man

For the first time in weeks he was alone, and frightened. This was a different sort of fear. All of them were afraid – of sudden death, a hideous wound, slow torture and above all, perhaps, of showing fear.

But to these routine fears was now added fear of loneliness in an unknown forest which could hide men with guns waiting to kill him. Perhaps like the childhood fear of a wolf, but he had always known with part of his mind that the wolf was just something out of a story book.

Today the wolf was real; any second a bullet could blot him out. That he could face, he thought, but if he was only wounded he would lie there in pain, with nobody to put a merciful bullet through his head as he had done for a friend a few days back. Nobody would know he was dead; his comrades might even think he had gone on the run.

The battle had lasted for ever. Apart from their fear they had their weariness, hunger, thirst, filth. Nobody had spoken for weeks of their ideals, their noble aims. They had a job to do – to kill the enemy – and they were doing it with full determination.

Just a few minutes ago the sergeant in command of their dwindling, ragged, starving company had called him over. The sergeant, because all officers had long been dead: 'first in attack, last in retreat' the book had said. The sergeant suggested – orders had gone out of fashion in their small half-dead community – that he might make a one-man probe on the left flank. 'I've no idea what is over there,' he said. 'Perhaps there's some of ours in the forest; perhaps the others. Try to find out.'

So now he was a lone scout. Big stuff on the screen, not such fun when it's you. If he stumbled on the enemy, they would get him if they saw him first; and one of his own side might shoot him first and ask questions later.

He carried his rifle on the ready, finger on the trigger, a round up the spout. For a city boy he moved skilfully through the trees. Darwin's survival of the fittest, he thought vaguely. Those of the company who had not adapted swiftly to playing Indian in earnest had been the first to go.

Before he could pursue the thought – bone-weariness seemed to slow the brain – he noticed that the trees were thinning, and he slowed to a creep. Had he been fighting this war according to the book he would have dropped to the ground and entered the clearing on his elbows, but they had thrown away the book ages ago, and he kept on going.

Suddenly the trees ended and he was out in the burning sun, and saw he was not alone. Twenty yards away, on the other side of the narrow clearing, a man faced him. For a moment the lone scout felt like laughing; it was like turning a corner and facing yourself in a mirror. The other man stood still, frozen by shock; his uniform too was stained and ragged, and he held his rifle at the ready, finger on the trigger.

For a short eternity they just stood, nothing moving but their eyes. Just like a corny western when the sheriff faces the bad man, the scout thought.

There had never been much difference between the uniforms of the two sides, and in the long-drawn agony of battle such differences had practically disappeared.

Both of them must be thinking the same; friend or enemy? But both of them were clothed in rags; any insignia which had once marked their sweat-sodden caps had long been lost.

Then the scout recalled he was wearing abandoned trousers he had picked up in an overrun enemy camp, in bad shape but better than his own. And they were easy to identify, for they buttoned at the ankle. If the mirror-man was a friend he would be drawing his conclusions, bracing his muscles to fire first; if he was a foe he might miss the significance of the button; or he might be a deserter, no matter from which side, just aimlessly running away and ready to kill somebody who might try to take him in.

The permutations were endless. He did not know and could not guess, and the man across the clearing would be in the same fix.

There was only one thing to do; the scout must shoot first. Not just for the sake of survival, but for the sake of the men of his company, the men he knew and loved – yes, loved, because for weeks, for ever, they had been his only reference point, the only family he had.

But as he thought, he realised it was a rationalisation. If he raised his gun and fired he would do it simply because he did not want to die, though there did not seem to be much future in surviving.

Then, not suddenly but very slowly, the lips of the mirror-man bent into what might have been a crooked smile. His eyes locked with those of the scout, he slowly, very slowly, lifted his finger from the trigger, stretched it so that the scout could not miss the movement. In slow motion he bent his knees and laid his rifle on the ground, slowly and ceremoniously as one might lay a tiny baby in its cradle.

For a fraction of a second, as the other began to smile, the scout felt his trigger-finger brace, ready for the shoot-out; but the mirror-effect took over, and they pantomimed, unrehearsed, the same slow gestures of disarmament. An observer in the clearing would not have been able to tell who initiated it.

Inch by inch, like hunters avoiding all sharp movement which might scare the game, the two men straightened up, and when they were erect again they both made the same gesture, turning their hands forward to display empty palms.

Perhaps we shall now stand here till we drop, the scout thought; then he saw with relief that the mirror-man had raised one foot and was stepping forward.

They advanced towards each other like wary wrestlers. The scout felt an impulse to slow down, for then he would be nearer his gun. But the other trusted him – did he? – and forgotten conventions of honour and fair play – cowboy films again? – took over, and he matched the other step for step.

A pace or two apart they halted. The other raised his hand and fumbled in the pocket of his filthy shirt. A knife, perhaps. But the hand emerged holding two bent and mangled cigarettes, one of which he held out wordlessly.

They stood and smoked in silence. The sun beat down; their tense

84

muscles relaxed; finally they sat facing one another. In the distance they could hear the plop and splutter of rifle and machine-gun fire.

After a few puffs the scout nipped out his cigarette and stowed the butt, and the mirror-man did the same. The scout had nothing to offer but a little muddy brackish water in his canteen. The other drank, but only one careful mouthful, handing back the flask with a scarcely perceptible gesture of thanks.

And during this age-old ritual exchange of gifts the two men sat peacefully, too weary and too ever-frightened to try to analyse who was a friend to be helped or a foe to be killed. Finally they were both lying on the ground, limbs collapsed in exhaustion, drifting abruptly into deep unconsciousness.

One hour or two: then a random shell crumped dully near the clearing. As on a signal, the two men staggered to their feet, somehow embarrassed that the other was there, and stumbled back across the clearing to their rifles.

The truce was over, and once again they stood, half shaded by the trees, finger on the trigger.

For the last time, the mirror-effect took over, and simultaneously they stepped backwards into the shelter of the trees. And as the other faded from sight, the scout saw him take his finger from the trigger and slowly raise his hand in a gesture of greeting and farewell.

The battle continued.

The first story, 'Almond Blossoms', was published in *Citadel* in Cairo in January 1943. *Citadel* was an interesting literary magazine apparently sponsored by the British military authorities and circulating mainly in the Eighth Army in North Africa. The editor – or one of the editors – was John Willott, later noted as a writer on theatre with Bertolt Brecht as one of his main subjects. In making the story vague as to time and place I was presumably still worried that identification with Spain might make the editors shy away from 'premature anti-fascism'.

The story is strictly factual in most details, but I should fill in a few gaps. The events took place in mid-April 1938. In the preceding weeks a large part of the Republican army had been routed by Franco's troops, and thrown back into Catalonia north of the Ebro River. Now the shattered remnants of the Republican divisions were fortifying the north bank of the river, and stragglers from their ranks were still filtering through after hiding out behind the fascist lines. The exhausted escaper described in the story was brought into our reserve lines early one morning by soldiers of the Spanish anarchist unit stationed directly on the river bank a couple of hundred yards ahead of our positions. He was a German anti-fascist, and since I was the only German-speaker available I was the one to hear his story. He did not in fact die, but gasped out his tale as I escorted him on mule-back to brigade HQ, and I promised him I would personally try to bring his comrade over that night.

The second story, 'Mirror Man', was written much later, in 1980, and published in a shorter form in *Broadsheet*, the quarterly journal of English PEN, in its spring 1981 issue. It is placed in the fierce fighting in September 1938, when Republican troops had successfully recrossed the Ebro, but were unable to withstand Franco's arms superiority. This battle was the last action of the International Brigades.

14

Letters Home

It was only after completing the manuscript of this book that I discovered that many of the letters which I had written home from Spain had not been lost or destroyed. When I came to examine the letters, almost all scribbled in pencil on odd pieces of paper, it seemed to me that they constituted one of the very few primary sources revealing what I had thought, or at least what I had written, fifty years ago. They are certainly not great literature or rousing political essays, but they are genuine. In reading these letters today it must be remembered that I was writing under strict wartime censorship, and that I was constantly anxious to reassure my parents that I was well, or, in those periods when I was sick or wounded, that I was well looked after and getting better. Almost all the letters were addressed to my mother, a few to other members of the family.

The first letter, tantalisingly undated, names my location rather melodramatically as 'Somewhere in France':

Dear Mother,
I am not returning to Prague but going to Spain to do what I think is the right thing. I know that you and father do not agree with me on this, but I regard the fight in Spain as vital for the whole future of civilisation. Please don't worry about me. It is very interesting here. About 18 different nationalities represented. As a matter of fact I have just been interrupted by a Frenchman speaking only French, who asked me to translate for him into German for a Bulgarian who would translate into Roumanian. The Roumanian was the man he wanted to get at. Excuse the paper, but it is a part of the tablecloth. I'll let you know as soon as I have an address.

The next letter gives my address as 'SRI, Plaza del Altazona, Albacete, Spain'. Albacete was the base of the International Brigades, and all mail from abroad had to be addressed there for censorship and onward dispatch. Mail home from the volunteers was collected in Albacete and dispatched unfranked in sacks to Paris, where it was finally mailed. This awkward procedure was intended to protect relatives in the fascist or semi-fascist countries of Europe from reprisals by their authorities. My letter is dated 29 September 1937, and was obviously written from Tarazona:

Dear Mother,
I am sorry I haven't written before, but it has been quite impossible. I have arrived here quite safely, and everything here is o.k. I expect I shall be staying here for quite a time before moving on . . . We are having wonderful weather, and as it is fairly late in the year it is not too hot. The food is as good as one could expect in a country at war, and there are unlimited quantities of superb grapes. Apart from the fact that Spanish cigarettes are pretty vile, they are so scarce that you can't buy them at most places.
    The contrast between this army and the British Army is astonishing. The officers are real comrades of the men, and although discipline, on a self-imposed basis, is not as good as it should be, people who have been here a long time say that things have improved colossally in that respect. Letters take about four or five days, so you can't expect an answer too soon . . . I must stop now because we have to go on parade in a moment.

The next letter, dated 22 October, was received in London on 9 November, so my information about the time taken was badly out. Later in the war letters in both directions sometimes took months to reach their destination. This one is scrawled in a letter-card in faint pencil and is only partly legible:

I am terribly sorry I haven't written for so long, but I have been lying peacefully on my back with pleurisy. I still have quite a lot of waiting coming, I guess, before I am really fit again. At first I was in a little hospital with about ten beds of wood which were not exactly comfortable . . . I got eggs and milk galore, which was wonderful. After 13 days I was loaded into an ambulance, and taken on the worst two-hour journey I ever had . . . Finally we arrived at this hospital which has spring beds, trained nurses and so on, but as it is in a large town it is difficult to get special food. Most of the staff seem to be German anti-fascists, which is very useful for me. The time doesn't pass very quickly because my breath is too short to talk for long . . .

The following letter, dispatched on 12 November, had obviously been written in fits and starts over the previous days.

I am still lying on my back, but I hope to get up fairly soon; I expect to be sent to a convalescent home at the seaside as soon as I can travel . . . People are pretty good to me here. There is a typical little Frenchman sleeping in the bed opposite to mine who seems to have appointed himself my official keeper. For instance this morning at about half past five he saw I was struggling with my bed clothes, so he sprang from his bed and made my bed for me. In this ward now there is an American called Raven, who lost both his eyes and one foot, and the other foot severely injured . . . Now he sits here perfectly cheerful, playing a cello of all things . . . I had to break off the letter as my temperature suddenly shot right up again. Now it is five days later and it is getting more normal again. As a special favour now I am getting condensed milk in tea to drink. Not just a drop but really a lot; it seems like real nectar . . .

I don't think I mentioned it before, but if you had seen the masses of refugees in Valencia station, you would agitate for the Friends' Relief to receive more help from England. Can't you bring it up in Sunday meeting or the Meeting for Sufferings? Especially the children need help . . . I don't know how much the Quakers are doing to help here now, but there is scope for any amount of work, especially among the children . . .

A letter from hospital on 13 December 1937:

My hopes that I was finished with my lungs and only needed to get fat again are blasted today. After hanging around normal for nearly three weeks, my temperature has buzzed up to 102, and the doctor says, with a manner sweet and calm, another little bout will not do you any harm . . . It only means that my recovery is held up for a week or so . . . When I look around in the hospital I am amazed what a human can stand without grumbling. Next to me in bed is a French comrade. He was wounded twelve months [six lines were censored here] . . . Things have improved enormously since then, but the need for medical supplies is still colossal. I have absolutely no complaints about the treatment I am getting. It is the best possible under the circumstances . . .

One piece of treatment I had received was unorthodox but, I feel, effective. When I was at a low point, and moaning that I would never get better, one of the doctors, a Jewish volunteer from Vienna, decided on shock treatment. On his daily rounds he stopped for a moment at my bed and said, 'What, are you still alive? Don't you realise we need your bed for the wounded?' His callousness made me so furious that I took a sharp turn for the better.

My next letter was written on Christmas Day 1937:

> Somewhere the hospital has dug up some eggs, and I am getting one nearly every day, and I am now definitely gaining weight. What is sending me crazy is that every time I think that I am getting near to being sent to a convalescent home I start a new fever. When I start to pity myself I have to think of others I know who are living in the trenches with little protection against snow or rain . . .
>
> Our capture of Teruel has been another excitement. Everybody feels it is the turning point in the war, and will have consequences far beyond the capture of a comparatively small town . . .

On 6 January 1938 I was finally able to write from that convalescent home I had been longing to reach:

> I went to the station at an unearthly hour in the middle of the night, only to find that my travel papers had not come through, so I had to go back to the hospital for one more day. It was snowing heavily at the time, and when I finally left there was nearly a foot of snow. I had very good luck in the train to Valencia – a first-class carriage, with glass in all the windows, and all the cushions on the seats, something unusual here today. Wonder of wonder, there was a buffet car on the train where we got a hot strong coffee and good meat sandwiches . . . In Valencia between trains I went to a news cinema and saw a series of Mickey Mouse films . . . In the evening I went on down the coast some hours ride to the place I am staying now. The train was crammed full and I had to stand, but after a few minutes an old peasant noticed I didn't look very happy, and when I explained I was just out of hospital he gave me his seat. Not only that, but he explained to all the others on the seat that I wasn't well, and they all got up so I could lie down. Then they all insisted I must eat something, and gave me bread, fish and wine.
>
> Early in the morning – in the middle of the night really – I arrived at the convalescent home amidst orange groves on the shores of the sunny Mediterranean. Several inches of snow on the ground, and an icy wind blowing. It is the first snow they have had for seven years, but that isn't very helpful . . . Everyone says it will soon be warm again: I hope so.
>
> We have a group of villas which used to belong to rich people who have left the country or been arrested, and they are rather fine, though built in the most abominable style. The artistic appreciation of the Spanish bourgeois must have been nil. Their great disadvantage at the moment is that they are summer villas, and have no heating facilities . . .
>
> There is one disadvantage to this place. As you know, the Fascists are trying to blockade the coast here, to prevent us getting food and materials

from outside. And they have the pleasant habit of bombarding the coastal towns, presumably to terrorise the civilian population and to scare off ships which might try to run the blockade. The town here has been shelled a number of times, and yesterday we could hear the booming of artillery up the coast. There is no danger here as we are well outside the town . . . There is no possible military objective here, it is sheer terrorism. The only result of one of the bombardments a little while ago was to kill a mother and her four children . . .

The town was Denia, halfway between Valencia and Alicante. For some reason, probably to avoid censor trouble, I failed to mention that when our train drew into Denia station at about midnight on 2 January 1938 we had immediately to take cover in snow-filled ditches, because a German warship was shelling the town. It was the first time I was under fire.

My letter dated 6 February came from Tarazona, the base for English-speaking volunteers, though I could not mention this:

I have just got back to work, and for the next few weeks I expect to be working on the Cultural Commission, which means mostly helping to run the duplicated news bulletin, wall newspaper and so on. Could you possibly sent me a copy of 'World Radio', as part of our work is to listen to news bulletins, and it is difficult to find out when all the different stations give the news . . .

A letter dated 27 February announced that I had been transferred to Albacete (though I could not mention the place-name) and was working in the central post office of the International Brigades:

My work is quite interesting, and I have an impetus, when I think of the way some of my letters have been held up, not to let it happen to other people. There is a pretty big job here sending out the mail, as people keep moving around a lot . . . We have [one line censored] . . . and every day the addresses of hundreds of cards have to be changed, but the complication is the names. First there is the mixture of nationalities to consider – names like Wyzesowski are a commonplace – and the fact that nobody can ever spell a foreigner's name right. If a list comes from a hospital of the men there, it is a safe bet that half the names are not spelled exactly right, and a good number incredibly wrong . . .

By the time I wrote my letter dated 31 March the military situation of the Republic had become grave. Franco's forces, with massive Italian reinforcement, had broken through the Republican lines on the Aragon front and were driving for the Mediterranean to cut the Republican area in two. In the course of the drive the British Battalion had been almost wiped out as a fighting force:

> I left the post office a few days ago, so I don't expect I shall get mail quite so regularly now . . . I am back at the training base now, and with the great drive for reinforcements which is being conducted just now I expect it is not long before I shall be sent up. Everybody seems to have realised how serious the position is, and thousands of people who have been working in the rearguard after being wounded or sick are volunteering to go back to the front again. At the moment I write the advance on the Aragon front appears to have been stopped, but with fresh supplies for Franco coming in all the time he may try to break through any time . . .

A few days later, Franco's forces did break through to the Mediterranean, cutting Catalonia, in the north, off from the main body of the Republic. Before this happened, the mass of International Brigaders in the southern zone had been evacuated to the north. I was one of them, and my next letter, dated 12 April 1938, came from Catalonia where I had now finally joined the remnants of the British Battalion:

> I never thought I would become a cave dweller, but now I am one. We are lying at rest in a reserve position near enough to the front to hear the rumble of guns, and as it gets rather cold at night most of us have cut out caves in the side of the hill and made quite decent dug-outs. At the moment of writing things are pretty good for us – plenty of cigarettes, good food, magnificent scenery (if anyone is interested), and so on. But nobody knows how long this will last. The last letter I got was dated March 18, but naturally everything has been disarranged by Franco's drive, so letters may be more delayed . . .

Mail was in fact wildly disorganised by the military situation. The two previous letters both took over five weeks to reach London. My next letter, dated 14 April, reached my parents in a record six days, since it was taken back, together with letters from the whole Battalion, by Harry Pollitt, secretary of the British Communist Party, who had paid a short visit to see how the British Battalion was recovering from the terrible losses of the great retreat:

> As I expect this note will reach you more quickly than usual, I am just writing a line or two to let you know I am alive and scratching – due to lice. I don't suppose Keatings is any good against them, but you might put a tin into any further parcel you send. We are lying in a reserve position just behind the lines, but nothing is happening at the moment. A few shells

scream overhead, but otherwise all is quiet. If there are any pictures in the Daily Worker or elsewhere of Harry Pollitt's visit to Spain, you may be able to make me out. I am wearing a black chauffeur's cap.

My next letter dated 23 July was written on the eve of going into combat in the offensive on the Ebro, probably the most audacious, and certainly the most costly, Republican operation of the whole war:

I suppose at any time now we may be leaving the training here to go into action – we have been in reserve for a long time. If we go in it will have to be decisive. The war cannot drag on indefinitely, and the rebel drive against Valencia will have to be stopped. They are only making progress at a terrific loss, but they are advancing all the same. I am receiving the 'Prager Tagblatt' by post regularly every day now, from a friend in Prague, and it is encouraging to read there the 'Times' article on two years of war in Spain. Their correspondent does not seem at all inclined to give Franco much chance of an early victory, and I don't think the 'Times' is exactly in favour of 'Red' Spain . . .

My next letter, dated 1 August, has a familiar ring: I was back in hospital. We had crossed the Ebro, and advanced deep into Franco-held territory, and after a few days I was wounded:

I am writing this letter on International Anti-War Day, though at first sight there doesn't seem to be much Anti-War to celebrate. Still, right or wrong, we believe that we are fighting here in a positive way against future and even more terrible wars which the victory of fascism would inevitably bring.

I expect that you have read about the crossing of the Ebro and the advance we have made. In the course of the third or fourth day, I am not sure which, I managed to run my leg against a bullet. It skidded round everything important, and just made a neat little hole in the flesh. As I was sliding down the hill to the dressing station, a shell dropped quite near and a small fragment made a neat crease across the other side of the same leg. So now I am living in luxury, in a huge building that used to be a college, lying, incredible though it seems, in a bed with springs, with white sheets on it, eating well-cooked food off plates sitting up at a table, and washing with water out of a tap. It is a good many months since I had all this. I can walk quite easily, though slowly. I don't expect I shall be here very long, as my pin-pricks will soon be healed . . .

By 6 September I was back at the front:

I am back with the battalion now, and feeling all the better for the five weeks holiday from camping out in the rather crude form which we practise here. At the moment we are in reserve, doing nothing but listen to the shells buzzing overhead in an artillery duel which is going on. As a matter of fact, the noise they make reminds me of the little cars on overhead wires which they used to have in the Penge Co-op running to the cash desk. There are lots of planes of all sorts wandering round the sky, doing nothing in particular except make it awkward for us to walk about . . . I believe just as much as ever in what we are fighting for, but the foulness of war makes me all the more determined to do everything to stop another one breaking out, or rather an extension of the present one.

My last letter from the front, dated 23 September 1938, amazes me when I read it today, for this calm and chatty letter must have been written in the midst of one of the most bloody days of combat in the whole Spanish War:

Pardon the writing, but I am sitting rather cramped up in a little trench to be out of harm's way. There are shells bursting every few seconds on my right, but about 60 yards away, so the only danger is flying fragments and stones thrown up by the explosion. They have been bursting all day, but never nearer than 30 or 40 yards, so I think where I am must be protected by a bit of a hill. Incidentally it is surprising the number of shells or bombs that have to be used to do much. They plough up the ground, but if you are in a bit of a trench, it is practically impossible to be hit. During the past few days the Fascists have been including leaflets in the ordinary diet of bombing and strafing, but most of the stuff has been merely puerile.

There is some prospect of getting taken out of the line on rest now. I hope it comes off, everybody is a bit on edge now from the constant bombing and shelling.

The letter ends with a short PS dated 24 September: 'We have been withdrawn for rest now. No more. I must sleep.'

All of us were certainly more than 'a bit on edge' as I stated in my letter. What I failed to mention in the letter was that before we went into battle on that terrible day we had been informed that the Republican Government had decided to repatriate all members of the International Brigades immediately. I probably omitted the news because I, like most others, did not really believe it. To indicate the ferocity of the fighting, here are two sentences from the official history of the British volunteers: 'When the battalion moved up on the night of September 22 its strength was 377, of whom 106 were British. When it withdrew on the night of the 24th it was 173 strong of whom 58 were British.'

94

A letter dated 28 September:

Amidst all the rush of crisis news I expect you have seen the news of Premier Negrin's speech at Geneva. Now Spain feels itself strong enough to fight on without us, and wants to remove any possible cause for a worsening of the international situation, so we are to be sent home. It would be silly to say that we do not want to go home – anybody would want to get away from a war – but at the same time it is a pity to have to go away before the final victory is ours and before we have avenged our dead.

We are out of the line now, some way behind the front, waiting for repatriation to be arranged. It will probably be some time before we are home – I have no idea whether it will be a matter of weeks or months.

We are living in a church in a small village, and at the moment it is pouring with rain. It is unpleasant, but we think of those at the front who will be blessing this rain which grounds the Fascist aviation and bogs down their tanks and artillery. I don't think any of us who come back will ever forget the Spaniards who will continue the fight when we are safely at home (always providing there is not a general conflagration), and until this struggle against Fascism is finally won, none of us will be able to rest.

The references in this letter to 'crisis news' and 'general conflagration' refer to the crisis about Czechoslovakia, which reached its high point in September 1938. Hitler was claiming large areas of Czechoslovakia, and threatening to take them by force. Britain and France were preparing to appease Hitler and give him what he wanted.

A letter dated 7 October:

Three days ago, a parcel rolled up for me – it was one you sent in April – the 20th century age of speed. Everything was in pretty good condition, though a little battered, and quite a number of us enjoyed the contents, especially the Keatings powder, since the straw we are sleeping on is pretty full of fleas.

At first, people here simply could not credit the betrayal of Czechslovakia by Chamberlain. Although the British Government only followed the same road of concession to fascism which they have been following for years, people had a hope that someone would wake up before it was too late. War has been postponed, but nobody can possibly believe that Hitler will rest content with the Sudeten German areas, when apparently he can have anything for the threatening – as long as it isn't 'our Empire'.

I wish I had been there to witness the change of Czechoslovakia from a proud, free, advanced state into a vassal country with about the importance of Latvia. It makes me sick to be an Englishman, and proud to think that I have at least tried to do my best till now in fighting Fascism.

One thing that cheered me up was the fact that I saw a letter in the 'News

Chronicle' of September 26 from four former colleagues on the British Institute in Prague. Before they had no interest in politics, but circumstances have woken them up. I hope a lot of other people have learned from the events of the last fortnight.

My letter dated 1 November was in answer to a letter from my mother:

You ask what we find to do during the time of waiting. Actually I think the last fortnight is almost the busiest time I have had in Spain. First I was on a delegation going round the hospitals, visiting the wounded comrades, making lists, taking particulars, and so on. As soon as that was over we moved to Barcelona, and I was on a delegation which attended various fiestas and so on, given in honour of the International Brigades. Then the whole of the Brigades came to Barcelona for the magnificent parade of which you may have seen pictures. I think it was the most moving ceremony in which I have ever taken part. Now we are in camp, waiting for final arrangements to be made, and there is still plenty to do, filling out forms for this and that, writing articles for the wall newspaper, and so on . . .

Re-reading the above letter today, I am again surprised at the sparsity of the information I gave, although it would all have passed the censor, and I had plenty of time to write. I was appointed to the various delegations I mention mainly because I could converse with some fluency in several languages. The fiestas I mention so casually were in part newsworthy, for instance a state banquet given by Premier Negrin, with all the big names of the Spanish Republic – La Pasionaria, Generals Lister, Modesto and El Campesino and so forth – pouring praise on us. There were, I think, two delegates from each battalion of the Brigades, which would have meant some seventy-five delegates in all. What I remember most vividly is the food. It was nothing remarkable, a plate of soup and then the main course, consisting of three thin slices of ham. But this was accompanied by *unlimited* quantities of bread, something unheard of at this stage of the war. We all wolfed incredible quantities of the bread.

But I am particularly surprised at the paucity of my information about the farewell parade in Barcelona on 28 or 29 October. The remnants of the International Brigades – for there were only a few thousand left of the 45,000 volunteers who went to Spain – formed up outside the bullring at one end of the broad boulevard Diagonal. The 15th Brigade, composed of British, American and Canadian volunteers, marched last, as the last brigade to be established. Out ahead of our brigade marched one solitary figure, carrying a large and very heavy Spanish flag: I was the one. This time I had been picked out, not because I knew several languages, but because somebody remembered that I had been in the Grenadier Guards, and thus presumably knew something about formal parades.

Keeping in step proved difficult, because bands all along the route played different marching tunes. Dipping my flag in salute as we passed the main platform was a major problem, since I had firmly in my head the British Army maxim that the sacred folds should never brush the earth. But the real trial started a minute later. All the girls of Barcelona apparently wanted to kiss and embrace 'the heroes', and it was very difficult to accept this tribute and still keep the flag flying. At one point I was actually forced to my knees as the girls embraced me. It apparently happened to all of us, but I got the full blast since I was marching alone ahead of the column. Not a word of all this in my letter.

On 6 December we boarded a train for Britain. A final entry in my Spanish Army paybook states: 'Authorised to leave for France with 200 French francs' – which was a little over £2 sterling at the time. So much for the mercenaries of the International Brigades.

15

Back in Blighty

On 8 December 1938 we arrived at Victoria Station to an enormous welcome, with Clement Attlee, leader of the Labour Party, shaking all our hands. So there we were, back home. It was an odd feeling. We had left a war-torn and starving country, a land in the death throes, though most of us refused to recognise the fact, and had suddenly landed in the midst of peace and moderate prosperity.

The most baffling phenomenon we had to face was that the ordinary British citizen appeared to be completely blind to the fact, which seemed clear to us, that a second world war could be only a few weeks or months away.

And probably a majority of the surviving British members of the International Brigades had guilty consciences. We were back home in safety, but we had been ordered to leave Spain in its hour of greatest need. If a call had gone out for us to return to Spain a large proportion would, I think, have gone.

In fact, when Franco's troops stormed through Catalonia up to the French frontier only two months later, the demobilised men of the International Brigades still there – the Italian and German anti-fascists and others who had no homes to go to – mobilised themselves again voluntarily, and helped to hold up the Franco advance for a few days while hundreds of thousands of Republican civilians sought refuge in France.

In Britain we could not fight, but we threw ourselves into the campaigns to help the Republic, mainly in the 'Food for Spain' drive, but also to raise funds for our disabled comrades, and for the dependants of the roughly 600 British volunteers killed in Spain.

In April 1939, only four months after we returned to Britain, the last resistance in the Spanish Republic came to an end, and I had to look around for a way to earn a living. I had toyed with the idea of returning to Prague to teach English again, but after Hitler occupied the rump of Czechoslovakia in March 1939 there was obviously no future in that. So I advertised rather optimistically in a London paper offering my services as a German–English translator.

The only reply came from a Viennese refugee writer, with fluent but shaky English, who had a pile of short stories she hoped to place with British magazines. I tailored some of the stories for the British market with no success, but in the meantime my authoress had managed to wangle a very lowly piece-work job in Fleet Street for which she also needed my help.

At that time several big magazine chains published cheap weekly papers for 'working-class girls', filled with indescribably dreary wish-fulfilment stories about girls meeting Mr Right – affluent and often aristocratic – and living happily ever after. All these magazines – *Peg's Paper* was the best known – ran 'Advice to the Lovelorn' columns and 'What Your Dreams Mean' pages: and apart from the published replies, they sent personal answers to all the letters received if the necessary coupon was enclosed. These personal replies had to be handwritten, and each had to be varied in text, and 'personalised' as much as possible.

My Austrian acquaintance had managed to get the job of ghosting these letters for the 'Aunt Sonia' of one of these magazines (he turned out to be a beery and bleary hack). Her imagination was up to the job, but her English was not, so for a number of weeks I toiled as her sub-ghost.

To anyone with a slight acquaintance with the works of Sigmund Freud, the dreams submitted for elucidation were predominantly phallic: and the lovelorn letters, with very few exceptions, could be reduced to the simple formula: 'My young man wants me to: should I?'

If we had had a free hand we could, perhaps, have played havoc with the pre-pill morals of a section of the British public, but our hands were bound, for all our dreary replies had to be submitted to editorial censorship. As a result we had to invent endless variations of the sentiment: 'No, dear, you must keep yourself pure for the fine young man you will one day marry'; and the spires and snakes of the dreams had to be explained away in terms of unexpected letters and interesting new friends. All in all, it was certainly sweated labour; if I recall rightly, we received ninepence per letter, which we shared.

A few other odd jobs followed, including a short term as warden of a home for Spanish Republican refugees in Hove, on the south coast. But in the meantime, throughout the summer of 1939 it became increasingly clear that a European war was just around the corner. With one rather exhausting war just behind me, I began to consider how I would, in later years, answer the famous question: 'What did you do in the great war, Daddy?' (In the end, nobody asked me; they just aren't interested.)

At that time the RAF began advertising for young men of good education to take up short-service commissions as pilot officers. Flying seemed preferable to going to war on foot, once again, and I applied. Almost by return of post I was summoned to appear before a board. Three or four affable officers questioned me on my qualifications, nodding agreeably when they heard I was fluent in German and had considerable first-hand knowledge of central Europe. My favourite sport? Skiing seemed appropriate, as a thoroughly upper-class pursuit, and it had the additional advantage that the chances of being asked immediately to show my prowess were fairly low.

In giving biographical details it seemed wisest to omit the Spanish episode. So, without stretching the truth unduly, I gave the impression that I had continued teaching in Prague until rudely interrupted by Hitler in March 1939. It was a short and friendly interview, and the senior officer concluded by saying that of course he could not give a final answer right off the bat, but it might not be a bad idea if I started considering how to wind up my private civilian affairs at short notice.

A week or two later an official letter arrived: we have to inform you that you are unsuitable for a short-service commission. I showed the letter to a senior man in our organisation, the International Brigade Association.

'So you are another of the rejects,' he said. 'It seems that all applications for commissions in the armed forces are now being screened by the Special Branch at Scotland Yard, to keep out anybody who has actually been through a modern war.'

It was only a year later that I realised that the Special Branch had probably saved my life. Otherwise I might well have been one of the pilots thrown into the Battle of Britain in summer 1940. They won the battle, but few survived.

Next to the RAF advertisements in the quality newspapers there appeared regularly in those days ads inserted by the Crown Agents for the Colonies offering enlistment in the Palestine Police. I wrote in for details purely out of curiosity; it would be interesting to see whether the Special Branch was keeping an eye on this service too.

Soon the Crown Agents sent me a long application form and some rather dry details on terms of service. The pay did not sound too bad; 'good chances of promotion'; generous home leave every two years. Most interesting was a clause which allowed recruits, as in the army, to terminate the engagement during the first three months of service.

So I could join up for three months, see an interesting part of the world and perhaps write a book about it – something I never managed to get around to until now. I filled out the form and sent it in.

While all this was going on, in August and September 1939, world events intruded rather forcibly. Stalin signed his non-aggression pact with Hitler; a few days later, on 1 September, the Wehrmacht invaded Poland, and two days later Britain slipped rather hesitantly into war.

Like so many other Communists or near-Communists at the time I was dazed by Stalin's volte-face. For years the international Communist movement had made 'Hitler means War' one of its rallying cries, and called for an anti-fascist alliance against him; now Stalin had signed a pact with the devil incarnate. Lots of people explained his motives at length, and some of the explanations made quite good sense; but it was hard to take.

This confusion is certainly part of the reason why I decided to go to Palestine when I received notification that my application had been accepted. The contract I signed assured me of the right to withdraw from the agreement during the first three months of service, but if I stopped to think I should have realised that under wartime conditions such escape clauses could easily be cancelled. And so, some time in October 1939, I arrived in the Holy Land, which I was unable to leave until six years later.

The last few paragraphs do not tell the whole story, however. In fact, I was also running away from a commitment to the Soviet Union which went well beyond the normal manifestations of support and sympathy.

It all started in Spain in October 1938, when the International Brigades had been withdrawn from the line and were waiting to leave Spain. We were stationed in an out-of-the-way Catalan village, and one day a comrade stuck his head into the battalion office where I was working on battalion records. I was needed urgently, he said, and it was all very hush-hush.

In a sparsely furnished peasant cottage a thickset middle-aged man in khaki uniform without insignia or badges of rank was waiting for me. Speaking fluent but heavily accented German, he interrogated me fairly thoroughly on my background, education, political affiliations and dozens of other subjects.

Then he launched into an interminable speech about how the world-wide popular front was the only force capable of standing up to fascism and reaction, and how vital it was that the popular front should be fully informed about political and military developments in every country, including confidential developments: and at this point I finally realised what he was getting at.

Then he asked me if I had listened carefully and understood what he was talking about. I replied, 'If I understand you rightly, you are asking if I would be willing to be a Soviet spy.' He looked shocked, and assured me he meant nothing of the sort. But the broad popular front needed bright young assistants to provide information in the fields he had indicated, and would I be willing?

I had already decided on my answer. For many months I had been fighting against fascism with rifle and machine gun: intelligence work for the Soviet Union, the only power which had effectively aided the Spanish Republic, and apparently the only reliable anti-fascist bastion, was obviously a continuation of the struggle in a different field.

To my relief he then dropped the oration and got down to hard tacks. When I returned to Britain I should slowly and discreetly sever any links I had with Communists, and establish myself as a humdrum normal member of society, with a proper job, paid-up health insurance and a bit of money in post office savings. In particular, I should be patient and wait until I was contacted; under no circumstances should I get in touch with any Soviet agency to find out what was happening. He fixed an exchange of code words by which my contact would identify himself.

Then that was that, and I was out on the street of the little Catalan village once again.

Back in London a couple of months later, this unusual interview soon took a back place, for there was so much else to do. I did not actually forget my commitment, but the whole thing seemed a trifle unlikely. Only if some anonymous character came up and gave me the recognition signal, then it would be time to think about it.

Finally, in August 1939, as Europe dithered on the brink of war, the phone rang. The caller refused to identify himself, but urgently suggested an immediate meeting on a nearby street corner. I was reluctant. Finally he said, 'This is against all the rules, but do you like Spanish watches?' Since this was the agreed code word, I went to meet him.

A very normal middle-class Englishman. Tweeds, a moustache and a pipe. He told me he was there as my teacher, and I should pay strict attention to his first lessons, which would be confined to the technique of conspiratorial meetings and communication: how to change buses and tubes to shake possible tails; dead-letter drops; apparently innocent messages on picture postcards. Then he fixed the place and time for the next meeting and jumped on a passing bus.

Our subsequent meetings, two or three in the following weeks, consisted of more of the same, and an absolute refusal on his part to discuss 'the work' to which I would be assigned. My contact constantly chided me for not having a proper job, but finally I was able to assure him that this was now fixed. I had just signed on with the Palestine Police, and would be leaving Britain in a week or two.

He was rather taken aback, and suggested an emergency meeting the following day, at which he informed me that 'the firm' saw no objection. Contact would be resumed in Palestine, and my contact gave me the new recognition signal. In fact, the next contact came, totally unexpectedly, fourteen years later. To keep things in some sort of chronological order, further details in this very unthrilling spy story will be found at the end of the chapter entitled 'Peet's Progress' later on in this book.

16

Not a Happy One

As Gilbert (or was it Sullivan?) wrote, a policeman's lot is not a happy one, and I certainly cannot claim that my three years in the ranks of the Palestine Police were a high point of my life.

At the end of the First World War, Palestine was a country with an overwhelmingly Arab population under British military rule. The British Government, without fully realising the implications, had promised to aid in the establishment of a Jewish National Home in the country: one of its reasons was the hope of setting up a pro-British 'white' colony to protect the Suez Canal, then the lifeline of the Empire.

When I arrived in 1939, twenty years later, the country was still predominantly Arab, but there was a flourishing Jewish community which was taking over more and more of the country, and the Arab majority was feeling threatened. The Palestine Police, a force first raised after Britain had been granted the mandate over Palestine by the League of Nations, was planned on the pattern of the British colonial police forces in other parts of the world: a handful of white sahibs would run the forces of law and order, and 'natives' would provide the rank and file.

The plan soon failed, for the Palestinian Arabs, feeling menaced by Jewish immigration, were soon in opposition to the colonial authorities; and the Jewish immigrants were interested in working for a Jewish state, not for the British Empire. Since neither section of the population provided convenient and obedient mercenaries, more and more police had to be recruited in Britain, and they were a very mixed bag.

The group with which I arrived included two men who had been cashiered from the British Army, apparently for fiddling the mess accounts; a very competent trumpet player sacked as a drunk; and a largish group of what may be best described as 'failed grammar-school boys' who had lately been hawking vacuum-cleaners and 'Kleen Eezi' brushes from door to door. The last group, incidentally, contained several young men who chatted knowingly together about the jolly days they had spent as Blackshirts in Sir Oswald Mosley's British Union of Fascists. (The drunken trumpeter was the only man with whom I felt really comfortable.)

Then came three months' training at the police school in Jerusalem. This was a curious mixture of normal police schooling with the classical Judges' Rules on arrest and interrogation on one hand, and military anti-guerilla training on the other; for the Palestine Police served both as fairly normal constabulary and as gendarmerie troops.

Near the end of this training period came another of those fantasy episodes which seem to have punctuated my life with fair regularity. Without much warning, I suddenly found myself, in full police uniform, with a tin hat on my head and holding a loaded rifle, guarding the exact spot where, according to tradition, Jesus Christ had been born 1939 years earlier.

At the police school there had been rumours for several days that we were going to be sent out on special duties, and at midday on 23 December 1939 we were loaded on to lorries and driven down the few miles from Jerusalem to Bethlehem, where a senior police officer – one of the few learned men I encountered in the Palestine Police – gave us a briefing on what it was all about.

Everybody knew about the Jewish–Arab conflict, he told us, but though the numbers involved were fewer there was just as much chance of mayhem between the various Christian factions. Then followed a meaty and very complicated summary of the situation, running quickly through the various and intricate schisms in the Church over the past 1,500 years: not only Rome and Constantinople, but dozens of other splits which most people have never heard of.

Then he got down to the point. Over the centuries, the two most holy places in Christendom – the Church of the Nativity in Bethlehem and the Church of the Sepulchre in Jerusalem – had been portioned out, more or less *ad hoc*, and with no discernible system, between at least a dozen segments of the Christian faith; but there had been, also for centuries, continued and often bloody squabbles about which few yards belonged to them.

The Turkish Empire, responsible for Palestine until the British conquered it, had tried with some success to make hard-and-fast delimitation rulings. These rulings had been taken over as a solemn obligation by the British Mandatory authorities after a solemn and learned League of Nations Commission had provided a vast and very detailed report on the subject in the mid-1920s. (This would appear to be one of the few positive things ever accomplished by the League, and one must assume that the Israelis still apply the League rulings today.)

That was why we were there in Bethlehem, the police officer said. He wouldn't bother us with details, like which of the Armenian confessions was entitled to polish up to the third step, but no further, on the flight on the right at the end of the nave; or whether the Syriacs were allowed to drive nails into the east walls. Our main problem would be tomorrow morning, Christmas Eve, when the Catholics (Roman) and the Orthodox (Greek) regularly tried to change the rules.

He explained that the narrow main entrance to the church led into the Greek Orthodox nave, lined on both sides with enormous internal pillars. On the left, inside the Orthodox portion, was a doorway leading to the Roman Catholic nave. The point was that by immemorial tradition the Catholic monks had the right, on Christmas Eve, to enter the church in procession by the main entrance, then swing smartly to the left to get to the Catholic precincts.

There was agreement on this between all parties: but there was serious conflict as to how far up the Orthodox nave they were allowed to go before turning smartly left. The Greeks claimed that from time immemorial – everything was naturally immemorial in those fields – the Romans had to pass between pillar three and pillar four from the entrance, and not tread one inch further on the hallowed ground of the only true Christian faith. The Romans, on the other hand, claimed they could produce documents of immense antiquity to show that they had always, practically from the days of Saint Peter, entered their home territory between pillar four and pillar five; the whole trouble had arisen because the Turk who got the ruling down in writing could not count.

So, said the officer, we had to be on duty bright and early next morning, our buttons polished, our tin hats on and our rifles ready, to see fair play, ensure that the Romans never got beyond pillar four, that they were not driven back behind pillar three and that the number of maimed or mutilated monks was kept to a minimum. We should not worry about keeping our hats on in church.

So there we were in the church next morning, a thin blue line of slightly apprehensive under-trained policemen, suddenly hurled into this East–West religious confrontation. We took our stand in line with the vital fourth pillar in the nave, with half the constables facing the main entrance ready to handle the Catholics and the other half facing the Orthodox line of battle.

For a while we were alone, except for isolated ecclesiastical figures who scampered in corners of the nave, polishing votive lamps, sweeping flights of stairs (but only up to the third step) and generally getting ready for the pilgrims. Then, very slowly, the Orthodox clerics started drifting into their immemorial preserve, looking very exotic to the western eye in their inverted top hats, and arrayed themselves near to our peace line.

Outside the main entrance we could hear sounds of chanting, and then suddenly, on the stroke of ten, a massed phalanx of brown-habited Catholic monks came charging, at the half-run, through the doorway. To be quite exact, the phalanx was probably not as massed as the Papal warriors might have wished, for the main entrance to the Church of the Nativity is very low and narrow – legend has it that Saladin or someone had it half bricked-up to prevent his cavalry from riding into the church on their horses – so that only two or three monks could squeeze through at the same time.

They did not actually attack us, but peacefully lent on us fairly hard, and there were muttered requests in strong Irish accents: 'Just a step back, my boy', and 'Give us a little space now for the Bishop who is just on his way.'

On the other side the black-habited Greeks were chanting holy verses, and pressing in on us too; but our officer had given us firm instructions how to act. 'You mustn't lay a finger on the holy men,' he had said, 'not unless things get really sticky and I order you to use your rifle butts. But,' he added, 'we have one great tactical advantage. Both sides wear sandals, and if, in the confusion, one of you should happen to loosen his grip on his bundook, and the butt hits the floor, or something, sharply, then I don't expect I'll dock that man a day's pay.'

So shortly there were grunts of pain from both sides, and the Romans processed away in relatively good order through the gap between the third and the fourth pillars, though some of the Irish were muttering, just loud enough to be heard, 'Just what you'd expect from the British.'

The rest of Christmas Eve was filled with odd guard jobs in and around the church. Underneath the Church of the Nativity lies the supposed site of the stable where Jesus was born. This is approached by a narrow flight of steps and a low corridor, and on Christmas Eve it is naturally jammed with pilgrims of varied confessions, mostly with lighted candles. The actual site of the birth is marked by a silver star set into the rock. This was guarded by a Muslim, armed with a long baton, obviously in the role of a neutral observer. To back him up, at least in my time, a British constable tried to keep the crowd moving. Which is how I found myself mixed up in this rather curious crowd scene.

Soon after this odd experience I was sent off to Haifa, assigned to a normal beat in a mixed-population area in the north of the city. Patrols were always composed of two men: one British constable and one 'native', either Jewish or Arab according to the area to be patrolled. As I write, I recall the anecdote popular in Czechoslovakia after the events of 1968: 'Why do the police always patrol in threes?' – 'Don't know' – 'One can read, one can write, and the third man keeps a sharp eye on the two intellectuals.' In Palestine, the local policeman had to deal with any actual police work which turned up, and I was there to keep an eye on him.

I can recall few details of those dreary months. There was an apparently rabid dog to be shot. In the Jewish quarter of Neve Shanaan one could sometimes feel like the helpful constable of British tradition when, on a Friday evening, some forgetful and despairing orthodox Jew invited one into the house to turn on the light in the lavatory, since to kindle a light on the sabbath would have been a breach of Mosaic law. But two episodes deserve fuller treatment.

One evening, probably in May 1940, when the nazi invasion of western Europe was in full swing, the British station sergeant at Haifa North Police Station felt too lazy to tour the area checking on whether the foot patrols were on the job, and detailed me for the duty. It made a nice change, and off I sped in the station car with a Jewish constable – a perky boy from Vienna – as driver. We located all the patrols, who had all got nice and vigilant and buttoned their tunics properly as soon as they saw the lights of the sergeant's car far off down the road.

The last British constable we encountered, a Glaswegian, whom I had long identified as a Mosleyite, wanted to chat. 'Have you heard what Lord Haw-Haw said last night on Berlin Radio?' he asked. In Palestine, as in Britain, the most astonishing rumours circulated about Haw-Haw's omnipotence in knowing that the town hall clock in Wigan had stopped that very day at half past four, so I asked him what the latest rumour was.

'A pal of mine heard him say last night that Hitler regards the Palestine Police as a fine body of men, and when the nazis take over Britain we'll all get good jobs in the police back home,' he said cheerily. I knew him as a fairly dim type, not very responsive to logical argument, but luckily I had a sudden inspiration.

'I don't believe a word of it,' I said. 'But's let's just assume it really should be like that. Do you know what would happen to you? You'd go back to Glasgow, and get taken on in the police, and then you'd go out on the beat. And with you would be a great big clumping SS man in jackboots, and he would be the "British constable" and you would be the native policeman and he would bugger you about and treat you like dirt like you treat the poor Palestinian copper with you now.' His face fell. 'Christ! I never thought of it like that.'

As we drove away, my Jewish driver turned and shook my hand. We became good friends.

The second memorable incident came a few weeks later. I had been taken off the regular beat and assigned to a special squad detailed to guard vital spots on the oil pipeline running from the oilfields of Iraq across the desert to the refineries at Haifa. It was a tempting target for saboteurs, and two police sentries on twelve-hour shifts guarded all those points where the pipeline crossed nakedly the narrow wadis. I had expected a huge pipe, and was disappointed to encounter something like a water main, about eight inches in diameter.

The day shifts were not arduous, for there was always some shade from the narrow bridge over which the pipeline crossed the wadi, and all we really did was to keep an eye open for the armoured car which drove past on inspection at irregular intervals. The German-speaking Jewish constable from Czechoslovakia who regularly shared the shift with me was glad to be able to lecture me on the aims and achievements of the socialist wing of the Zionist movement to which he belonged, and helped me patiently to spell out at least the headlines of the Hebrew daily paper he always had with him.

One day in July 1940, as we were discussing the consequences of the Fall of France the previous day, we spotted far in the distance the cloud of dust which heralded the approach of the armoured car. Stowing away our newspapers and books, we leaped to our feet and started guarding the pipeline.

The British police sergeant popped his head out of the turret, and received my report that everything was quiet. Then he said, 'Oh, have you heard the news? Churchill's just announced he is suing for peace.' With that he clapped down the lid, and the armoured car rolled on.

It seemed only too possible. In the previous few weeks the phoney war had suddenly ceased to be phoney, and in breathtaking succession Denmark, Norway, Holland and Belgium had fallen, quickly followed by France.

Sitting out all alone in our sunny wadi, the Jewish constable and I discussed what was going to happen now. For a few minutes my colleague withdrew a few yards to consider his problems. In our long discussions he had come to realise that I held views somewhere on the left of the political spectrum: but could he trust me? Could he trust any British official? Then he came back, and said very seriously, 'I have no alternative but to lay my cards on the table, but I shall absolutely deny this conversation if I am ever queried, and you had better forget it too. I am an officer in the Haganah. We have discussed this problem at low level in our company in the past few weeks, and have decided that whatever happens we shall take to the hills and fight on. I have heard that other groups feel the same.'

It was like a sudden ray of sunshine. I told him that if there was the slightest chance of organised resistance I would do anything I could to help; I could think of one or two other British constables who might help. What could we do?

So, for the next hour or two, we made some tentative emergency plans: how we could maintain contact, and all the other dreary details of conspiracy, but above all the ways and means of raiding one of the main police armouries and getting rifles, machine guns and ammunition to improve the armament of the mainline Jewish underground army. It was all in dead earnest. Once or twice he warned me what I was letting myself in for, and he looked considerably happier when I finally revealed that I had fought fascism in Spain.

We were so deep in discussion that we almost missed the cloud of sand heralding the armoured car. It slowed as it came nearer. The sergeant popped his head out of the turret with a silly grin on his face. 'April Fool!' he shouted. 'I bet I got you worried that time.' And he drove on. I would happily have shot him.

For a long time we sat there silently, a dozen miles from anywhere. Then the Jewish constable looked at me with a crooked grin. 'Forget it,' he said.

'Forget what?' I replied, and after a pause for breath we went on with our Hebrew lesson.

17

Little Green Hats

Only a few days after Churchill had thrown in the towel I suddenly found myself translated from the uniformed force into the plain-clothes department. Today I cannot recall exactly how or why, but it appears that word had reached the Criminal Investigation Department that there was a British bobby wasting his time on the beat who could not only read, write and make himself understood in several languages, but who appeared to be at least a marginal officer-and-gentleman.

For the CID was very much the preserve of the gentlemen rankers, the remittance men, who felt themselves a different race from the council-school boys. The plain-clothes angle of our work (for I now have reluctantly to identify myself with the CID) was farcical, since none of us could hope to be mistaken for a member of either of the two Palestinian communities, even in the plainest of plain clothes. This was taken so much for granted that nobody tried; and practically all of the British detective constables and detective sergeants dressed in a uniform non-uniform consisting of suede shoes, rather baggy grey flannels and very long jackets with two slits, all topped by narrow-brimmed pork-pie hats, usually green.

During my period in the uniformed ranks, I had drifted into the cast of a police concert party as one half of a monocled 'silly-ass' couple modelled on the then-popular British entertainers called the Western Brothers. Naturally we chose for ourselves the name 'Near Eastern Brothers'. I wrote most of the lyrics for the act, and one verse sent up the CID. I can actually recall this verse, which I present with muted pride as my only contribution to modern song:

III

We're plainclothesmen, just plainclothesmen,
We can pass as an Arab or Jew.
We could even get by as Estonians or Lats,
If we didn't all have to wear little green hats,
We're plainclothesmen.

Most of the time I and my colleagues were excessively under-employed, sitting around in our comfortable mansion waiting for something to happen and playing bridge or Monopoly. All normal detective work – breaking and entering, pilfering in Haifa Port, thefts of supplies from British Army camps – was naturally done by Arab and Jewish detectives.

But a few off-beat tasks and incidents stick in my memory. Some time late in 1940 somebody, somewhere, probably in Middle East Intelligence in Cairo, decided that in a key port like Haifa the ladies of the town could be a valuable source of information to enemy agents. With vague memories of Mata Hari, orders were given that the CID should assemble a card index of all the local prostitutes.

The Assistant Superintendent (CID) called in a specially selected vice squad, presumably men with moral stamina, and gave us our instructions. The whole thing was slightly outside legality, he explained, because, as we knew, prostitution itself was illegal. But under the special conditions of wartime security, this would have to be ignored, and we would have to track down all such persons, obtaining personal details and photographs for a card index, but at the same time make it quite clear that we were not conniving in their work or issuing licences.

The Assistant Superintendent, a curiously shy and unworldly man for a police officer, stammered and blushed as he briefed us, reminding me of all those stories and sketches of a father telling his son about the birds and the bees. The climax of the briefing came when he mumbled more than usual, pulled himself together and read out one sentence from his orders received by radio in code from Jerusalem.

'It says here, quote, all active prostitutes comma female and male unquote. That doesn't seem to make sense. Perhaps it was mutilated in transmission.'

So somebody explained, and he looked bewildered and shocked.

For the first few days the operation was mildly amusing. The madams of the larger establishments were very accommodating, showing us round proudly, serving coffee and beer, assuring us they were delighted to co-operate in every way, inviting us to drop in any time and producing their girls one by one for a short interview. Things got trickier when we moved on to the individual operators. Addresses and telephone numbers were easily gleaned from hotel porters and taxi drivers, but when we found them, most of them naturally tried to convince us that we had made a grave mistake: we only had to ask the local rabbi, or the mayor of Haifa, or Lieutenant-Colonel Smith, for a character reference.

After a few days on this sort of job I was relieved to be taken off for a more august assignment as one of the bodyguards of a member of the British royal family who was making a tour of British forces in the Near East. The British Army in all its majesty might have been thought able to guard its own, but CID help was called in because of our alleged familiarity with the personnel and *modus operandi* of the local pistol-packing scene, which was just beginning to become active again.

My particular job, apart from mingling with the crowd and keeping my eyes open during the two days the Royal Personage spent in Haifa, was to ensure his safety during his overnight stay in a rather superior officers' billet on Mount Carmel. My instructions were clear. Firstly, the ducal bedchamber was to be thoroughly searched for infernal machines, and after the search nobody but the Duke was to be allowed to enter. Secondly, the door was to be closely guarded all night. Thirdly, and apparently most important of all, the Duke, who was allergic to bodyguards, must under no circumstances notice that he had protection.

Searching the Duke's bedroom was fun. Under his pillow were his pale-blue pyjamas, the first I had ever seen with short instead of long trousers. Leafing through some papers on the night table (after all, they might have been threatening letters), I discovered, rather to my surprise, that the royals too were subject to UK clothes rationing. Shortly before leaving on his trip the Duke had been appealing rather desperately to his relatives to lend him a few coupons to buy tropical wear.

On his table lay his appointment diary for the next day. One of his chores was to inspect a unit of the Free Czechoslovak Forces stationed near Haifa. A special note was attached: 'The Czech troops would especially appreciate being greeted in traditional fashion in their own language. The inspecting officer is humbly requested to greet them with the Czech word "Nazdar".'

But there were no infernal machines. For my duties as an invisible guard there was a comfortable toilet diagonally across the corridor. With the door slighly ajar I could keep the ducal door under constant observation through the hinges, and I settled down for a long wait.

After protracted revelry in the mess on the floor below, I heard confused stumbling on the stairs, and two full colonels appeared, assisting the Duke, who was obviously over-tired, to bed. My instructions had been explicit that nobody but the Duke was to enter the bedroom, but it occurred to me that the colonels might react negatively if I suggested they should drop their burden on the floor in the corridor, and leave him to creep into bed under his own steam. So I stayed in the lavatory.

After a couple of minutes the colonels, looking relieved, clattered their spurs downstairs, and I settled in for the night. But noises from the bedroom a few minutes later appeared to indicate that the Duke's sense of duty had triumphed over his exhaustion, for something crashed loudly to the floor, and there were incoherent snatches of song.

Clearly my duties as bodyguard included the obligation to prevent him from hurling himself out of the window. In addition, I was simply curious as to what members of the royal family did when dead drunk, so I moved quietly across the passage to his door.

For a while the noises were indistinct, but then something obviously attracted his full attention, for there was a sudden dead silence. Then he began hoarsely to read aloud his programme for the coming day: '. . . to greet them with the Czech word "nazidar".' Then another long pause. 'Odd, that,' muttered the august voice. 'Thought the Czechs were on our side, not cheering for the nazis.'

But the word, or at least his interpretation, had caught his fancy. He began to chant, rather tunelessly, 'nazi-dar, nazi-dar, nazi-nazi-nazi-dar', and it was clear he was dancing to his song. Finally, with a tremendous crash, he fell, apparently on to his bed. There was peace, and I could return to my lavatory seat.

With some forethought, I had earlier slipped into my pocket a copy of Bertolt Brecht's *Threepenny Novel*, a prose adaptation of his famous *Threepenny Opera*, and I was delighted to read some of Brecht's rather snide references to the British royals while sitting in a lavatory guarding one of the family. I told Brecht the story in Berlin some ten years later. He murmured, 'Very fitting, very fitting.'

18

The Bad Templars

Everybody knows something about the clashes between Jews and Arabs over Palestine; some people are aware of the undignified squabbles between various Christian denominations over the Holy Places; but very few of them have even heard of the flourishing nazi Party group in Palestine.

This unexpected group was based upon a number of farming communities which had been established in Turkish Palestine back at the turn of the century by a fairly obscure German sect called the Templars. They appear to have been encouraged by Kaiser Wilhelm, who had some vision of himself as a defender of the Holy Places.

These small farming colonies prospered, but made no particular impact on the country as a whole. Then, when Hitler came to power, the colonists, like many other groups of overseas Germans, decided that he was a good thing. So most of them became nazi supporters, and a very large number joined the nazi Party. On the outbreak of war, all the German farmers of military age were interned by the Palestine Government.

Then came the War in the West and the Fall of France, and in panic reaction at the often exaggerated stories of nazi fifth columnists the British Government decided to intern most male German citizens in the UK. Very many of them, of course, happened to be Jewish refugees, most unlikely to give aid and succour to the nazis, but that is another story.

Simultaneously with the big round-up in Britain, cables were sent out to the various British colonies and dependencies ordering similar action. It was presumably easy to round up all German nationals in, say, Jamaica, but the position in Palestine was quite different. Many thousands, or possibly tens of thousands, of the Jewish community still nominally held German citizenship, and their internment would have posed enormous problems. So urgent cables passed between Jerusalem and London. I have no idea in what way the British Government modified its original 'intern them all' ruling, but the way the order trickled down to the Haifa CID was a message saying: 'Intern all German citizens unless they can prove they are Jews.'

So our unfortunate Assistant Superintendent was faced with a question which has baffled greater minds: 'What is a Jew?' He called the whole department in to ruminate on the problem – there were only about a dozen of us, for 'native' detectives were naturally excluded.

Most of the cases were quite clear, the Super thought. They were obviously Jews, integrated in the Jewish community, members of the Jewish trade unions (which only accepted Jewish members) and so on. But what about the borderline cases? There were the German Christians who had accompanied their Jewish wives to Palestine, and vice versa, and all sorts of odds and ends who, for one reason or another, had failed to assimilate in the fairly tight-knit Jewish community.

'Any ideas?' he concluded.

Racialist suggestions abounded: they should be made to take their trousers down, or their noses should be measured. So I got into the discussion with a suggestion which seemed bright at the time, but does not appear so brilliant today.

'Well, sir,' I said, 'what about standing the nazi ruling on its head? Hitler has ruled that anybody with a Jewish grandmother is a Jew. So if the borderline cases can produce a Jewish grandmother they stay out of internment.'

Luckily my suggestion never had to be put into practice. For in the meantime somebody in the Palestine Government had made a more precise ruling, and only a very small scattering of people of dubious antecedents were actually rounded up and interned. But a few months later it turned out that several perfectly bona-fide nazi Party members were still alive, well and uninterned, in various parts of Palestine.

Some time in late 1940 I was sitting in a café in Haifa when I was approached by a young man who looked vaguely familiar, though I could not place him. He sat down at my table and said, 'You probably don't remember me, but I remember you well from Ripoll.'

Then I recalled him. When the International Brigades were being withdrawn from Spain, all the British Empire citizens were concentrated in a demob camp at Ripoll, a small Catalan town in the Pyrenees. Apart from those from the UK we had a smattering of Australians and New

Above: Hubert Peet, John Peet's father, at work as a journalist c. 1909

Left: John Peet, aged about nine, on holiday in the Isle of Wight.

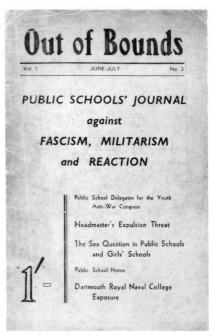

Above: The author's membership card for The Friends of the Soviet Union, 1931, and (*right*) the second number of *Out of Bounds*, the controversial public schools' magazine founded by Esmond Romilly in 1934. *Below:* school photograph, Bootham School, York (John Peet is in the front row, extreme right).

John Peet as a First Battalion Grenadier Guardsman (*above left*) in June 1935 (he enlisted in order to spread the revolutionary word), as an English teacher (*above right*) in Prague 1936, **and** (*below*) on holiday in England, c. 1937, just before going off to the Spanish Civil War.

Above left: John Peet (left) in Barcelona in October 1938 for the disbanding of the International Brigades. *Above right:* in the C.I.D., Haifa, 1942. *Below:* pages from his accreditation as Reuters correspondent in Vienna, 1945.

Identity Card
for Foreign Press Representatives

Mr. *John Peet*

is the representative of the

Correspondent Reuter London

and enjoys as such the full assistance of the Provisional Government.

    All authorities and police officers are duly requested to lend him every support in carrying out his press work and not to interfere with his freedom of circulation.

Vienna,

УДОСТОВЕРЕНИЕ
для иностранных журналистов

Господин *Иок Теет*

корреспондент *корреспонд. Рейтер, Лондон*

пользуется в качестве корреспондента широкой поддержкой Временного Австрийского Правительства.

    Предписывается всем властям, учреждениям и полицейским органам оказывать ему всякое содействие при исполнении его обязанностей журналиста и никоим образом не чинить препятствий свободному передвижению его.

г. Вена,

Above and *left:* the author addressing peace rallies in East Berlin, after his defection there, summer 1950.

Above: leaflet advertising the appearance of the ex-Reuters correspondent at a peace rally.

**NATIONALES AUFBAUPROGRAMM
BERLIN 1952**

Front cover of Peet's booklet, *I Choose Peace*, published in East Germany after his arrival, and (*above right*) his record card for voluntary community work on war-damage in East Berlin, 1952. *Below:* the author helping to clear rubble on a Sunday in January 1951.

Anniversary issue of the highly acclaimed magazine which Peet published from January 1952 to December 1975.

Above: on holiday on the Bulgarian Black Sea coast, c. 1970, and (*below*) a few months before his death in June 1988.

Zealanders and large contingents of men with Cypriot and Palestine passports.

'I'd like to tell you something,' he said hurriedly, 'but I can't be seen talking to a cop, and you can't be seen talking to a Red.' So we fixed up a more discreet meeting for that evening.

There he explained that he had some important information. As I knew, the official Communist Party line in 1940 was that the Second World War was just another imperialist war and we shouldn't take sides, but he had fought against fascism in Spain, and would help anyone to bash the nazis. He had seen me sitting in that same café a few days earlier, made a few quiet enquiries to find out what my job was, and would like to give me some important information if I could swear to keep quiet about the source.

His information was certainly interesting. An Arab Communist had given him the tip. A peasant from his village had told him of something strange which had happened a day or two before Britain declared war on Germany in September 1940. This peasant had been working for one of the German Templar farmers. On this day, the farmer had suddenly loaded him and a couple of other Arab day labourers on to a lorry and driven them into Haifa, where, after nightfall, they had dug a hole under the foundation of a house belonging to another German.

When the hole was big enough, they had dragged a heavy box into the empty space under the foundations and refilled the hole. When the operation was completed, the German farmer had driven them home, given each of them several pounds – much more than they had expected – and warned them to keep their mouths shut.

The box was probably still there, my friend from Spain said, since all the German farmers had been interned a day or two later. I could make any use I liked of the information.

My first impulse was to go on a treasure hunt myself, but then I decided I had better do it by the book. So I went to see our CID Inspector, ascribing the story to a source I had promised not to disclose. The Inspector was sceptical. 'Johnny Arab loves to invent romantic stories. Look at this,' he said, and pulled the latest Military Intelligence report on public reaction to the war in Arab rural areas. The main item ran something like this:

From many areas we have reports of an identical rumour which is receiving much credence. A man on a motor-bicycle suddenly appeared in X [always a named village some distance away] and delivered a speech in Arabic declaring that Hitler would soon arrive in Palestine and drive the Jews into the sea. After his speech his motor-cycle turned into an aeroplane, and he flew away.

In brackets the reporting officer had added his comment: '(Sounds like a useful invention.)'

When, however, I gave the Inspector the exact address of the house where the box was said to be buried, he conceded it might be worth looking into. Within a few minutes six of us, armed with picks and spades, clambered into an armoured car and went to take a look. The armoured car was rather superfluous in peaceful wartime Haifa; it was a left-over from the 'Arab troubles' of previous years, when thin-skinned police transport invited Arab bombs. Jewish bombs came later.

Our hopes that we had not been garden-pathed rose when we inspected the outer walls of the target house, which was unoccupied. The soil had quite obviously been disturbed at one point. The digging was relatively easy, and we were soon under the foundations. Torches showed a coffin-like box of unstained wood at the other end of the foundation area.

The question now was how to get it out. We were all rather hypnotised at the time by stories of wily booby-traps set by nazi agents during the recent War in the West, and nobody was very keen to approach the box.

'Come on, Peet,' said the Inspector. 'You brought us here, so you can volunteer to get the bloody thing out.'

Reluctantly I crawled across the builders' rubble and tied a rope round the box, trying not to shift it. Then we all got out of the foundation space, retreated to the end of the tope, and gave a number of sharp tugs. The theory was that this should set off any possible booby-trap. When nothing happened, we manhandled the coffin out of the cellar and into the armoured car, and raced back to the CID office.

When we had unscrewed the top, we realised we had got Pandora's box. The lead-lined coffin was stuffed with papers – documents, certificates and even rubber stamps – all from the files of Ortsgruppe Palestina der Auslandsorganisation der NSDAP (the Palestine Local Group of the Foreign Organisation of the National Socialist Party).

The most superficial scrutiny showed that the material was of very considerable interest, and far outside the scope of a provincial CID office. But before the booty was duly handed on to higher quarters, the Haifa CID brass wanted to know just what we had got, in some detail.

So through the rest of that day and most of the night I toiled, skimming through routine papers, secret reports on 'unreliable' Aryan Germans in Palestine, full lists of nazi Party members and a very bulky file on one local member who had been arraigned before a nazi 'court of honour' in the

Brown House in Munich on charges of treacherous conduct in the First World War and drummed out of the nazi Party, but later reinstated.

It would be nice to be able to report that I found in those files some reference to a visit paid to Palestine by an SS officer named Adolf Eichmann about 1938. He certainly paid such a visit, and there may well have been such a reference. But the name Eichmann meant nothing to the outside world at that time.

Next day, the proper quarters were informed. An excited senior Intelligence officer arrived a few hours later, and after I had given him a quick summary of the contents he carted the coffin away. Later we heard that information in the files had led to the detection of several nazi Party members still at large.

After my first few months in the CID I realised that the Assistant Superintendent was taking a lot of interest in me, calling me in to have a cup of tea and chat with him about local affairs, the world situation and whatever. Colleagues soon noticed the development, and a long-service sergeant explained, 'They've spotted you as officer material. Pretty soon you'll be running around in a high black officer's kalpak.' The kalpak, a rather sensational piece of headgear inherited from the Turks, was a high brimless tea-cosy made of black Persian lamb – or at least sheepskin.

I was not very happy about the idea. It would mean a lot more money than a constable's pay, but it would certainly involve me much more closely and responsibly in colonial administration. There may be no great moral distinction between carrying out orders and giving orders, but still . . .

Time passed, and nothing happened, and I began to think that the uncertain joy of promotion had passed me by. Then, one day in early 1941, I was summoned to the Super's office. As soon as I arrived I knew that the black kalpak was out. The Super glowered at me, and made no move to ask me to sit down. As usual, he hummed and hawed a lot before getting down to business.

There seemed to be some unclarity about just what I had been doing before I enlisted in the Palestine Police, he finally explained. He had got my curriculum vitae on his desk, and perhaps we had better go through it, he said.

I put him out of his agony immediately, explaining that I had feared that my service in the International Brigades in Spain might prevent my enlistment, and so I had fudged the dates a bit. The Super looked relieved that I had made a clean breast of it, played a straight bat and all the rest of it. This might mean I would have to go back to the uniformed branch, he said, but that was up to Jerusalem.

And that was the last I heard of it.

19

The Patria

Not all the work in the Haifa CID was comic opera. After Hitler had overrun western Europe in summer 1940, the Balkans were practically the only escape hatch through which people fleeing from the nazis could hope to save themselves. Jews in particular saw Palestine as a possible refuge. Bulgaria and Romania were already well within the German sphere of influence but were ready, at a price, to let refugees through.

The only way to Palestine was across the Mediterranean, so a small procession of ancient tramp steamers, long ready for the wrecker's yard, set out from the Black Sea ports loaded to the gunwales with desperate men, women and children. They faced not only a perilous voyage in unseaworthy vessels but also a British naval blockade; for the British Government, fearing pro-Axis reactions in the whole Arab world if Jewish immigration to Palestine continued, had sent in the fleet.

A few small vessels evaded the blockade; the *Struma*, even more unseaworthy than the other vessels, put into Istanbul. The Turkish authorities, under British pressure, forced the limping ship to leave, and it sank, with an almost total loss of life, a few miles out of port.

In November 1940 within the span of a few days the Royal Navy intercepted and brought into Haifa Port three of the refugee vessels, *Milos*, *Atlantic* and *Pacific*. The British plan was to send the refugees onward for 'internment for the duration' on the island of Mauritius, but the vessels on which they had arrived were obviously incapable of the voyage across the Indian Ocean. While a sturdier vessel was being sought to take them to

Mauritius, the refugees were to be held in a special internment camp for illegal immigrants some miles south of Haifa.

In my capacity as universal interpreter I was always on the dock when the Navy brought the vessels in, to help get the refugees lined up and marched away to internment. There were, of course, many Jewish police officers far more competent to speak to the bewildered masses and give them instructions as they staggered down the gangway. But the authorities had ruled that as far as possible contact should be avoided between 'free' Jews and illegal immigrants.

One day came one of those incredible double coincidences which defy all statistical probability. The story needs a short flashback.

In hospital during the Spanish War, I came to after a long period of insensibility, and turned my head weakly to the bed on my right. The man lying there, heavily bandaged, grinned and said in Czech, 'Good day, professor.' It turned out that he had been studying English at the school in Prague where I had taught. That alone was a fairly wild coincidence.

But now, on the quayside in Haifa, lightning struck again. Down the gangway, filthy and weary from the voyage, came a gaunt figure. He saw me, did a double take, shouted out 'Good day, professor!' in Czech, broke ranks and embraced me before he was marched away by some rather puzzled British constables. I have long forgotten his name, but every now and then I have a feeling that he will greet me once again in some odd corner of the world.

This, however, was the one and only light touch in the miserable story of the illegal immigrants. After some search, the British authorities finally located a fairly large old French liner, the *Patria*, to take them to Mauritius. While the liner was being fitted out for the trip it was tied up at an isolated spot on the Haifa Port mole. Several hundred refugees had already been escorted aboard. The vessel was in strict quarantine, with a strong police guard on the mole, and two police launches off the stern.

On 25 November 1940 I was doing some routine work in CID headquarters, which looked out over the port, when a colleague called me over to the window. The *Patria* was listing quite distinctly to one side. As we watched, the list increased rapidly, and small figures on deck could be seen scrabbling uphill to the upper side. Everything happened very fast, and within one or two minutes the liner was on its side like a beached whale, half covered by the sea.

At first we could not grasp the extent of the catastrophe. The sea was calm, the sun bright, the liner was only half under water, the mole was only a few yards away. But when we reached the scene, the first bodies of the drowned were already being carried into an empty warehouse; within a few hours, the bodies of over two hundred men, women and children were laid out there in long rows.

What had caused the catastrophe? A British Naval Board of Enquiry was convened a few days later, and once again I had an inside view, since the British authorities insisted that there should be a British and not a Jewish court interpreter. The Board heard convincing expert evidence that a large hole had been blown in the bottom of the vessel by a powerful explosion inside the hull, but none of the survivors who were called as witnesses could – or would – explain how the explosives had been brought aboard, or who had detonated the charge.

I am afraid that British naval officers who made up the Board took a poor view of my interpreting talents. (I would like to note here that the members of the Board were very considerate and polite to confused and frightened witnesses, many of whom had lost their families, a pleasant contrast to the hectoring tone of most British officials in Palestine when dealing with 'natives'.)

Right at the start we ran into a problem. The naval men naturally phrased their questions in the language of their trade; like so many non-mariners, I have never been able to grasp which side is port and which is starboard, let alone more complicated nautical terms. Even if I had known, I certainly did not know the German translation; and had I known the right words it appears unlikely that most people in the witness box would have known what they meant.

So after the very first question to the first witness I had to hold up the proceedings while I asked the presiding officer whether the port side was the right or the left. After a stunned silence, he explained; and for the remainder of the proceedings the court, the interpreter and the witnesses talked about what had happened 'on the right side of the boat looking towards the sharp end.' Even this did not always help, for many of the witnesses had not been long enough aboard to note which end was the sharp end.

But all the interrogation brought no clarity; all that was clear was that there had been an explosion, an inside job, which had torn out part of the bottom.

Over twenty years later, on holiday in the Soviet Union, I happened to meet a Haganah officer I had known slightly in Haifa; he was now on the staff of the Israeli Embassy in Moscow. He gave me his version of what had happened.

'We wanted to wreck the engines of the *Patria* so it could not sail for Mauritius with all those people who had just escaped from Hitler,' he said. 'I am not going to tell you how we got the explosives on board, but we managed it. We tried to get an explosives man on board, but it proved impossible; all we could do was provide written instructions. We never discovered exactly what happened, but obviously the charge was wrongly placed.'

I should like to note that other versions of the *Patria* tragedy have been published. I won't argue. I simply don't know.

The British Mandatory Government in Palestine regarded Jewish refugees from Europe as an unmitigated nuisance. But British Military Intelligence realised that some of these people, who had left enemy territory only a few weeks earlier, might have valuable information. So once again as an interpreter I accompanied a very competent British major to the internment camp south of Haifa, and sorted through the refugees for those who might have something to tell. British Intelligence was particularly interested in those who had come straight from industrial areas in Germany, where they had been employed in various forms of pressed labour.

To interrogate these people in depth, Intelligence very sensibly decided to call in the help of the Haganah, which had an excellent intelligence network of its own. This led to an immediate clash between the Palestine Adminstration and the military; but in this case the War Office must have overruled the Colonial Office.

Once again I was called in by my Assistant Superintendent (CID), who was very cross.

'These bloody soldiers are mucking things up again,' he said. 'Now we've got to take some of these bloody Jewish illegals out of their bloody camp, and bring them into Haifa under armed escort: and what do you think we have to do with them?'

Knowing the Super, I kept quiet.

'Then we've got to take them to a bloody Haganah officer – officer, mind you, a bloody man who ought to be in clink – and he's going to interrogate them. But I've managed to get Jerusalem to insist that a German-speaking British CID man sits in on the interrogations to make sure they don't plot a mass break-out from the camp, or something – and that's you.

'And just one more thing. Those lunatics from Intelligence insist that you treat this Haganah bastard as an officer! Luckily you won't be in uniform, or they'd want you to salute him.'

'Sir,' I said smartly, as I had learned to in the Grenadiers, and left him to smoulder.

So every day for several very interesting weeks I drove out in the morning to the internment camp in a police pick-up, with two armed guards from the uniformed branch, and brought small parties of interrogatees into Haifa. Here, in a furnished apartment, the 'Haganah bastard', a soft-spoken central European intellectual (I would guess from his accent and manner a lawyer from Prague), went to work, and I watched him with growing admiration.

He did not, of course, have the job of extracting information from an unwilling witness: for all the interviewees were willing and anxious to provide any details which could help to defeat the nazis. On the other hand, a number of them had a very understandable psychological block against co-operating with the authorities – any authorities.

So he gave them cups of coffee, and encouraged them to talk to him about anything and everything. When the immigrant had talked himself out, the interrogator started guiding him.

'So you have been living in Duisburg all your life, right? So where were you living just before you got away? And where were you working?'

Then he slowly got down to the details. Where was the factory exactly? Could he pinpoint it on a street map of Duisburg? (The Haganah officer had a wonderful collection of urban street maps.) Was there any building activity in the factory area? What was being produced? And often the person under interrogation could suddenly remember little details which perhaps could pinpoint a target for future British air raids.

After a few days the Haganah officer decided he might be able to trust me, and asked rather hesitantly whether I would mind looking the other way if one of the interrogatees wanted to hand him a short personal note to relatives of his already in Palestine. I assured him I could be as blind as a bat if he would censor the note himself to ensure it contained nothing contrary to the Allied war effort.

20

Anonymous Journalism

All this time, inside the colonial CID constable there was a journalist struggling to get out. As a government official I was not permitted to write for the press, but I had a lot to say, so I sent several articles on life in Palestine to my father in London for possible publication under a pseudonym.

First success came when the London *Spectator* published a one-page article entitled 'Palestine Problems' on 10 September 1943. If anyone should take the trouble to check, they will find that the article appeared under the name 'Eustace Gordon'. Wilson Harris explained in a subsequent letter to my father how the name came into being. 'Why I called him Eustace Gordon I cannot tell you. "Gordon" was taken from the square close by [the *Spectator* office]. "Eustace" I think probably struck me as a melodious name.'

Re-reading this ancient article today I was pleased to see that it reads quite well forty years later. Here is a short extract:

> Whatever fair words and phrases with regard to the solution of the Arab problem may be used by Jewish leaders in speeches and articles for external consumption, the fact remains that no serious proposal to ensure that the Arabs will have a fair share in post-war Palestine has come from any of these leaders . . .
>
> Not only is the Arab population to all intents and purposes ignored, but any body or individual who makes a concrete proposal for mutual understanding is denounced as a traitor to Zion. Dr Magnes, Chancellor of Jerusalem Hebrew University, founded in 1942 an organisation called

'Union', the declared aims of which are:
1. The government of Palestine to be based upon equal political rights for
   the two peoples.
2. A federal union of Palestine and the neighbouring countries to be
   created.

Such a programme appears innocent enough, but Dr Magnes and his
associates were violently attacked on all sides, apparently for suggesting that
the Arabs might be treated other than as 'untermenschen'.

Apart from the openly fascist and terrorist Stern Group, which was,
according to the Jerusalem correspondent of *The Times*, in touch with the
Italians, incredible though that may sound, and which seems to have
disappeared, totalitarian methods are increasingly coming into favour in
Jewish politics . . .

The picture must not be painted too black, however. In spite of the
illiberal and undemocratic attitude taken up by the old parties, there is a
great body of progressive feeling, though largely unorganised. Arnold
Zweig with his paper *Orient*, Henrietta Szold, the 'grand old woman' of
Zionism, and a large proportion of the new immigrants from Central
Europe, abhor the progressive 'junglisation' of political life, and are conscious that, as a free and democratic Palestine could not exist in a Fascist
world, so an ultra-nationalistic Jewish Palestine will not be tolerated in a free
and democratic world.

Most of the Hebrew press in Palestine worked itself up into a frenzy
about Eustace Gordon's article. I do not think anything else I have ever
written aroused such a tempest, though admittedly in a small teapot.

The conservative daily *Haboker* stated: 'These charges bear the mark of
tried and tested anti-Semites, and like all veteran anti-Semites, the
Spectator contributor also finds that there are a few good Jews who are
unfortunately without influence.' *Hatzofeh*, organ of Orthodox Jewry in
Palestine, said: 'The *Spectator* found "junglisation" not in nazi Germany,
fascist Italy, or nazi-fascist Japan, but in Palestine.'

And so on, in most of the rest of the press. But the papers studiously
ignored one sentence in the story, the report that the Stern Group had been
in touch with the Italians. In my article in the *Spectator* I could only cite
The Times as a source, since I could not very well quote from confidential
police documents on the story.

In the course of my duties at Haifa CID I often had access to the
periodical reports drawn up by Police HQ in Jerusalem on 'subversive
activities' in the Jewish and Arab communities. One of those documents
struck me as so interesting that I made a private copy, and this yellowing
sheet of foolscap, which I typed back in 1941, lies before me as I write.

It is dated, rather vaguely, 'Autumn 1941' and is entitled 'Notes on the Stern Gang'. The document opens with a short summary of the founding of the right-wing underground movement Irgun in 1937, and the armistice concluded between Irgun and the Palestine Mandatory Government on the outbreak of war in 1939. It continues:

Most detainees were released, including in June 1940 Abraham Stern and Hanoch Strelitz, implicated in the murder of Cairns and Barker [CID officers killed in August 1939] . . . With a group of approximately 50 ex-Irgun members they set about overthrowing Irgun and part of the leadership, starting by seizing money and arms. Large quantities of arms were stolen from a Haganah cache at Herzlia. This was organised while Stern was still inside. It was followed by a £5,000 bank robbery in Tel Aviv.

The group posed to the Italians as a Jewish fascist party, so that if the Axis won the war they would have Italian backing, while if Britain won the country would go to the Arabs and there was nothing to lose.

In September 1940 the question was raised as to internment. On November 5th there were detentions all over the country, with GOC's approval. Proof of contact with the Italians was only forthcoming in March 1941, when a search in Rehovoth in the room of Itamar Ben Haroeh revealed plans of military value. In early April 1941 Stern was reported in Beirut having conversation with the Italian Armistice Commission.

Abraham Stern was shot dead by police in Tel Aviv on 12 February 1942 'when trying to escape', and I put the words very advisedly in inverted commas. Axis documents which came to light long after the war showed that the Stern Group had been in touch not only with the Italians but with the Germans too; and the story is not all that dead, for Yitzak Shamir, Israeli Prime Minister in the early and late 1980s, was a member of the leadership of the Stern Group when it made those contacts back in 1941.

Some time in the spring of 1941 I got married for the first time; several subsequent marriages will be duly noted in later chapters.

Getting married in the Palestine Police involved overcoming several difficulties. In many parts of the British Empire obstacles were erected to prevent marriages between British colonial officials and 'the lesser breeds without the law', as Rudyard Kipling put it so tactfully. In Palestine, the definition of the lesser breeds was not so simple: it was, for instance, a little difficult to classify as a 'native' a British girl from Leeds who had emigrated to Palestine with her Zionist parents.

The aim of the operation in Palestine was mainly to prevent British officials from contracting marriages with members of the Arab or Jewish communities, and before the war British members of the police force who contracted inconvenient marriages were apparently asked to leave the service. Under wartime conditions this could not easily be done: quite a number of policemen eager to get out might have contracted marriages of convenience.

As a result, Police HQ had to introduce a new ruling, which was formalised in a very intricate instruction from the Inspector-General of Police on 3 June 1942 (the instruction, marked 'confidential', bore the reference number K84/68/2). This curious document was a revised version of an earlier similar instruction, of which I have not got a copy, which was in force at the time when I got married. It laid down that there were two categories of marriage. 'Authorised marriages', to a white Anglo-Saxon Protestant (or Catholic) – though this was not spelled out – would receive full benefits, such as married quarters and marriage allowance. 'Unauthorised marriages' could not be prevented, but would have some negative effects on the man concerned – no promotion, no quarters and so on.

Then the instruction sheet got down to the complicated problem of defining the unwanted brides, and this section deserves quotation in full:

As there are various classifications of the unauthorised marriage, it is necessary to define them as follows:
1. The 'local' marriage, which I define as marriage with persons of Palestinian, Cyprian, Egyptian, Arab, Syrian, Armenian or Circassian nationaliity, or of long residence in these countries or of Eastern race.
2. The 'foreign' marriage, which I define as marriage with persons, resident in Palestine or otherwise, who have retained European nationality but who are not of the Christian faith including those who have
(a) changed their religion in order to marry, and
(b) changed their religion prior to any suggestion of marriage with a British police officer.

When I submitted my application for permission to marry in early 1941, our Assistant Superintendent informed me bluntly he did not like his men getting married to Jews, that the application would have to go to Jerusalem, and I ought to have more sense anyway.

But Jerusalem reluctantly authorised this 'unauthorised marriage', and

Suzanne, a girl of German Jewish origin, became my wife. Looking back, I think we came together mainly because she was rootless in the Jewish community in Palestine, and I was ill at ease in the British police community. We were moderately happy together for about four years. She divorced me soon after the end of the war when I was working in Vienna for Reuters and informed her that I could see no future in the marriage.

21

News from Jerusalem

My record as a 'premature anti-fascist' appeared to doom me to a cushy war as a listless and unproductive colonial cop in Haifa. Sporadically, I tried to get out of the force. Resignation was impossible, for we had been classified as part of HM Forces, and all my efforts to get transferred to the real army were in vain.

But finally I did manage to get secondment to a job where I really felt I could be more useful. Arnold Zweig, the exiled left-wing German writer who achieved world fame in the 1920s with his book *The Strange Case of Sergeant Grisha*, was a neighbour of mine on Mount Carmel, a Haifa suburb, and I translated into English for him a number of short stories published in a Jerusalem English-language weekly. When I told him of my efforts to disengage from the police force, he gave me an introduction to the man in charge of the English-language section of Jerusalem Radio, run by the Palestine Government. Reggie Smith, the official in question (later immortalised by his wife Olivia Manning in a series of books), listened to me with sympathy, but no offer of a job.

'Just leave me your autobiographical details,' he said. 'Something might turn up some time.'

As I disappointedly trudged up the dusty Jerusalem alley between the broadcasting headquarters and the Central Police Prison, I heard the *clop-clop* of sandals behind me.

'Come back, old man,' panted Reggie Smith. 'I've just read your biography, and I'm pretty sure I can find you a job.' It turned out that Reggie was a committed progressive; noting that I had fought on the right side in Spain, he soon found a notch for me in the radio news department.

Since I knew quite a lot about world affairs, and a few of the basics of journalism, and since most of the scratch staff in the news department were willing enough, but knew little about either, I soon found myself pratically running the whole show. This was one of the most satisfying jobs which have ever come my way, and certainly one of the most exhausting. With a tiny staff, mainly unqualified, we were turning out – for this was in 1943, in the middle of the Second World War – a stream of news bulletins in seven languages.

It was a time of headline news from the battlefronts every day, and to my great satisfaction I discovered that with our very limited resources we were often able to scoop the mighty BBC, particularly on news from the Eastern and Balkan fronts. Apparently this was due precisely to the fact that we were a tinpot radio station.

Right in the newsroom we had an extraordinarily capable and reliable monitoring official, an unflappable young multilingual Jew from eastern Europe. Our first scoops – they were not very devastating, but we regularly beat the BBC by two or three minutes – came from Moscow Radio in late 1943. When a special announcement was due, Moscow Radio interrupted its normal programme, and put on a distinctive interval signal. We notified the studio announcer that a special bulletin was coming up shortly. The news could often be anticipated, and we drew up a two- or three-line announcement, leaving open the name of the city liberated. When the Moscow communiqué was read, my monitor simply shouted across the room, 'Kharkov liberated!' I immediately filled in the name, and the announcer, standing by, simply interrupted the programme and read the flash perhaps ten seconds behind Moscow. The BBC, which was very quick on the ball, but had to go through channels, generally tailed us by several minutes.

When the war moved down into the Balkans in summer 1944, things became even more exciting, since we could monitor local stations in Romania and Bulgaria which were inaudible to BBC radio monitors in London. When the Red Army was approaching the Bulgarian frontier, for instance, our talented monitor brushed up his Bulgarian, and provided us with a stream of intercepts showing the way the wind was blowing. The best illustration may be a short excerpt from an article I wrote on the subject for a Jerusalem weekly on 22 September 1944:

> Radio Sofia has come on the air regularly every day, reflecting to the world the succession of sudden changes in Bulgarian policy.
> On September 2, Sofia announced that a new government, under Mr Muravieff, had been set up. For the next few days, the news section in Sofia

was obviously out of its depth. They were not at all sure which side they were on, and the news consisted of a curious mixture of Allied communiqués, German propaganda hand-outs, and local announcements of a harmless nature.

On September 9, when Kimon Georgieff set up his popular front government, the announcers heaved a sigh of relief, and really went to work with a will. A careful analysis of the news broadcasts from Sofia since that date shows that this was by no means simply another reshuffle of cabinet members, but far more like a revolution.

The seven languages in which we broadcast news were English, Arabic and Hebrew (the three official tongues), and in addition we provided the news of the day in French, German, Polish and Greek. This wide range of languages was, like most things in Palestine, totally unplanned. News in French had been put on the programme in 1940 when the pro-German Vichy Government of France took over control of Palestine's neighbours, Syria and Lebanon; the Vichy governors had been ousted in 1941, but the broadcasts continued. German-language broadcasts had ostensibly been initiated for the benefit of Marshal Rommel's Afrika Korps when it menaced Egypt in 1941; by 1943 the Wehrmacht had long been driven out of range of Jerusalem Radio's medium-wave transmitter, but the broadcasts continued. This appears to have been based on deliberate policy to meet the needs of many recent Jewish immigrants to Palestine who understood little Hebrew but were fluent in German. The fiction of broadcasts for the Wehrmacht had been made necessary by the ferocious opposition of the Zionist establishment, which worked for the immediate eradication of the languages of the Diaspora, incidentally including Yiddish.

The Polish news bulletins, similarly, were claimed to be for General Ander's Polish Army in the Middle East, but found an eager following amongst Polish Jews. The Greek news needed no alibi: Jerusalem was almost the only medium-wave transmitter under British control audible in most of nazi-occupied Greece.

As acting operative head of the multilingual news section I found myself in a tricky position. I had to write the bulk of the news bulletins – a basic service was provided in English, which had to be translated and edited by the various language departments – and at the same time I was supposed to ensure that all the various language desks complied with the wartime censorship regulations.

In fact, of course, I had to rely on the good sense of the language desks. I knew only German and French with any degree of fluency, and three of the remaining four languages even used alphabets which I could only decipher very slowly with my lips moving. As it turned out, in the twenty-four months I spent in this slot there was only one serious bloop, and to this day I have been unable to determine whether this was not in fact a bit of devious misinformation launched by some spook organisation on our own side.

It happened like this: apart from the world news items provided by the central news desk – my direct responsibility – the Arabic and Hebrew news sections were permitted to originate 'non-controversial' news items about their respective communities. At the end of 1943 preparations were under way for a summit conference somewhere in the Middle East. There were real fears that the nazi secret services might make a desperate attempt to blow up Churchill, Roosevelt and Stalin at one fell swoop, so disinformation was launched on an enormous scale.

Three presumptive sites were selected for the meeting, and given the code names of 'Cairo One', 'Cairo Two' and 'Cairo Three'. Cairo Three was Teheran, where the conference was actually to be held; Cairo Two was Jerusalem; and Cairo One, as a stroke of intelligence double bluff, was actually Cairo. The drill was to prepare, in utmost secrecy, the necessary accommodation and security arrangements in all three cities. The idea appears to have been that busy-beaver nazi agents in all three places would learn of the preparations, and Berlin would be suitably baffled.

This was where the Hebrew news department of Jerusalem Radio got into the picture. One bright day the final item in the main Hebrew news bulletin was an interesting piece of 'non-controversial' local news: General Dwight D. Eisenhower had that day paid a visit to the Kotel Ma'aravi, the Wailing Wall.

One of the basic and sensible wartime censorship rules was that troop movements or the location of high-ranking officers were never to be mentioned unless officially announced, and rockets of all calibres started flying. I was the obvious candidate for the high jump, since I had clearly failed in my duty to prevent the leak. But then, as suddenly as it had started, the flap stopped, and it was never mentioned again.

The only logical explanation would appear to be that some disinformation expert, acting on the highest authority, had planted the leak, acting on the rather unlikely assumption that the nazis monitored Jerusalem Radio in Hebrew, and would jump to the conclusion that the summit meeting, just about to start in Teheran, was really being held in Jerusalem.

By and large, however, we managed to get along very nicely by ignoring the flood of mainly outdated, and often lunatic, censorship directives which flowed in from the Middle East Forces HQ in Cairo. To judge by the directives, the censors there were elderly officers still vainly trying to relieve Mafeking.

Today I can recall only one of these dotty directives, which read roughly as follows: 'The Yugoslav insurgent known as Tito has recently conferred upon himself the rank of Marshal. Since this title is self-conferred, he shall continue to be referred to as General Tito.' Not, however, by Jerusalem Radio. Nobody seemed to care.

Apart from running the news service, I occasionally took a couple of hours off to act as a film censor. The Palestine Board of Film Censors was slightly surrealist, like so many bodies and situations in Palestine under the British Mandate. Backbone of the Board was a clutch of clergy – a rabbi, an imam, heavily bearded priests of various Orthodox churches, a Roman Catholic and a mild representative of the Church of England who for some obscure theological reason also represented more exotic Christian rites such as the Armenian. The dog-collar contingent was supplemented by a few laymen, including a representative of the Palestine Government Information Office, sometimes myself.

The declared aim of the film censorship was to protect public morals and to watch out for subversion or scenes likely to promote interracial enmity. An oddity was that some films, adjudged to be borderline cases with regard to morals, were licensed for public showing throughout Palestine with the exception of Jerusalem, the Holy City.

At an earlier date the censors had made a great point of protecting Palestine against the Communist menace, although this had been toned down now that the Soviet Union had become the Great Ally. But before Stalin became Uncle Joe, the anti-Communist tic had sometimes produced peculiar results. In the late 1930s Soviet film-makers had produced a film entitled *Professor Mamluck*, based on a story by Friedrich Wolf, the German anti-fascist author. The film, playing in the first months of the Hitler regime in Germany, dealt mainly with nazi anti-Semitism; the Communist underground had a marginal role.

As was usual with films playing to the multilingual audiences of Palestine, this film too was multi-captioned. The sound was in Russian, subtitled on film in English and French by the Middle East distributors. On special display screens on both sides of the main screen, additional subtitles were provided, in Arabic and Hebrew and in some cinemas in German.

The censors – this was before my time – had been unable to write the Communist underground fighters out of the film, but had come up with what they obviously regarded as a happy solution: just call the Communists 'anarchists' in the captions, and the whole thing would be sanitised.

So when an actor on the screen said clearly and distinctly on the Russian soundtrack, 'I am a Communist' (understandable even to those with no Russian), the multilingual subtitles proclaimed: 'I am an anarchist.'

The audiences rolled in the aisles.

There were still problems on the censorship Board even now that the Commie menace had faded. All this happened, of course, long before the days of permissible nipples, let alone pubic hair, but many of our clerical members could get vastly excited by deep cleavage or damp bathing costumes, and often managed have quite mild scenes mutilated. I fought for the cleavage once or twice, but capitulated before the massed modesty of the Monotheist Bloc, united probably on this issue only. However, in once instance I did find it necessary to insist upon the complete banning of a film – curiously enough a Soviet film.

This happened in the year 1944, when right-wing Zionist underground groups had launched a bombing campaign against the British administration, blowing up with alarming efficiency a number of police sections, including Haifa CID headquarters, where I had spent such dreary years. The Soviet film in question dealt with partisan activities in nazi-occupied areas, and a large part of the action consisted of rather detailed technical instructions on how the partisans blew up nazi installations, particularly railway lines.

I felt, possibly rightly, that a handy handbook on explosives and sabotage was not exactly helpful to the war effort in the particular atmosphere of Palestine at that time, and had the film banned.

After an underground has shown that it can deliver the goods it can wreak almost as much confusion with a telephone call as with a sackful of explosives. All over Palestine, government offices were evacuated with hectic urgency when a bomb warning was phoned in. After a series of false alarms, somebody would decide that work should continue as usual, despite a warning; and then, of course, another real bomb went up.

One day the shadow of the gunman loomed on my doorstep. I received a phone call asking me to look in at the offices of Jerusalem CID at my earliest convenience. My conscience reasonably clear, I walked across to Police HQ, where an officer of the anti-terrorist squad received me.

'We thought you ought to see this,' he said, and flipped across the desk a small file-card neatly typed in Hebrew. I could decipher my name typed in the top right corner, and a passport photo of myself was pasted top left. Attached to the card was an English translation, which I studied with interest. My name and address, age, height, colour of eyes, languages spoken and then a few chillingly accurate notes on my daily routine: which bus I took to work and where and when; restaurants and cafés I frequented; the route I walked home after late-night work. The back of the card named a number of friends and associates. All in all it was the sort of file the police would try to assemble on a suspect.

'A couple of days ago we turned over the flat of a terrorist suspect,' said the CID man, 'and we found a boxful of cards like this. Somebody seems to have fingered you as an easy target. You'll understand we can't do a damn thing about it; we are overstretched trying to guard the sensitive targets, but it might be a good idea to switch your daily programme a bit. Since you are still nominally on the police strength, I have been authorised to issue you with a personal weapon.'

So I picked up a short-barrelled Smith & Wesson 0.38 from the police armoury. For the remaining year of my service I regularly cursed Menachem Begin and the filing-card bureaucrats of his Irgun. Even in a cool climate, carrying a gun in civilian clothes is uncomfortable, during a hot Palestine summer, when most men wear only a shirt and slacks, it forces you to wear a jacket at all times.

Anticlimactically, nothing ever happened. I never supposed very seriously that the Irgun had any particular reason for trying to gun me down. I just happened to be a government official about whom they had gathered rather good information. But there was always the possibility that they might try to take me out as a target of opportunity. Before I left the CID office the terror-squad man asked whether I had any idea as to who might have fingered me. I told him truthfully I had no clue.

Thinking it over afterwards I wondered vaguely whether it might not have been a very charming girl whose father, I knew, had been on the extreme right of the Zionist movement, but I had no real reason to suspect her. Walking down Oxford Street in London some ten years later I bumped into the charming girl from Jerusalem, now a handsome matron. On an impulse, I asked her whether she had put me up as an Irgun target.

'Oh, yes,' she said with a beautiful smile. 'I wondered whether you might guess. But I'm glad they didn't shoot you. It was nice to see you again.' And she turned into Marks & Spencer.

During my period in the police I had been involved in continual conflict between my personal convictions and my official task, though it was not entirely a rationalisation when I explained to myself that ensuring internal security in a pivotal base area like Palestine was in fact a contribution to the war effort. On Jerusalem Radio the situation was much simpler: we provided the news, as quickly and factually as possible, and since my term on the radio stretched from mid-1943 to soon after VE Day, it was mostly optimistic news.

But tricky situations did arise, particularly as the war front moved to Greece in late 1944. The resistance movement inside Greece was split, as in so many occupied countries, into a right-wing nationalist faction and a left-wing progressive faction which wanted not only to drive out the occupiers but also to build a better and more equitable post-war society.

In Greece, again as in so many other parts of Europe, the progressive partisan movement was largely under Communist leadership, not as the result of Moscow machinations, but because the Communists had proven themselves the toughest fighters with a clear-cut programme.

By late 1944 the left-wing liberation army ELAS had taken control of the greater part of Greece as the Wehrmacht withdrew northward to avoid being cut off; and this was not viewed favourably by the British Government, which looked forward to a Greece firmly within the British sphere of influence.

After complicated manoeuvres, Winston Churchill decided to use force to overthrow ELAS, which had begun to organise a progressive Greek Republic, and at the end of 1944 open fighting broke out within the Greek resistance, and British troops rushed to the Athens area. I was naturally firmly on the side of ELAS, but my very considerable freedom of action as news editor could not really be stretched to commit Jerusalem Radio to ELAS rather than the British Army.

Instead our news bulletins remained severely neutral, running both the official British hand-outs on the fighting and the parallel negotiations, and the official ELAS communiqués on the same subjects. These ELAS communiqués were either ignored or distorted by the main wire services which provided the bulk of our news; but in Jerusalem we were in the lucky position of being able to pick up the low-power ELAS transmitter in Greece. It is my guess that Jerusalem Radio was the only station in the world outside Greece which carried the extended text of ELAS bulletins.

Palestine was naturally the staging base for British troops bound for Greece, and ELAS supporters in Palestine made great efforts to get the truth about the situation to the troops. In this effort they received the support of a shadowy left-wing organisation in the British forces, and large numbers of explanatory leaflets were circulated. I had seen a number of such specimens of 'subversive propaganda' in the confidential files of the Government Information Office.

Many British troops were less than happy when they discovered they were to be sent into action against anti-nazi partisans, and the military authorities had countered with some success with the story that the Greek opponents were merely bandits, with many Wehrmacht soldiers in their ranks.

In this situation I was suddenly approached by a British sergeant with whom I was slightly acquainted, and who had obviously been tipped off that I was a Red. Without beating about the bush he explained what he wanted. Their only illicit printshop in Palestine had been raided by Military Police, and they needed a few hundred leaflets right away; I was the only person who might be able to help. Since I had access to an official government duplicator, I could obviously run off a few hundred.

I asked him what the leaflet should say. 'It should blow up this official lie suggesting that ELAS is somehow nazi-penetrated, and I've been assured you can easily write it,' he said. So that night I stayed at work even longer, and after the rest of the staff had left I ran off, rather smudgily, for I am a poor duplicator operator, about two hundred copies of a leaflet on the subject, which I handed over furtively at midnight to the sergeant on a dark street corner.

In accordance with good conspiratorial practice, I failed to keep a copy of my one and only underground leaflet, but I think I can recall its contents. After a short introductory paragraph explaining that the Greek resistance movement ELAS had liberated the country by its own efforts, the leaflet continued:

> Now you are being told that ELAS has been penetrated by nazi agents, and that former members of the Wehrmacht are fighting in its ranks.
>
> Yes, there are Wehrmacht soldiers with ELAS: they are not nazis but tried and true anti-nazis, our allies inside Germany.
>
> How did they come to be in Greece? When Hitler began to run out of manpower, he drafted concentration camp prisoners – Germans who had been fighting nazism from the word go – into special punishment units, identified by the code name Battalion 999. Those sent on occupation duty in Greece soon contacted ELAS, and went over to the Greek partisan army.
>
> These particular German soldiers are among the best anti-nazis you are likely to find anywhere: they fought against Hitler inside Germany, some of them fought Hitler and Franco in the International Brigades in Spain.

A few days later I knew that my leaflet had achieved a wider circulation than my smudgy two hundred: four or five different properly printed versions turned up in the daily crop of 'subversive propaganda' sent to the Information Office by the British military authorities.

Since the story of the Wehrmacht Battalion 999 has, I believe, never been told in English, I should explain that this special penal formation was in fact very mixed in composition, including a proportion of common-or-garden criminals as well as anti-nazis. The true position of the Wehrmacht deserters in the ranks of ELAS was well known to the British military authorities, for British liaison officers had been parachuted into Greece many months earlier, and had given full and truthful reports of the situation. My own knowledge came from one such liaison officer. Several hundreds of German anti-fascists who had given valiant help to the Greek partisans later languished for several years in British POW camps in Egypt.

22

Dateline Vienna

As soon as possible after the end of the war in Europe, I hurried to sever my various connections with the Palestine Government, and I arrived back in London a few days before the atomic bomb fell on Hiroshima. Full of confidence in my ability to handle news after more than two years on Jerusalem Radio, I walked into Reuters' office in Fleet Street, and was immediately engaged for a trial period as a sub-editor on the European news desk.

Apparently I gave satisfaction, for some six weeks later the news editor rambled over to my desk, enquired offhandedly whether it was true that I spoke fluent German and to my astonishment suggested that I should fly immediately to Vienna to take over the post of Reuters correspondent there.

The whole appointment was vague in the extreme. Nobody gave me any sort of briefing on what my job would be, and I scratched together for myself a few hints from former foreign correspondents now working in the head office. Nobody even bothered to test my fluency in German. In fact, I was very much reminded of the way in which the hero in Evelyn Waugh's novel *Scoop*, a humble gardening correspondent, was sent off to cover a war in Africa because of a confusion over names.

So back into uniform again, this time in battledress with shoulder flashes proclaiming me to be a British War Correspondent. I was rather tickled to discover that the fairly senior British official who issued me with the necessary visas and documentation was an old acquaintance: the young man with whom I had sold the *Daily Worker* at Deptford Tram Depot ten years earlier. Both of us discreetly ignored the episode.

Two or three days after I had been plucked off the desk, I found myself winging my way to Vienna in a battered Dakota. Most of the other passengers turned out to be leading members of the Austrian Socialist Party who had spent the nazi years in Britain and were now going home.

Our arrival in Vienna was unexpectedly spectacular. The city airport at Schwechat was completely fogged in, so the plane would have to make a blind landing. In preparation, we circled through the fog to use up fuel. Next to me in the bucket seats which lined both sides of the fuselage was a rather attractive young WAAF officer, who turned out to be an Irish Catholic.

While we droned round and round for what seemed like hours, the WAAF girl became convinced that we were going to crash, and she would die unshriven. Clinging to my arm nervously, and in the absence of any more suitable father-confessor, she poured out her sins, which were numerous and rather repetitive. However, they took my mind off our predicament; at the same time I was searching my memory for a suitable Latin phrase which might make her feel better.

Finally the pilot announced that he was going in to land; it might be bumpy, so we should brace ourselves. We touched down, bumped alarmingly, and suddenly the plane came to an abrupt halt, and loose articles were hurled to the front of the cabin. That was unsettling enough, but a few seconds later there was a sudden burst of flame outside the left-hand portholes, and we were ordered to get out at the double.

As it turned out, the danger was over. During the blind landing the pilot had missed the runway, and while he was taxiing the plane had fallen into an unfilled bomb crater. The sudden stop had torn off one of the wings, and it was the burning motor which had given us the impression that the whole aircraft was going up in flames.

The only sufferer was one of the Austrian socialist leaders. The abrupt halt had torn his dentures from his mouth, and they had been flattened in the rush to evacuate. In the military bus which took us to the famous Hotel Sacher in the heart of Vienna, now a billet for British officers, the WAAF officer ignored me studiously, and I never saw her again.

Becoming Reuters' man in Vienna from a standing start turned out to be a good deal easier than I had feared. At that time – it was only five months after the end of the war in Europe – foreign correspondents from the media of the four occupying powers lived a life of cushioned ease amid the ruins and hunger of the Austrian capital. The British, American and French military press detachments, which had housed and fed and supervised the genuine war correspondents behind the various fighting fronts, continued to function even more smoothly now they were firmly established in more permanent comfortable quarters.

The British Press Camp – that was the official name – was ridiculously unlike a camp. It was situated in the 3rd District, quite near the city centre, in the Palais Salm, one of Vienna's numerous minor palaces, which today houses, I believe, the Yugoslav Embassy. The Camp was headed by a very affable colonel, rich landed-gentry type, who regarded the journalists under his care as rather unusual house guests at his country seat. He had managed to gather around him, in the form of junior officers and other ranks, all the Victorian prerequisites for gracious living – private secretaries, major-domos, butlers, footmen and all the rest. This made it very comfortable for the correspondents, though for most of us it was a way of life we had never seen except on the stage. At any moment Bertie Wooster might have toddled in.

Even the purpose of our presence – news-gathering – was catered for, though in a slightly offhand way. Conducting officers, who had previously taken the war correspondents to see suitable portions of the front line, were now available to drive us in their jeeps to interview senior officers of the British Element of the Allied Control Commission for Austria in their unpractical but highly ornamental offices in Kaiser Franz Josef's palace at Schönbrunn.

We could just as easily have gone by tram, but tram-riding was unnecessary even if no conducting officer was available. A couple of days after I had settled in at the Press Camp, our affable colonel asked me how I was fixed for transport. I could always get the loan of a jeep and a military driver, he said, but perhaps I would prefer a car of my own. In that case I should go round and see the sergeant in charge of transport (presumably the head groom), and he would fix me up.

Recalling the parting warning from Reuters in London to keep down my expense account, I asked what the hire costs would be. 'But you don't understand the position, my dear fellow,' said the colonel. 'In the last weeks of the war we picked up such a lot of private cars which had been requisitioned by the Wehrmacht that we really don't know what to do with them. The best ones have all been allotted by now, I expect, but the sergeant will certainly be able to find you one that runs. Then it's all yours.'

So I suddenly and unexpectedly found myself provided with a private car. My first car, a clapped-out Opel Rekord, only held up for a few weeks, but a judicious bottle of whisky for the transport sergeant produced a sturdier vehicle, an Austrian-made Steyr. A few months later our colonel, working on some military old-boy network, got his hand on half a dozen brand-new Volkswagen Beetles, which had just started coming off the production lines in the British zone of Germany, and I was able to buy one for the enormous sum of £160.

Most of the correspondents in the British Press Camp at the time I arrived in October 1945 were veteran genuine war correspondents, some of whom had covered the entire long march of the British Army from El Alamein right up the Italian peninsula and into Austria. Among them were several outstanding journalists whose names had become household words to the British public when they wrote of the Eighth Army. A few had adapted quickly to reporting the confused affairs of central Europe in the first months of uneasy peace, but others, battle-weary and with little interest in central European politics, were just coasting along, filing little except human-interest stories on how Private Joe Doakes of Huddersfield got along with Viennese waltzes and Viennese girls, and dreary hand-outs from the British Control Commission.

Though I had no experience at all as a foreign correspondent, I could read the Austrian press and talk to Austrians without an interpreter, and I knew quite a lot of the historical background. This gave me a head start.

Luckily at about the same time a few British correspondents who knew the form better than I did begin to trickle in. In particular, I was taken under the friendly wing of the *Daily Express* correspondent, Peter Smollett, who quickly introduced me to all the Austrians who mattered; from Chancellor Karl Renner, who had been a leading Austrian socialist since before the First World War and had headed the Austrian delegation to the peace conference in St Germain in 1919, to Leopold Figl, Catholic politician and later Chancellor, who had spent a long term in a nazi concentration camp for his Austrian nationalist opposition to Hitler.

Probably the most useful contact provided by Peter Smollett was Ernst Fischer, a one-time young socialist leader who had joined the Communist Party in the mid-1930s and spent the war years in Moscow as a radio propagandist. He was now back in Vienna as Minister of Education in the Provisional Austrian Government, and joint editor of a daily published jointly by the three licensed Austrian political parties: the rightist People's Party, the Socialist Party and the Communist Party. Inevitably these emergent parties were more or less openly sponsored by one or other of the occupation powers. The USA favoured the People's Party, the British the Socialist Party, and the Soviet Union the Communist Party. By some oversight, the French were left without a satellite of their own.

Chancellor Karl Renner, a distinguished old man with a sense of humour, was obviously delighted at having been suddenly promoted from obscure old-age pensioner to head of government. He not only leaked news readily if he thought it was to the advantage of Austria, but was also a source of anecdotes.

Asked how he liked being Austrian Chancellor, he replied, 'How would you like to be rowing a leaky rowing boat with four elephants as your passengers?' – referring of course to the four occupying powers. It was a nice crack, but like so many witty sayings did not really meet the situation. It would have been nearer the truth to say that Karl Renner, representing Austria, was the passenger, and the four elephants were at the oars, furiously rowing in increasingly differing directions.

Sitting in a quiet corner with Chancellor Renner and several other journalists at an official reception, I asked him what had launched him on his meteoric new career at the age of seventy-four.

'The story actually starts in 1910,' he said, 'but we had better skip a few years. During the nazi years they left me alone. I was an old man out of political life, living in the village of Gloggnitz, south of Vienna.

'After the Red Army arrived at the beginning of April there was a lot of confusion, so I set out to find a Soviet command post. I thought I might be able to help to restore order locally, as a village mayor, or something like that.

'I finally found the command post in the nearby village of Köttlach, and enquired if they could use me, as an anti-nazi and old socialist. They weren't very interested – dozens of "instant anti-nazis" were offering their services. But then a senior officer glanced at my papers. "Karl Renner?" he said. "You wouldn't be the Renner whom Generalissimo Stalin attacked in one of his books?"

'For a moment I thought of denying it,' Renner continued. 'Having been publicly attacked by Stalin didn't seem much of a recommendation at that time and place. But it had happened a long time ago; so, choosing my words carefully, I said to the Soviet officer, "I am very proud that Comrade Stalin did me the honour, back in 1913, of studying my book on the problems of the nationalities in the Austro-Hungarian Empire, and I read with great interest his criticism in his book *Marxism and the National Question*. The Comrade Colonel (I think he was a colonel) will certainly recall that Comrade Lenin gave great praise to Comrade Stalin's book."

'The colonel sent me home in a jeep, with a big parcel of food, and stationed a Red Army soldier at the door, either to guard me or to keep an eye on me. And a few days later I was rushed to Vienna, which had just been liberated, and asked if I would agree to head the Provisional Government of the Austrian Republic. Which just goes to show what comes of writing a widely-ignored political polemic when you are a young man.'

Although selected on such a haphazard basis, Chancellor Renner did a good job of getting the new-born Austrian state off to a relatively good start, though his work was hampered by the fact that the western powers refused to recognise the Renner Government for the first six months of the occupation. In a small country devastated by war and occupied by four different armies with differing aims, the Austrian Government found itself in an almost untenable semi-puppet position with four different hands trying to pull the strings.

A rather hilarious but not very dignified exhibition of this semi-colonial status was played out in public. At the end of 1945, after the usual four-power wrangling, general elections were held to replace the *ad hoc* Soviet-appointed provisional government. On 19 December the newly elected Parliament, in which the People's Party held a small margin over the socialists, leaving the Communists a bad third, met in solemn session to proclaim the restoration of Austrian independence. The distinguished strangers' gallery was jammed with officers of four nations in their very best uniforms; the press were there in force. Flashbulbs popped as press photographers jostled for good shots of Karl Renner making the solemn declaration.

He had just finished and was beginning to sit down when there was a commotion at the rear of the chamber, and two belated American photographers erupted into the hall. Before anyone had really grasped what was happening, the two men, hung with cameras like Christmas trees, had clambered on to the dais, raced round to the centre, loomed over Renner and shouted, 'Do it again, Mr President!' So the dignified old man, bowing to the Allied instructions, proclaimed once again the re-establishment of the Republic.

Peter Smollett of the *Daily Express* taught me a lot about the job, including the necessity of asking people awkward questions, something from which I shrank, possibly as a result of my early Quaker surroundings. Smollett's real name was Smolka, and he was a Viennese who had spent the nazi years in Britain. After I had left Vienna he settled down in his old home town again. Struck by paralysis, he spent his last years of life almost totally immobilised in a wheelchair, but amazingly remained so alert and witty that one forgot, after a few minutes, that only his brain was in full function. Until his death a few years ago he was one of the closest advisers of Austrian Chancellor Kreisky.

In the notorious Slansky trial in Prague in 1952, in which a large part of the leadership of the Czechoslovak Communist Party was framed on treason charges, Peter Smollett was fleetingly mentioned in evidence as a notorious British spy. Since such noted British spies as Noel Coward were also dragged in, and since a large part of the evidence was transparently fraudulent, I tend to regard this as fairly conclusive evidence that my friend was not a British spy.

Apart from his other friendly services, Smollett introduced me to my second wife. She came from the impoverished Austrian aristocracy, and rejoiced in the title of Countess: the Count, her father, had apparently gamed away the family fortunes in his youth. As a progressive I have never had much time for titles, but I should admit that when we got married I felt slightly aggrieved that when a count marries his wife automatically becomes a countess, but not vice versa. She was a jolly plump girl with great charm, who got along well with everybody – except eventually with me. We parted and got divorced quite amicably about three years later.

But life in Vienna was not all country-house-style living, presidential anecdotes and aristocratic marriages. I worked hard, learned a lot and apparently satisfied my London bosses. In December 1946 they suddenly switched me to Warsaw.

23

The Chink in the Iron Curtain

By December 1946 the weapons had been silent in Europe for over eighteen months, but conditions were still unsettled in many places. Cross-continental travel was still a considerable undertaking.

First I flew back from Vienna to London for a short briefing on my new job, which looked considerably more daunting that the Vienna assignment. For a start I could speak no Polish, and had only a superficial knowledge of the very complicated Polish political scene; for another thing I would no longer be able to rely on British military rations and accommodation, but would have to fend for myself with regard to bed and food and news transmission facilities in what was certainly the worst-battered capital in Europe.

Even getting from London to Warsaw appeared to be a complicated operation. Thomas Cook informed me that there was said to be a through-train from Paris to Warsaw two or three times a week, but the breakdown in international traffic information had been so complete that even Cooks had no reliable information on the route taken or the timetable. They would be grateful if I would drop them a line with a few details if or when I actually arrived. A few useful hints for travellers would be nice too, for instance whether it was advisable to provide oneself with food and drink for the whole journey.

Then I needed a transit visa for France, a special stamp from the Allied Control Commission for Germany allowing me to pass through the British and US zones, a Czechoslovak transit visa and of course a Polish visa.

As it turned out, the trip was relatively uneventful, though I was glad that Thomas Cook had raised the question of iron rations. Unsurprisingly,

148

there were no restaurant cars all across sharply rationed post-war Europe, except for a short stretch in Czechoslovakia. For much of the journey I appeared to be the only passenger on the train; for few people wanted to go to ruined Warsaw, and even fewer had a legitimate reason for the trip which was necessary to collect assorted visas.

I should have known better than to choose a train which landed me in Warsaw late at night on 24 December 1946. Reuters had cabled the Polish News Agency asking them to reserve me a room, and had received a reply saying I should check in at the Hotel Polonia, one of the only two hotels then operating. From the railway station I rode rather grandly in a four-wheel horse cab through the wintry streets to the hotel; but at the reception desk they looked blank: no reservation. And there was no room at the inn: it was, of course, Christmas Eve.

Luckily there is a very substantial freemasonry among foreign correspondents as long as a scoop is not involved, and I managed to locate a colleague from the *New York Times* staying in the hotel. He immediately fixed me up in the room of another American correspondent who was away over Christmas. When the holiday season was finally over the press department of the Polish Foreign Ministry found me more permanent quarters in a small *pension* near the Polonia, which had apparently earlier been a Wehrmacht brothel, and had thus escaped the general destruction of Warsaw's remaining buildings when the nazis left.

The rather down-at-heel Polonia, with its various annexes like my *pension*, was at that time one of the busiest centres in sorely stricken Warsaw. It was inhabited almost entirely by foreigners, for there was a complete lack of alternative accommodation, and functioned rather more like a large office block than a hotel. It housed twenty or thirty journalists who lived and worked in their rooms, and also several embassies and a number of consulates, where business was done over half-made beds and on small tables set up in bathrooms and halls.

The hotel corridors were choked all day long by queues of people from all parts of the world who had been marooned in Poland since Hitler invaded in 1939, or who had been washed up there by the vast movements of populations across Europe in the closing months of the war and the first months of peace. Now they hoped that their consulates could help them to go home. The situation was naturally complicated by the fact that many had no proper documents.

One of the more unexpected features was the long queue of persons claiming Chinese citizenship. These people waited, rather less than impassively, outside the office of the Chinese consul, who at that time represented Chiang Kai-shek's government. Many of them were apparently

Chinese seamen who had jumped ship somewhere in eastern Europe many years previously, and had managed to establish themselves in a small line as laundrymen or restaurant keepers: during the war most of them had survived inoffensively as exotic waiters or servants in Wehrmacht officers' messes. The Chinese consul was inevitably known to the Anglo-American section of the Hotel Polonia as the Chink in the Iron Curtain, a crack which I report with some reluctance.

As soon as I had a bed of my own and a table for my typewriter, I set about the task of trying to provide Reuters with a decent news service from Warsaw, but there were considerable obstacles. For a start there was my complete lack of Polish, and a big further complication was provided by the poor communications with London. Theoretically there was direct phone and cable contact, but there were few telephones, few international lines and almost total incomprehensibility if you managed to get through.

In addition there was the frustrating 'hard currency barrier', which needs a little explanation. Reuters, which was bound by post-war British exchange restrictions, and was anyway strikingly parsimonious, had insisted that I should pay for my living and working expenses from the vast stock of non-transferrable Polish currency accumulating to Reuters' account from the sale of the international news service to the Polish News Agency.

This may have seemed right and reasonable to the bookkeepers in London, but on the ground the situation was different. The Polish zloty, like the Polish economy, was in desperate straits. I could pay my hotel bill and eat off-the-ration hotel food by drawing enormous sums of zloties, but even handfuls of zloties were useless for bribing the telephone girls, who wanted nice hard dollars. Many foreign correspondents had them, and they inevitably went to the top of the queue.

About four months later, the zloty gap would cause Reuters to withdraw me from Warsaw. The London bookkeepers, alarmed at the fact that I was literally eating up their zloty mountain at the rate of well over £100 per week – at that time my salary was £700 a year – demanded an explanation. When I showed them, with a detailed financial statement, that I would need a cost-of-living supplement of at least £5,000 a year, a vast sum in those days, they decided to close down the Warsaw office.

On the news-gathering front I had some luck, for General Grosz, head of the Foreign Ministry press department, suggested I should try to engage as assistant an experienced journalist who had just got back to Warsaw from emigration in Sweden. Immanuel Birnbaum, a dour tall man who never appeared to smile, was a real acquisition. He was a first-class journalist in the best central European tradition, and without his guidance I would have made a lot of nasty mistakes.

But there were disadvantages too. Mr Birnbaum's idea of a story was a measured and well-informed leisurely essay on trends and developments, illustrated with well-chosen historical parallels and spiced with Latin or even Greek tags. He would have been absolutely at home writing editorials for *The Times* in late-Victorian days.

Though he tried very hard, he never managed to master the news-agency style demanded by Reuters: a concise tailored message reporting the facts, presented in short paragraphs and in its ideal form written in such a way that it can be 'cut from the bottom'. This means that all the salient facts should, if possible, be crammed into the first short paragraph, and then fleshed out in the remainder of the story. A textbook example of such a dispatch – actually fairly rare in the competitive haste of most agency work – would consist of perhaps ten short paragraphs, but would still constitute a coherent story if a sub-editor cut away paragraphs from the bottom until he reached the number of column inches which he needed.

Since Mr Birnbaum simply gathered and explained the events of the day to me, and I prepared news items for transmission, this did not matter too much. However, I had to listen patiently while he lectured me at length on the various partitions of Poland, the exact configuration of the Curzon line or the complicated history of the early Polish Socialist Party (which bore the rather unlikely but memorable name of 'Social Democracy of the Kingdom of Poland and Lithuania', though that kingdom had vanished long before the party was formed).

When I left Warsaw I appointed Mr Birnbaum as Reuters' stringer after explaining to him at great length the virtue of brevity in a news-agency story. I am sure he tried hard, but Reuters told me some months later that they had had to dispose of his services because his dispatches were generally unsuitable. I am glad to report that this was by no means the end of his journalistic career. He later moved to West Germany, where he became foreign editor of the *Süddeutsche Zeitung*, which he helped to build into a first-class and balanced newspaper for the literate reader. He only retired from a post on the editorial board at the ripe old age of eighty.

Mr Birnbaum – I find it impossible to think of him simply as Birnbaum – taught me a lot about history and kept me well posted on current events, but I and other foreign correspondents were treated to very high-level instruction on the same subject in the first months of 1947. One day the Foreign Ministry press department informed us that Boleslaw Bierut,

President of Poland, would like to see the western press the next day, not for a press conference but for an informal chat.

Since top government figures were relatively unapproachable, the press corps turned out in force. The President, a stubby man with a tiny dark moustache, was a veteran Communist who had spent the war years in Moscow. He greeted us very cordially, and explained that he had asked us round because he had been upset by the misapprehensions and misinformation in many western press reports. He had concluded, he said, that much of the misreporting was not due to ill-will, but had come about because most of us knew so little about his country. Nobody, he said, could understand the Poland of today without some knowledge of Polish history, so he had decided to give us three or four short talks on the subject.

And so, on that Sunday afternoon, and several subsequent Sunday afternoons, he chatted to us on the subject. He did not speak from a prepared manuscript, but simply referred from time to time to a few notes on a small piece of paper. Some of the correspondents were restive at first, murmuring about being sent back to school, but President Bierut did so well that quite a high proportion returned the next week for another instalment.

There was, of course, the added attraction that after his chat the President responded fairly freely to questions on affairs of the day, which provided a few of those news items which state, slightly tendentiously, 'The Polish President told me today' – as if the reporter had been the only person in the room.

Early in my collaboration with Mr Birnbaum, before I really had a chance to appreciate his acute nose for news, I ignored one of his tips, thus missing not only a good exclusive story, but also the chance of being present at one of the more remarkable finds in what might be called contemporary archaeology.

A short excursion into history is unavoidable. Soon after the nazis occupied Warsaw in 1939 they quarantined the mainly Jewish quarter of the city, walled it in very efficiently and concentrated there not only the large Jewish community of Warsaw, but also Jews from other parts of Poland. By summer 1942 the Warsaw Ghetto had a population of some 500,000, living in conditions of the utmost squalor, and trying to survive on rations far below the starvation level. Huge deportations to the death camps, coupled with 'natural' deaths, quickly reduced the population to well under 100,000, and in April 1943 Hitler ordered their total liquidation.

But when SS units backed up by Wehrmacht detachments moved in to liquidate the Ghetto, they were shocked to run into determined armed resistance, and for over three weeks poorly armed Jewish partisans fought back. Inevitably they were overcome, the last Jews were deported, and the epic Warsaw Ghetto Rising was over.

Just for the record, and because it does not appear to be mentioned in most of the many books on the subject, it may be worth recalling that the first steps to build the Jewish Fighting Organisation in the Warsaw Ghetto were taken by a survivor of the Polish section of the International Brigades in Spain. In autumn 1941 a young Warsaw Jew named Pinkus Kartin (who had fought in Spain under the name Andrzej Szmidt) was parachuted into nazi-occupied Poland from a Soviet plane. He had been charged with possibly the most suicidal mission of the Second World War: to organise armed resistance in the Warsaw Ghetto.

He was caught and killed by the Gestapo in May 1942, but before that he had managed to overcome some of the deep traditional divisions between various parties which were ready to fight back – in the main the Hashomer (Zionist socialists), the Bund (anti-Zionist socialists) and Communists – and to organise small resistance units with a pitiful armoury of pistols and explosives mainly purchased on the Warsaw black market and smuggled into the Ghetto through the sewers. After his death the main work of organising the resistance was taken over by Mordechai Anielewicz of Hashomer, commander of the Jewish Fighting Organisation in the rising.

Since the inhabitants of the Warsaw Ghetto were wiped out almost to a man, in the first post-war years there were practically no reliable or detailed accounts either of everyday life in the doomed Ghetto or of the armed resistance. Among the few survivors – a handful of Jews had found refuge with friends on the 'Aryan' side, and others had escaped to the forests to join the partisans – there were rumours that Dr Ringelblum, a historian, had collected details both of daily life in the Ghetto, and of the organisation of the resistance. But it was generally believed that any such records must have been lost when the Germans dynamited the remaining ruins of the Ghetto after the rising.

Now, from a friend in the Jewish Community Council, Mr Birnbaum had learned that they hoped that day to unearth some of Dr Ringelblum's papers. A message giving the exact location of the hoard had been received from a Ghetto fighter who had escaped, fought with the partisans and then made his way to Palestine. We ought to go along and watch the search, Mr Birnbaum suggested. It should make a good story.

I had never heard of Dr Ringelblum, and could not believe that his records, even if they could be located in the huge expanse of broken rubble, would be of any particular interest. It was one of my big mistakes. Dr Ringelblum must have been one of the most far-sighted and determined historians of modern times, for he had not only collected every scrap of evidence of life in the doomed Ghetto, but had also taken great precautions to see that his archives survived. As soon as he had accumulated enough material – his own diary of daily events, copies of underground leaflets, copies of Yiddish schoolbooks produced illegally, a painstaking record of current rumours and jokes and much more – he would seal it in a large zinc milk-can, and bury it at a spot which could probably be located even if every house was smashed. When the end was near he notified a few trusted friends of the exact locations in the hope that the news would survive the war.

The excavation which I missed was the first of a whole series during the subsequent months and years, finds which have filled in what would otherwise have been almost a blank page in history.

I did see another, appalling, excavation, for gruesome finds were common in Warsaw. Wandering rather aimlessly through the ruins one bright winter Sunday morning, I and a colleague chanced upon a small group who had dug a shallow trench, and were now stacking along its rim the corpses they had disinterred – the bodies of over a hundred men, women and children, frozen solid in the harsh winter cold. They were Poles, executed by the Wehrmacht when it 'pacified' the city following the abortive Warsaw Rising of 1944, not to be confused with the earlier Ghetto Rising. All over the city similar work was in progress, and thousands of corpses were disinterred, identified where possible and buried again on hallowed ground.

A number of men responsible for the mass slaughter in Poland had been caught, mainly in the British and US zones of Germany, and in that early period, when East–West co-operation still functioned in certain fields, some had been handed over to the Polish authorities for trial, in accordance with an Allied wartime agreement that war criminals should be sent to stand trial at the scene of their crimes. One of these trials in Warsaw remains clear in memory. The man tried was possibly the greatest mass murderer in history, though the title might also go to Adolf Eichmann. He was a relatively unknown minor nazi official named Rudolf Hoess, and he had been Commandant of Auschwitz concentration camp for a large part of its history.

Here is my report on Hoess, as it was sent out by Reuters in London on 31 March 1947:

From John Peet, Reuters correspondent, Warsaw, Monday – Rudolf Hoess, 47-year-old ex-commander of Auschwitz Concentration Camp, now awaiting sentence on charges of murdering 4,000,000 people, told me in an interview today: 'If I had been ordered to gas and burn my wife and five children I would have done it. Of course, I would then have killed myself too.' Hoess, stocky and well-nourished, wearing a neat but well-worn Wehrmacht uniform without insignia, stood strictly to attention between two Polish guards armed with tommy-guns as he answered questions intelligently and precisely.

Asked why he had not followed Hitler's example and committed suicide, Hoess, who had gassed tens of thousands of children, said: 'I and my wife considered this, but felt we could neither kill our innocent children nor leave them alone in the world.'

Hoess said: 'I admit fully my guilt for all that wanton Auschwitz killing now that I realise our ideology was false. I joined the nazi Party in 1922 after hearing Hitler speak in the Munich Beer Hall. From then until the collapse I believed implicitly in his promises and statements.

'After the collapse, when I was free for eight months, I read the papers and heard the radio, and realised for the first time that the foundations on which my belief was built were thoroughly false.

'Specifically, it became clear to me that Germany was the aggressor and had not been brutally encircled and attacked.

'I was amazed at the magnanimity the Allies have shown towards the Germans after the way we behaved.'

When he, as a high SS officer, left Berlin and travelled westward in the days just before the German collapse, he said, 'we believed implicitly Hitler's and Goebbels's promises that a new wonder weapon would save the day.

'During the journey we were drawing up plans where to establish a new seat of government and how to organise further arms production. Doenitz's declaration that the war was lost was like lightning from a clear sky.

'If I had my life again I certainly would not behave in the same way, because I realise now that the foundations of my entire belief were wrong. I should, instead, buy a little farm which would provide future security for my children.

Asked whether he considered he had had a fair trial, he said: 'Absolutely, though I was in no position to produce defence witnesses.'

Then, with German bureaucratic thoroughness, Hoess proceeded to 'correct' the statement of a witness who said the 80,000 people were gassed in a single night. 'This would mean 40 train loads,' said Hoess. 'Even the most modern marshalling yards could not handle 40 trains in one night.'

At the end of the interview Hoess, who appears neither as a figure of horror nor as a pathetic tool, but simply as a well-educated, intelligent, precise little German official, clicked his heels and marched out between the guards. End.

A few minutes after I had interviewed Hoess, the court reassembled and very predictably sentenced Hoess to death. He was hanged on the parade ground at Auschwitz some days later.

Perhaps I should add a few details omitted for reasons of length from my Reuters dispatch. After Hoess had been convicted, and the court had been adjourned while the judges deliberated on the sentence, I buttonholed the Polish State Prosecutor and asked rather diffidently whether it would be possible to have a few words with the convicted man.

'No trouble at all,' he said, rather to my astonishment, and led me to a room at the back of the court.

Hoess was standing against one wall, very straight and a little nervous between the two Polish soldiers, looking slightly confused by the bustle and hurry as lawyers came and went. Court interpreters, glad to be released from the strain of the two-week trial, were smoking cigarettes.

After asking Hoess a few questions, I said, 'What did you want to be when you were young?' and received the astonishing reply, 'I always wanted to be a missionary, but my father would not let me.' At this point I automatically reached into my pocket for a cigarette, and just as automatically held out the packet to the prisoner.

But Hoess, who had been a disciplined official and a disciplined mass murderer, was a disciplined prisoner too. He clicked his heels, bowed slightly and said, 'The regulations do not allow me to smoke, thank you.'

24

All the Conspirators

Most European countries in early 1947, less than two years after the end of the war, were in a fairly parlous state, and Poland was one of the worst hit. Apart from the normal ruins left behind as the fronts lumbered to and fro across the country, there had been vast massacres by the nazis and enormous movements of population. From 1939 onward the German occupation power had driven millions of Poles eastwards across the new borders of 'Greater Germany', and then, with the end of the war, the victorious Allies had shifted the whole of Poland bodily a couple of hundred miles westwards. This meant that the eastern part of Poland, with a largely White Russian and Ukrainian population, was incorporated into the Soviet Union, and most of the Polish inhabitants moved westwards at the same time as some eight million people of German origin and language fled or were expelled over the new Polish western frontier into Germany.

Moving and resettling millions of Poles was only one of the problems. During the war, a large portion of the population had been involved in the resistance movement. It would be more correct to say 'movements', since the resistance was sadly fragmented. The most powerful was the 'Home Army', of which at least the leaders wished to restore the pre-war authoritarian regime. Very active, but considerably smaller, was the 'People's Army', under Communist leadership but taking in wide sections of the left. In addition, there were a multitude of smaller resistance organisations, often on a local basis.

When the Germans were driven out, the Soviets naturally favoured the left, and the first Provisional Government was mainly composed of

157

Communists and socialists. Many members of the Home Army, satisfied that Poland was again ruled by Poles, emerged from the underground and resumed normal life, inasmuch as any life was normal in Poland in those days. More intransigent right-wing elements, basing themselves on the widespread feeling that anything connected with Russia – whether Tsarist or Communist – was bad, kept their underground fighting units in being, waiting for the day when the British and Americans would arrive to drive out the Russians.

To prevent the new regime from stabilising itself, political murder was widespread. Practically every day reports came in of the assassination of local government officials in small towns and villages in the provinces, though Warsaw itself was relatively quiet.

Foreign correspondents in Warsaw got a glimpse of the quantities of arms still in the hands of the underground one day in spring 1947. The authorities, aware that many of the underground groups were ready to surface and return to normal life, but did not know what to do with their arms hoards, had proclaimed an amnesty. It was announced that, on a given date, anyone could surrender weapons at the nearest police station with no questions asked, and a bounty would be paid out, in cash, for every revolver, rifle or other weapon turned in.

I toured the suburbs of Warsaw early on the Sunday morning appointed, and it was an astonishing sight. Everywhere you looked, men were trekking to the nearest police station. Some were carrying one or more rifles, others were dragging behind them heavy Russian machine guns on their wheeled trollies – possibly trophies from the Polish–Soviet War of 1920 – and others had rucksacks full of small arms. I was sorry to miss the sight reported by colleagues: in one street they encountered a group manhandling a heavy German anti-tank gun.

Polish acquaintances assured me that evening that a good number of the weapons had never reached the police stations, for members of the 'no surrender' groups in the underground had often waylaid the surrenderers and offered them double the bounty they would have received from the police, then hurrying the weapons off to new places of concealment. It was officially announced that country-wide the arms surrendered included 10 pieces of artillery, 3,500 machine guns and tens of thousands of lighter weapons.

Early one morning, a far-out section of the underground paid me a visit in an episode taken straight out of a thriller. I was woken by a sharp rap on my door. Thinking it was the hotel porter, come rather earlier than usual to stoke up the enormous tiled stove which kept the room warm, I shouted that he should come in. The door opened, and a total stranger slipped quickly in and closed the door behind him. With a conspiratorial gesture he placed his finger on his lips and then cupped his ear to indicate that the walls might have ears, and I should say nothing. Intrigued, I waited to see what might happen next.

My visitor, a thin-faced young man wearing a short fur-lined jacket and riding boots, peered round suspiciously and walked quietly to my bed. There he cautioned me to silence once again, held out one hand and with the other forefinger drew the three letters U-P-A.

If he was telling the truth, I was confronted by a representative of possibly the most ruthless and effective of the various underground armies then operating in Poland: and it was not even a Polish outfit. The letters UPA stood (in Ukranian) for Ukranian Insurgent Army, a far-right organisation with a chequered, bloody and confusing history, dating back at least to the Civil War in the young Soviet Union after the First World War. The only clear aim of UPA was the establishment of a united 'Greater Ukraine' incorporating the Soviet Ukraine, eastern Poland and the eastern tip of Czechoslovakia, with their considerable Ukrainian populations.

In the 1930s elements of the UPA had been in contact with the nazis, hoping for their help in setting up 'Free Ukraine', and when the Wehrmacht invaded the Soviet Union in June 1941 the organisation went into immediate action. When the Wehrmacht, in its rapid advance, reached the city of Lviv (more usually known by its Russian and Polish name of Lvov or Lwow), it was rather surprised to discover that the local UPA units had taken the city over as the Red Army had retreated, had proclaimed a Free Ukrainian state and had already launched a pogrom against the considerable Jewish population.

The nazi political officer accompanying the first Wehrmacht units (Professor Theodor Oberländer, in 1953 a minister in Chancellor Adenauer's West German Government) told the insurgents firmly that a 'Free Ukraine' was not as yet on the nazi programme. Instead of setting up a state immediately they should concentrate on killing Jews. If they ran out of Jews, Polish intellectuals in the city would make a good target group.

The story of UPA during the Second World War is almost impossible to disentangle. Various feuding UPA groups intermittently collaborated with the nazi occupation forces in combating Soviet and Polish partisans, and between times fought each other and indulged in banditry. The nazis grew so tired of their irresponsible friends that they threw several of their leaders into concentration camps, only releasing them again in the closing stages of the war in an attempt to recruit last-minute allies against the Red Army.

In the general confusion at the end of the war the remnants of UPA managed to establish themselves in some force in a remote and easily defensible area of south-east Poland in the district of Sanok. Small-scale offensives launched by the Polish Army were beaten back, and it was apparently decided to leave them to stew in their own juice for the time being.

I nodded to the underground conspirator standing at my bed to show I understood 'UPA'. He proceeded to explain in pantomime that he would like to talk to me, but not in a hotel room. I signalled back 'Where?' and he whipped out a street map, indicated a street intersection in Praga, a suburb on the other bank of the River Vistula, mimed a rendezvous at eleven that evening, handed me a UPA leaflet as an indication of his bona fides, saluted smartly and left as silently as he had come.

The leaflet, written in English and rather smudgily cyclostyled, was addressed to President Truman and Winston Churchill and called upon them to rush to the aid of Free Ukraine, which was being oppressed by the Russians, Poles, Czechos and possibly a few others.

Over coffee and a cigarette I pondered what to do. Information from inside 'Free Ukraine' was obviously news whatever the merits or demerits of the UPA cause. On the other hand, the Polish authorities were understandably suspicious of contacts between correspondents and underground organisations, UPA in particular. Only a few weeks before I reached Warsaw a British correspondent had been given a conducted tour of UPA territory, and been cajoled into taking the salute at a parade of UPA troops. When the news got out, the Polish authorities cancelled his visa, and indicated that more serious action would be taken if there was any repetition.

But there were other angles to be considered too. My UPA visitor could easily have been a plant. Perhaps the Security Police wanted to clamp down on foreign correspondents generally, and in this case catching a British journalist at a clandestine meeting with a representative of a group engaged in armed rebellion would provide an excellent excuse. It would, for instance, be all too easy to inflate my service as a detective constable in Haifa CID into 'notorious agent of British intelligence'.

After a few more cigarettes I decided on a course of action, and trudged through the snow to the Polish Foreign Ministry, where I asked for a few words with General Wiktor Grosz, head of the press department. The general was not a professional military man, but a very intelligent and friendly pre-war journalist, who had served in the Polish Second Army, raised in 1942 in the Soviet Union.

To make matters easier for both of us, I presented him with a hypothetical case. What, in his opinion, would be the right action for a foreign journalist approached by someone claiming to represent a subversive organisation? Grosz, entering into the spirit of the game, said that it was not his job, in his official capacity, to give any guidance to journalists on how they did their work; but speaking as a journalist himself he would be inclined to go after the story; if the correspondent in question had a good record as a responsible journalist, he did not think the authorities would be unusually alarmed if he established unorthodox contacts in the course of his professional duties.

I was trying to frame a tactful question about the hypothetical frame-up of the hypothetical correspondent when the general himself came to my aid . 'If our very vigilant security authorities should happen to get wind of such a contact, I think you could assure your colleague – unofficially, of course – that our ministry would put in a good word for him. And if your colleague would drop by and tell me about the meeting – without fingering his contact, of course – I would be grateful.'

So late that evening I put on my warmest clothes and hired a droshky for the long cold ride to Praga. Before leaving my room I slipped into my pocket the heavy Walther automatic which one of the Vienna Press Camp officers had given me as a souvenir. I lugged it round with me conscientiously during my years as a foreign correspondent, but never used it. Once I brandished it successfully when I emerged late at night from the flat I had rented on the Stefansplatz in Vienna, and found a Soviet soldier busily unscrewing one of the wheels of my car.

Trying to remember some of the rules of conspiracy as set out in the spy novels, I gave the droshky driver an address several streets away from the agreed rendezvous, waited until he had clopped away over the frozen and rutted snow, and then back-tracked to the corner stipulated. On the stroke of eleven the man in riding boots popped up beside me, clutched my arm and led me in silence and darkness through a maze of back alleys. At that time there were a few street lights back in service in central Warsaw, but the suburbs were in total darkness.

After a few minutes of zigzagging, we slipped through a doorway and traversed what appeared to be a devastated warren of shattered tenements. Here and there a light flickered in a window, but otherwise there was no sign of life. Finally my guide, doing things by the book, rapped out what was obviously the agreed signal on a door. The door creaked open, and I found myself in a small room, unfurnished except for a small table and a couple of chairs. The only light came from an oil lamp in the far corner, and the window was blacked-out with a heavy blanket.

At the table sat a heavily built man in a bulky sheepskin coat. In the background hovered his bodyguard, also shapeless in a sheepskin, over which he had strapped one of those enormous Mauser pistols which you sometimes glimpse in early films of the Russian Revolution, and which turned up again in Spain. The automatic itself is not particularly large, but it is carried in a massive wooden holster shaped like a rifle butt. For long-range shots you draw the pistol, unhitch the holster from your belt, clip the pistol on to the bottom of the holster and use the whole unwieldy contraption like a carbine. It is not really a quick-draw weapon.

While I was taking in the details of the scene, the 'B' film in which I was apparently playing ran on its predetermined grooves. My guide, standing behind me, murmured 'Excuse me,' ran his hands over me, extracted the Walther pistol from my right coat pocket, glanced at it to see that the safety was on and placed it on the table. The thickset man looked at it and said, in heavily accented English, 'You are a wise man, sir. Warsaw nights are full of bad people. But here with us you are safe.'

Then he launched into a short prepared speech, introducing himself as the head of the Warsaw delegation of the Free Ukranian Nation. After a few sentences he asked whether I spoke French or German, and switched into German. He was delighted, he said, to have the opportunity to present the case of the Ukranian Insurgent Army to that great nation, headed by the great Winston Churchill, which had always in history stood side by side with the great and generous Ukrainian people who for centuries (or possibly millennia – I have forgotten the details) had been holding high the banner of Christian civilisation in eastern Europe against the rapacious Russians, the hordes of Tartary, the treacherous Turks, the decadent Poles, the murderous Germans and anyone else one might like to mention. It was quite a performance.

When he paused for breath I explained as tactfully as possible that I was not Winston Churchill's personal envoy, but just a newspaperman whose job it was to report what was going on in various parts of the world. Since UPA was creating a certain amount of alarm and confusion in south-eastern Poland it was news, and that was my business. Could he perhaps give me some details of how much Polish territory they controlled, and what they hoped to do next.

The UPA man interrupted with some heat. 'We do not hold Polish territory. All the land which our brave divisions have liberated is historic Ukrainian earth. And we hold this earth not only in what you call south-east Poland but also for hundreds of kilometres into that part of the Ukraine which is today occupied by Moscow. The GPU may hold some of the towns, but the countryside is ours. And you ask what we shall do next. We shall extend our liberated territory, build up our forces and stand ready to fight side by side with the British and American troops when they come to free the world from the Bolshevik plague.'

Picking my words carefully I said I had heard it said that in the Second World War UPA had collaborated with the nazis, and perhaps been involved in pogroms.

I had rather expected another outburst, but the UPA man was obviously prepared for the question. 'I am sure you are familiar with your own island history, sir,' he said. 'Was it not the Irish patriot Sir Roger Casement who said that England's enemies are Ireland's friends? We had no liking for Hitler, but when he struck against the Red imperialists of Moscow we gave him some help since we hoped to gain freedom for the Ukraine. When we saw we had been fooled we took to the forests again.'

I reminded him about the pogroms. 'All those stories are greatly exaggerated,' he said. 'Some of our boys who had suffered under the sway of the criminal Red Jewish commissars got out of hand at times. I must assure you that some of my best friends are Jews.'

Then he indicated that he had other work to do, expressing his confidence I would inform the world of the struggle of the unconquerable Ukrainian people, and see to it that Winston Churchill hurried up with launching the Third World War. Then he handed me a small packet wrapped up in a copy of the Warsaw Communist newspaper. 'This will give you more details for your story. And don't forget your pistol, for there are bad people on the streets of Warsaw.'

That was it. My guide took me back to the road crossing, and I found my way to my hotel.

Next day I told General Grosz the main facts of my evening outing, and showed him the contents of the package – an assortment of cyclostyled handbills in half a dozen languages, including Ukrainian, with sweeping claims of vast UPA victories and impassioned appeals to western leaders for aid. I don't think any of the leaflets suggested that the Americans, who at that time had the atomic monopoly, should actually drop the A-bomb on Moscow, but that was the general tenor.

The only printed item was an undated sixteen-page pamphlet in German outlining Ukrainian history as UPA saw it. General Grosz regarded it with interest. This one I know,' he said. 'It was published in Lviv early in the war when they were still in full co-operation with the nazis.'

For Reuters I filed a short news item on the encounter, reporting some of the UPA claims and quoting a few lines from one of the leaflets. As far as I know it was never published anywhere: it may well have been spiked as un-newsworthy in Reuters' office in Fleet Street.

At a government reception on 10 March 1947 – Czechoslovak President

Klement Gottwald was on a state visit in Warsaw – General Grosz introduced me to General Karol Swierczewski, the Polish Defence Minister. I had last seen him under very different circumstances some nine years earlier, on 24 July 1938. The whole of the 15th International Brigade was assembled in a canyon a few hundred yards north of the River Ebro, waiting to cross the river in the last great Republican offensive. While we waited, a small group of American volunteers from the Lincoln-Washington Battalion performed, as the evening light faded, a few scenes from Clifford Odet's play *Waiting for Lefty*. We had been cautioned not to applaud or sing, for Franco's front lines were only a short distance away across the Ebro, so there was silence as the actors took their bows. Then a heavy-set figure in general's uniform appeared on the improvised stage. It was General Swierczewski, at that time known as 'General Walter', our divisional commander, and he gave us a short pep talk in Spanish.

When I recalled the scene for the general nine years later, his reserve lessened, and we chatted for a few minutes. Somehow we got on to the subject of UPA – I think he mentioned that one of his officers from Spain had recently been killed in a skirmish with the Ukrainian insurgents. I told him I had seen some of their literature claiming huge expanses of liberated territory.

'They exaggerate, of course,' said the general, 'but at least at night they still hold quite a lot of ground. It will take a fairly big military operation to clean them out.'

Just eighteen days later, on 28 March 1947, General Swierczewski, who had survived service in the Red Army in the Russian Civil War, more than two years' active service in Spain and service with the Polish Second Army on the Eastern Front in the Second World War, was ambushed and killed by UPA forces near Sanok in south-east Poland.

It was only several years later that UPA was finally routed. Some of the leaders managed to escape to West Germany, where, at least until a few years ago, they were still feuding among themselves in Munich.

It is only as I write these lines, over thirty-five years later, that I realise that among those with whom I chatted at that Warsaw reception there were several others who were fated to die abruptly not long afterwards. One of them was a talented Czech Communist journalist who generally wrote under the name of 'André Simon'. Under his real name, Otto Katz, he was executed in Prague in November 1952 together with Rudolf Slansky and eleven others, after conviction on charges of treason at the last of the Stalinist frame-up trials.

And it was Otto Katz who took me across the room and introduced me to Jan Masaryk, the Czechoslovak Foreign Minister, who on 10 March 1948 fell – or was pushed – from the window of his office in Prague.

During my few months in Warsaw I managed, unwittingly, to annoy the Vatican. On a short visit to Cracow, a United Press correspondent and I managed to get an interview with Poland's senior prelate, Cardinal Sapieha. He was an ancient, austere and sombre figure who would have been perfect in the role of a film cardinal, but he chatted to us pleasantly enough about his experiences during the war, and made some carefully worded remarks about the wish of the Catholic Church that all Poles should work together for the good of their homeland.

At that time there was much heated discussion among former Polish slave-labourers then living in camps for 'displaced persons' in the western zones of Germany as to whether or not they should return to Poland under its mainly Communist-oriented government. I asked the Cardinal his opinion. He considered the question for a while, and then said that for the laymen this must be a matter of conscience and personal decision, but that he felt that many of the hundreds of priests also in the camps really should return to Poland to strengthen the work of the Church there.

I filed the story for Reuters as just another routine dispatch, and forgot all about it; but the eagle eye of the Vatican was obviously upon me. A couple of days later I received a slightly worried service message from our London office, informing me that the *Osservatore Romano*, generally regarded as the Pope's mouthpiece, had been chiding Reuters for misquoting the Cardinal. He could not possibly have urged priests to return to Poland in its present state, the article said. Luckily the United Press correspondent had filed an almost identical story on the interview, and when I pointed this out to the London office they decided, possibly reluctantly, to believe me and not the Vatican.

My term in Warsaw was soon up. As I noted earlier, Reuters' bookkeepers in London had decided that it would be too expensive to keep me there, and I was instructed to return to Vienna to stand in for my successor while he went on holiday.

For the next few months I was shoved round the map of Europe while Reuters decided what to do with me next. When neo-fascist riots broke out in Rome, some bright editor in the London office apparently looked at an old school atlas, saw that Vienna was only inches away from Rome, and instructed me to hurry there. I rushed off in my car, only to discover that all the mountain passes between Austria and Italy were hopelessly blocked by landslides. By the time I finally got to Rome, driving the long way via Switzerland, the riots were long over. It would have been quicker to fly someone in from London – or from Sydney for that matter.

A few weeks later I once again became involved with a fairly unknown nationalist underground movement, this time in southern Austria. British Military Government, Austria, had indicated that it would be pleased if two or three correspondents could go down to Carinthia to report on how successfully the British forces there were dealing with some armed Yugoslav gangs who were roaming the area. So James Cameron and I set off.

Until that moment nobody had heard anything in Vienna about these gangs. In Klagenfurt, the capital of Carinthia, a British intelligence officer explained the situation. Southern Carinthia, which borders on Slovenia, the northernmost part of Yugoslavia, has a considerable minority population of Slovenes. During the war Slovene partisans who supported Tito had been active in Slovenia proper, the intelligence officer said, but there had also been another and smaller right-wing resistance group, which claimed to be fighting both the Germans and the 'Red-atheist Tito gang'.

When the war ended, elements of this right-wing armed group, calling themselves 'Soldiers of the Cross', had infiltrated across the mountain areas populated by the Slovene minority. It was bad enough having an unknown number of unpredictable armed men sitting up in the mountains of the British zone of Austria, he continued, but then things got worse: the 'Soldiers of the Cross' started raiding across the frontier into Yugoslavia, murdering and looting.

The Yugoslav authorities had repeatedly protested to the British military authorites in Austria, and recently they had indicated unofficially that if the British could not keep order in their own area, then Yugoslav forces would have to take the matter into their own hands. So, to prevent border incidents with all sorts of international repercussions, the British Army was going to try to smoke out the 'Soldiers of the Cross' in the next few days.

For the next day or two, James Cameron and myself sweated up and down the jagged mountain ranges of the Karawanken Mountains with several companies of British troops, raiding isolated farms and searching for the bivouac areas of the armed raiders. It was very good exercise, but the results were meagre in the extreme. In one farm we found a few traces – some crumpled leaflets in Slovene which turned out to be appeals to the people of Yugoslav Slovenia to rise against 'the Reds' and a few inoffensive scraps of military equipment – but that was about all.

Most of the local population – either sympathisers with the right-wing partisans, or afraid of them, or just working on the good old principle that we were bloody foreigners and should leave them alone – swore blind that they knew nothing about anything. So James and I and the disgruntled and foot-sore British soldiery clambered down the mountains again, feeling like the Duke of York.

The episode provided me with a short dispatch for Reuters, a rather longer story for *The Times* (for whose Vienna correspondent I was covering while he was on holiday) and a lifelong friendship with James Cameron.

Then Reuters in London had another bright idea as to what I should do next. The Paris bureau was short-handed, and I should move there immediately. So I loaded my goods into my Volkswagen and took off. My French was rudimentary – I had only reached the 'failed matric' level at school – but possibly the big minds of Reuters in London were going on the assumption that any Englishman who spoke good German must have learned good French first.

My stay in Paris was short, possibly a week. Harold King, the veteran chief of the Paris bureau, listened to my French for about thirty seconds and then said, 'Go away. I can't use you.' So finally, some time in summer 1947, Reuters dispatched me to Berlin, and there I have been ever since.

25

Scouts I Have Known

There seems no logical place to insert this chapter, so I put it in here. First, a word of explanation about the title. After a longish life largely devoted to press, publicity and propaganda, I have become rather sensitive about pejorative words and phrases, designed to make things appear in a negative light. The point I am trying to make was well summed up by a British academic, Norman Davies, writing in *The Times* on 11 April 1973:

'Our language is loaded against them. We are blessed with "governments", "alliances" and "security forces"; the Soviet bloc is burdened with "regimes", "satellites" and "secret police".

What should I do when I want to write about spies, undercover agents, spooks, counter-intelligence operatives and what have you? The Germans have the useful word *Kundschafter*, which means 'scout', to describe spies on their side, but unfortunately the English word 'scout' does awaken a certain vision of shorts and knobbly knees. Frankly, none of the intelligence operatives I have known ever wore shorts (with the possible exception of those in Palestine).

So perhaps we had better stick to the good old word 'spy'. It was only when I started accumulating notes for this book that it occurred to me that I had met, or nearly met, a very considerable number of spies, or more often ex-spies, who had worked for Britain, the Soviet Union and a smattering of other countries. Most of them I had met either when they had either retired gracefully or when they had finally been released from some gaol or another. Those spies on active service whom I may have met usually kept their mouths shut.

Nothing sensational is going to follow, I fear – just a few notes on some acquaintances over the past fifty-odd years. Spies whom everybody knows, like Malcolm Muggeridge, are obviously omitted.

One of the very nicest of my ex-spy friends was a fully-fledged German aristocrat named Gans Edler Herr zu Putlitz, who died in 1975 at the age of seventy-six. When he died, I published a short obituary in East Berlin, and I might as well quote that:

> Putlitz used to tell me his family looked down upon the Hohenzollerns – the Kaiser's line – as late arrivals. He had an extremely unusual and in many ways admirable biography. He served as a young officer in the Kaiser's army, and then looked all set for the orthodox life of an Establishment German, studying for a period at Oxford and then entering the German diplomatic service.
>
> When Hitler took over, Putlitz considered resigning because of his firm anti-nazi convictions, but friends urged him to remain at his post and 'bore from within' against the nazis. Quite a lot of his surviving contemporaries claim to have done something similar, but Wolfgang Putlitz genuinely did quite a lot, and at the risk of his neck. Because of his excellent knowledge of English he obtained an important post in the nazi embassy in London in the 1930s, and here he got in touch (through the offices of Iona Ustinov, father of the famous Peter Ustinov) with leading British politicians who were worried about the nazi menace to world peace. For a period of years he supplied British politicians (Lord Vansittart was one of his main contacts) with valuable and authentic information from within the nazi embassy. Transferred to Holland, he managed to escape to Britain at the last moment when the Wehrmacht invaded in May 1940.

The story should be completed with a couple of details I omitted at the time. Putlitz, taking the nazi embassy code-books with him, was whisked out of Holland by British Intelligence at the last moment, and with perhaps unusual perception the British operatives also saved his boy-friend, a handsome young German.

In the closing stages of the war he was employed on 'Black Radio' in Britain, a string of radio stations which pretended to be operating within Germany and which, by broadcasting a mixture of genuine and faked news, tried to confuse the Germans. (In the process, they sometimes confused other people too. Immediately after the 20 July 1944 bomb plot against Hitler, one of these 'black' stations appointed itself the mouthpiece of the anti-Hitler plotters, and broadcast totally imaginary but authentic-sounding reports of risings against the nazi regime in many parts of the Reich. On Jerusalem Radio we had never been warned of the top-secret

Black Radio network, and I fell for a few hours for some of these inventions, and included them in our news bulletins.)

Many years later, Sefton Delmer, who ran the Black Radio network, reminisced to me about Putlitz's work there. 'He was quite useful in providing juicy personal details about nazi diplomats,' said Delmer. 'But we did wish that he wouldn't insist on wearing silk stockings.'

After the war, Putlitz settled for a while in West Germany, where he re-entered government service. When he found himself working closely together with a lot of old nazis, who naturally regarded him as a traitor, he moved to the German Democratic Republic, where his main complaint was that he could not find any decent bridge partners.

In the 1960s I often lunched with Putlitz in the East Berlin Press Club, and picked his brains on nazi affairs in general, and in particular about old nazi diplomats who at that time dominated the West German Foreign Service. He often talked nostalgically about the old days when he had been doing a useful job as a British spy, and propounded at great length a whimsical idea about a neutral old-age retreat for spavined spies. 'Any old spies, as long as they could play bridge,' he would say. 'We could fight our old battles all over again.' The spies' retreat should be in the south of France, he thought, and perhaps it could be financed by the United Nations.

Some years earlier I had often lunched in the same place with another figure who had formerly been in the same line of business, though he had not perhaps been technically a spy. This was Dr Otto John, who for a few years in the early 1950s had been head of the West German 'Office for the Protection of the Constitution', which was the rough equivalent of the British Special Branch or the United States FBI.

Very unexpectedly, he suddenly appeared in East Berlin in July 1954, declaring he could no longer stand re-nazification in the West German Establishment and 'the one-sided attachment of West Germany to the American "policy of strength" which will lead inevitably to a new war on German soil.'

Seventeen months later, in December 1955, Otto John resurfaced in West Germany, and was later imprisoned there for four years on treason charges. The case of the here-again-there-again spy-master is so complicated, and so many conflicting stories have been told about it by almost everybody involved, that I find it impossible to summarise. I would refer any reader interested to the book *The Secret War for Europe* by Louis Hagen, which gives a fairly full account.

However, during his stay in the German Democratic Republic, Otto John became a habitué of the East Berlin Press Club; and apparently because he liked to exercise his fluent English and I was the only Englishman around, I often found him sliding into a chair at my table.

John would promptly order double brandies all round and launch into long and involved stories about his part in the anti-Hitler bomb plot of July 1944 and his conflicts with West German Chancellor Adenauer and in particular with Adenauer's personal assistant Hans Globke. The latter was rather a sinister figure who actually drafted most of the nazi anti-Jewish legislation, and then blandly later explained that he had only done it to tone down the harshness of these laws.

What struck me most strongly about Otto John was his obvious unfittedness as the head of an important intelligence organisation. He was very sensitive, and kept complaining about minor slights to which he had been exposed – slights which had come from leading nazis, from fellow-conspirators in the Hitler bomb plot, from British intelligence officers, from Chancellor Adenauer and Hans Globke and now, of course, from practically everybody he had come into contact with in East Germany.

Apart from this, he was a devotee of what we may call the off-beat sciences: telepathy, second sight and so forth. He told me how had been stricken by a blinding headache in England at the very moment when his brother was executed by the nazis in Germany, and many other stories of a similar nature. After a few weeks of exposure to Otto John's stories, together with the double brandies which kept on arriving, I found myself forced to find another place to have lunch.

During my few months as Reuters correspondent in Warsaw I got to know the British Ambassador, Victor Frederick William Cavendish-Bentinck (known to his friends as Bill). One day early in 1947 he left Warsaw abruptly and never returned, and Embassy officials were notably reticent about the reasons. Gradually in succeeding weeks, the story leaked out from both British and Polish sources, but as far as I know it has never previously been published.

Conditions in post-war Poland were not exactly settled. Armed groups, some politically motivated and some just bandits, were active, and all sorts of espionage flourished. Under these circumstances, police methods were sweeping. One method, which apparently produced good results, was the 'blockade'. When a suspect was located, his flat was very discreetly raided, and everybody inside bound and gagged. Instead of carting them away immediately, the police held them in the flat, and for the next twenty-four hours – or sometimes forty-eight – anybody who rang the bell was pulled inside and held too.

The rules were strict: everybody was taken, the postman, the lady next door who wanted to borrow a cup of sugar, the man peddling shoelaces. The theory was that any of them might be an accomplice, and the rights and wrongs could be sorted out later.

So one morning in early 1947 a blockade was set up in a Warsaw suburb. The flat-owner, a count, was caught red-handed in possession of stolen secret government papers, and was bundled into the bathroom. Soon there was a ring at the bell, and in walked a distinguished-looking foreigner in a well-cut blue overcoat.

The police promptly clapped on the handcuffs. When their prisoner stated very politely that they must have made a mistake, since he was the British Ambassador and had full diplomatic immunity, they fell about laughing.

Finally it dawned on them that they had caught a fish of unusual size, and called in a senior officer. Mr Cavendish-Bentinck left Poland quietly within a few hours, and never returned.

As the story spread, there was a lot of speculation in diplomatic quarters as to why the ambassador himself had gone out on a job usually performed by a low-grade agent. Only one theory offered made any sense. For the entire period of the Second World War, Mr Cavendish-Bentinck had been chairman of the British Joint Intelligence Committee – in effect the boss of all the spooks. After so many years of chair-borne spying he wanted to show he could be operational too.

A lower-ranking ex-spy I had the pleasure of knowing in the German Democratic Republic was a German Communist journalist who never tired of reminiscing about the advantages of British gaols over other prisons he had known.

Georg Hansen, who in the post-war period was director of the East German News Agency, and was later promoted to edit *Neues Deutschland*, the main East German newspaper, was always a little vague, as so many retired spies are, about the exact circumstances of how he got into the profession, what he did and how he got caught. It was, in fact, only when I lent him the book *Walls Have Mouths* by Wilfred Macartney that he learned that he had earned himself a minor niche in English literature.

For Georg Hansen had been the shadowy 'second man' in the once notorious case of Wilfred Macartney who, in early 1928, was sentenced at the Old Bailey to ten years' penal servitude for spying on behalf of the Soviet Union. Hansen received the same sentence, and spent his term in Maidstone Prison.

'It was lovely,' Hansen used to tell me. 'Long periods of solitary confinement, no fuss and bother, no decisions to be made. I could work out all those mathematical problems that have always been my hobby. Then I got promoted to working in the library, and that was good too. Best time of my life, I think.'

Walls Have Mouths is almost entirely devoted to Macartney's own prison experiences. During the two men's appeal it appeared that the judge was going to increase their ten-year sentence, and Macartney writes:

'I whispered to Hansen, "Good heavens, he's going to add that extra four years! He can do it." Hansen, humorous at all times, whispered back, "That is not so good. To appeal in English is poor arithmetic, I think."'

Macartney served his term at Parkhurst and this is his only mention of Hansen. But in a long prologue to the book Compton Mackenzie gives some details of the case. Since most of the trial was held in camera there are not many hard facts.

Apparently Macartney was trying to obtain details of British arms shipments to states bordering on the Soviet Union. He recruited an assistant named Monkland, who promptly reported to British Intelligence. Compton Mackenzie goes on:

Throughout the summer of 1927 Macartney was buzzing about between London, Paris, and Berlin, writing idiotic letters to Mr Monkland, all of which the Intelligence Department had photographed by the Post Office in transit. In November there appeared on the scene a young German, named Georg Hansen, between whom and Mr Monkland, Macartney, who himself had never met Hansen, arranged a meeting at the Marble Arch Cinema café. Hansen, who was to be called Johnson, and Mr Monkland were to recognise one another by carrying red books. Mr Monkland notified the Intelligence authorities of the proposed meeting, which was duly shadowed, and at this meeting, on November 16, an appointment was made for Macartney to meet Hansen at the Hampstead Tube station at three o'clock the next day. Macartney was to carry a red book this time, and Hansen was to make himself known by asking for a light for a cigarette.

The two were promptly arrested, and my friend Georg Hansen was sent off to spend his restful years in Maidstone Prison.

I might so easily have met Klaus Fuchs when he was forced to flee to Britain from nazi Germany in 1933, long before he became involved in nuclear espionage. By one of those coincidences my father had been a close friend of his father, Emil Fuchs, a prominent German theologian with many links with Quakers. When he came to England as a refugee, it would have been quite logical for Klaus Fuchs to come to stay with us in London, or at least to pay a visit.

As everybody now knows, Fuchs, who had worked in Los Alamos, was sentenced to a long term of imprisonment in Britain in 1950 as an atom spy. On his release he moved to the German Democratic Republic, where he continued his work as a nuclear scientist, this time in the peaceful field.

A small incident connected with the Fuchs case brought to light for the first time that in the 1930s the Gestapo was reporting to the British police on the political affiliations of German emigrants in Britain. The evidence? In *Hansard* dated 6 March 1950 you may read the statement made by Prime Minister Clement Attlee in the House of Commons: 'Not long after this man [Fuchs] came to this country – that was in 1933 – it was said that he was a Communist. The source of that information was the Gestapo.'

More precise details were given by Alan Moorehead in his book *The Traitors*. Moorehead had some access to official documents, and wrote: 'In November 1934 the German Consul at Bristol reported unofficially to the Chief Constable of the city that Klaus Fuchs was a Communist. The source of his information was a Gestapo report from Kiel.'

26

Assignment Berlin

The job in Berlin was quite a different matter from Vienna and Warsaw, where I had been thrown in the deep end, left to my own devices, and managed to swim quite successfully. Reuters' office in Berlin was a fairly large set-up, with three or four full-time British correspondents and three German journalists (two learners and an ancient pre-war Reuters employee who had been put on the pay-roll as an act of compassion), plus a roomful of typists and teleprinter operators, two cars with German drivers and, of course, an office manager. A large staff was needed, for in the early post-war years Berlin was one of the big news centres of the world.

Austria had been comparatively simple. Long before the end of the war the Allied powers had agreed that it should be restored as an independent country, and by the end of 1945 a central Austrian Government was running the whole country (under four-power supervision), though final independence and neutrality were only achieved in 1955. Austria was also a small and relatively unimportant country, unlikely to play a major part in the balance of power in Europe.

Germany was quite another barrel of sauerkraut. As long as the Second World War was still in progress, the Allied powers had been unable to reach agreement on what should happen to Germany when Hitler had finally been defeated, except that they were going to abolish once and for all nazism and militarism. The United States Government toyed with a variety of ideas, ranging from cutting the country up into a whole series of smaller states to Henry Morgenthau's suggestion that all heavy industry should be removed and the country 'pastoralised'.

The British Government also appears for some time to have favoured the 'small state' solution, with the addition of plans for the internationalisation of heavy-industry areas such as the Ruhr. Public Soviet statements on the problem seem to have been practically confined to Stalin's delphic utterance, made in 1942: 'Hitlers come and go, but the German people and the German state remain.' (After two separate German states had been established in 1949, a joke was current in Berlin that Stalin had been misquoted; he had really said, ' . . . the German people and the German states remain.')

When the war had come to an end at last, and the Allied armies had occupied the whole of Germany, some sort of common policy had to be worked out, and this was detailed in the Potsdam Agreement of August 1945. This agreement, signed by Britain, the Soviet Union and the United States, dealt at length with how demilitarisation and de-nazification should proceed, and then turned to the administration of the country. Local and provincial governments should be set up, but 'for the time being, no central German government shall be established', though certain essential central German administrative departments should be created, and Germany should be treated as a single economic unit.

The first year or two after the war were largely occupied by the demilitarisation and de-nazification aspects, and by efforts to get life in the shattered country, left without any authority but the occupying forces, back into some semblance of normality: water, power and sewage in the cities, homes for the homeless, the provision of food, though rations were dangerously low, and the selection or election of local German authorities, which were nominally, but not always, staffed by anti-nazis or at least non-nazis.

By the time that I got to Berlin in summer 1947 it was beginning to become clear in both East and West that the bland commitments entered into at Potsdam could not be implemented easily – the rulings that Germany should be treated as an economic unit, and that after a certain period a German central government should take over a united and neutralised Germany. It was also dawning on the people that almost nobody – except perhaps the Germans, and they did not count at that time – really wanted a united Germany. Or, to be more precise, neither the East nor the West relished the idea of a united neutral Germany unless it was clearly neutral on their side. So in all probability the solution reached in 1949 – the creation of two German states – was inevitable. I do not recall that in summer 1947 anybody in authority was seriously talking about such a Gordian-knot solution, though planners must already have been drafting position papers on both sides. In any case the journalistic community in Berlin was up to its ears in the confused and confusing daily details of the friction and clashes in the four-power Allied Control Council (which was supposed to hammer out the details of how to treat Germany as a whole) and the four-power Allied Kommandantura (which was supposed to be running Berlin).

It would be wearying and unproductive to rehash these daily details, or to try to allot responsibility for the gradual erosion of the wartime co-operation between East and West. There were constant western claims that the Soviet Union was taking too much out of its occupation zone as reparations; and repeated Soviet charges that the British and Americans were not carrying out demilitarisation thoroughly, but were keeping Wehrmacht units in being under various guises; there was the running story in 1948–9 of the Berlin Blockade (and I could easily get bogged down here with a long explanation that it was not strictly a blockade, since the Soviet Union had offered to provision the West Berliners); there was the unilateral western decision to carry out a currency reform in the western zones, which meant the end of any pretence that Germany was being treated as a single economic unit; and much more.

In any event, in Reuters' office in the British sector of West Berlin we worked all day long and far into the night, servicing the world with long-forgotten stories. I have pleasantly smug memories of a series of scoops over our main competitors, AP and UP. These came about because Reuters had wisely, and very early, concluded a news exchange agreement with ADN, the budding East German News Agency. This meant that an ADN ticker in our West Berlin office provided us with early news of Soviet Zone announcements and moves. Important announcements reached us many minutes – or sometimes hours – before they were broadcast by the East German radio, the main source for other western correspondents. Since nobody else in West Berlin had an ADN ticker, as far as I know, this made scoops easy.

But there was one snag. Whenever the Soviet occupation authorities had something important to proclaim (like the announcement of currency reform in the Soviet occupation zone) the story came very late at night or in the small hours. When there was a crisis on, which was often, we had to stay late at the office, waiting for the ADN ticker to stutter into life. Sometimes, of course, nothing of interest came over – corrections to local football results were not exactly world stories – but often enough there was a good solid headline sensation.

Since our teleprinter operators only worked fairly civilised hours, I got a lot of practice in sitting at the Reuters teleprinter linked through to the London office, peering at the story coming up on the ADN ticker a few inches to the left, and bashing out first a 'snap' and then a fuller version of the Soviet announcement.

With the story tied up and landed in London well ahead of the competition, I could drive around to the British Press Club and watch the other correspondents being called to the phone by their London offices and berated for missing the story. The Germans have a word for it: *Schadenfreude*, enjoyment at the discomfiture of others.

We sometimes speculated as to why the Soviet spectaculars always seemed to come in the middle of the night. There was a general consensus that since Stalin notoriously worked late hours, he only initialled things in the small hours, Moscow time.

There were lighter moments too in the work of Reuters' office. Berlin had a thriving black market not only in goods, but also in news and information, most of it phoney. A young lady claiming to be the sister of Eva Braun, Hitler's bride, charmed one of the Reuters team into advancing her considerable quantities of NAAFI cigarettes on her promise to reveal all; she just had to pop round the corner to pick up the family photo album, she said, and was never seen again.

I nearly got taken too. A very plausible young man, who produced papers to show he had been a driver in a Wehrmacht transport company, dropped into the office with a very fetching story. In the closing weeks of the war, he said, he had been one of the drivers in a top-security convoy evacuating a top-secret load from beleaguered Berlin to the West. Overtaken by a Red Army spearhead, they had buried this load at a location which he had noted very exactly.

Then came the exciting part: the load had included fifty-seven containers filled with heavy water (with which the nazis had hoped to make an atom bomb), crates of documents and gold bars and, to top it off, a number of Old Masters, including Rembrandt's priceless *Man in a Golden Helmet*.

The only difficulty, he explained, was that the treasure trove lay in what was now the Soviet occupation zone, and he could not get there to dig it up. All he wanted for his map pin-pointing the hoard was ten cartons of cigarettes down, and $1,000 in cash when the stuff had been dug up.

It was a good story, well presented, and he nearly had me hooked. But a certain caution, probably inherited from canny Scots ancestors, made me suggest he should come back next day at the same time. Then I fired off an urgent service message to Reuters in London enquiring whether the Rembrandt picture was one of the Old Masters which had gone missing during the war. The reply was prompt: 'Rembrandt's *Golden Helmet* currently on exhibition in US gallery.'

So the treasure hunt ended before it had begun. But the plausible young man was quite satisified with the single packet of cigarettes which I presented to him, for enterprise, when he called in the next day.

In a rather similar case at about the same time I may perhaps have missed a lifetime chance of making a packet. A respectable-looking caller offered me a large bundle of shares in the IG Farben Company, the vast German chemical concern. The price was low, just a few cartons of cigarettes, because IG Farben had been sequestered by the Allies; but it was bound to be back in operation in a few years, and then the shares would be worth a fortune, my caller argued. I was naïvely convinced at the time that the British and Americans really meant it when they said that they would break up 'the present excessive concentration of economic power as exemplified by cartels, syndicates, trusts and other monopolistic arrangements', as they had pledged in the Potsdam Agreement, and turned down the offer. Shortly afterwards the Americans 'broke up' IG Farben into three different large companies, and IG Farben shareholders were paid off with shares in the new companies which, with the coming of the West German economic miracle, paid enormous dividends. I can only comfort myself with the thought that the shares I declined were probably forged anyway.

One of the few things upon which the four powers occupying Germany had actually managed to agree was that Prussia and Prussianism were Bad Things and should be exorcised with bell, book and candle. The Allied Control Council formally proclaimed on 22 February 1947 that Prussia had ceased to exist.

In early 1948, when I had properly settled in, Reuters in London suddenly decided to send me back to Warsaw, a move which I had totally forgotten till I recently turned up some old papers. As far as I can make out from the fragmentary correspondence which has survived in an old file, one of the main reasons for the proposed move was that the accountants once again wanted to use up the Reuters stock of Polish currency, which they could utilise in no other way. A letter from London put it plainly: 'As regards your personal financing, we wish to pay yourself in zloty . . . In principle we want to cover the whole cost of the Warsaw correspondent out of our zloty funds.'

Having been through the whole thing only a few months earlier, I was not enthusiastic. My reply perhaps bears quotation at some length, since it is written in that curious old journalistic language known as 'cablese', designed to save words in any way possible:

> earnestly request reconsideration your proposals january fifteenth which represent considerable financial demotion stop appreciate necessity utilizing zlotys but since eyem marrying shortliest etits impossible take wife warsawwards eyem in unposition accept salary in unstable unconvertible currency stop addition would outpoint proposed living allowance lower than that granted british embassy typists getting free accommodation stop unwish create difficulties but extremely reluctant accept appointment on terms stated end

Had I been an experienced cable journalist I would undoubtedly have been able to make it even shorter.

Anyway, Reuters retreated, and a couple of months later I found myself promoted to head of the Berlin bureau. The impending wife mentioned in the cable was my Viennese countess, and with her arrival in Berlin, and the abandonment of bachelor press quarters for a large and comfortable flat, social life widened.

In those cold and rationed post-war Berlin months, almost any German was glad to drop in on an Allied friend, with the certitude of a warm flat, a cup of real coffee or a drink, and the probability of something to eat. So the house was often full; but by no means all of our visitors were free-loaders. Arnold Zweig, the prominent author from the inter-war days, who had been so helpful in Palestine, was a frequent guest. Probably the only real block-buster in the name-dropping line, however, was Bertolt Brecht.

His real interest was not the coffee or the food or the warmth which was provided in the Peet household, but it was also utilitarian: he wanted to use my telephone. At that time, under some obscure four-power ruling, Germans could not telephone abroad. Brecht, just back from exile in the United States (where he had been mildly harried by the Un-American Activities Committee), was trying to get back into European theatre, and needed urgently to have quick communication with Austria, Switzerland and other countries; once, I recall, he made a long call to the USA, probably to Kurt Weill the composer.

Many people who came into contact with Brecht at some time have written books or at least articles recalling the words of wisdom which dropped from the lips of the great man. I remember him mainly as the man who came past frequently to use the phone and never offered to pay. This did not worry me much, for the phone bills were an office expense; in one case, however, I sent an international telegram for Brecht. Reuters'

London accountants sharply spotted it, and charged me three shillings and tuppence-halfpenny.

In the course of 1949 the partitioning of Germany, which had been emerging from the shadows since soon after the end of the Second World War, became a fact. In September of that year, the Federal Republic of Germany was formally established in the western occupation zones, and just one month later the German Democratic Republic was set up in the Soviet occupation zone. In both cases the new states remained – in the early period – firmly under the control of the respective occupation powers; and in both cases the new states mirrored, with some modifications, their sponsors.

With the hardening of the fronts and the obvious abandonment for a long period of all plans to re-establish a united German as a neutral state, I began to assess my personal position. Professionally I was doing very nicely, and apparently giving full satisfaction, but I began to anticipate difficult times ahead. Ever since my schooldays I had regarded myself, despite my somewhat erratic course, as a committed Marxist, agreeing in general with the political line of the international Communist movement, though I was reluctant to become a card-carrying Red.

In my work as a correspondent in Vienna, Warsaw and Berlin I had endeavoured to follow the rule laid down by C. P. Scott, the renowned editor of the *Manchester Guardian*, that comment was free but facts were sacred, and I believe that I was basically successful. By reporting as impartially as possible the policies and actions of both sides in the emerging cold conflict on the confrontation line in central Europe, I had the vague hope that it might be possible to do at least something to redress the balance in the western media which by and large reflected the Anglo-American establishment view of the clash – 'We have governments: they just have regimes.'

However, as the creeping cold war atmosphere reached new levels of frigidity, I was faced with a decision, and high-level rumours in early 1950 made the decision easier. The rumours said that the western allies, and in particular the United States, were soon going to take the first steps towards re-establishing German armed forces in their part of Germany, thus finally tearing up the remnants of decisions taken at Potsdam less than five years earlier.

So I made up my mind to go east, to the young German Democratic Republic. It was not a step into the unknown. I had watched from close quarters and with great interest the efforts being made to get things back on to their feet again in the Soviet occupation zone – on to their feet again, but on a different footing.

De-nazification had been far more swift and radical than in the western occupation zones, and a far higher proportion of persons involved in nazi crimes and war crimes had already been tried and sentenced – in comparison with a population about ten times as large. All nazis had been eliminated from the police, the judiciary and education; the lack of teachers was made up by hastily training new ones, who were often only a lesson or two ahead of their pupils. The economic situation was still pretty rocky, but the basis had been laid for a new start by a thoroughgoing land reform which broke up the old Junker estates; and the factories of nazi supporters and war profiteers – which meant a very high proportion of the larger enterprises – had been nationalised.

As Reuters correspondent I had been present when the German Democratic Republic was established on 7 October 1949. Some years later, long before I had thought of writing a book, I wrote down a short account of the event, and here it is:

In early October 1949, something was obviously in the air; the West German Parliament had constituted itself in early September, and clearly the various parties and organisations in what was then the Soviet Zone could not, and would not, let the old gang in Bonn get away with its claim to be the only government for the whole of Germany. In the foreign press colony in West Berlin, which at that time was prosperous enough to maintain relatively luxurious British and American press clubs, the rumours grew wilder by the minute. A new East German state was going to be set up with its capital in Leipzig; East Germany was going to become a Soviet Republic; and many more. But for anyone who observed developments instead of listening to rumours, it was fairly obvious what was going to happen. So I was not surprised when I received, on October 6, a press card for 'an important meeting of the German People's Council' (an *ad hoc* constituent assembly) at what is now the House of Ministries in Leipziger Strasse in East Berlin.

October 7 was, if I remember correctly, a grey cool October day. Not very many of the foreign correspondents working at that time in West Berlin had bothered to come, and the rows of seats reserved for the press on the eastern side of the hall of the first floor of the House of Ministries were not crowded.

The members of the People's Council who filled the hall – about 400 delegates, and possibly 100 spectators, including press – mostly looked thin and overworked; and though they had put on their best suits for the meeting, many of the suits were threadbare. For this was a meeting of the Activists of the First Hour (men and women who had tackled the job of getting the country back on to its feet almost before the guns fell silent), and for many of those present there had scarcely been a pause to take breath since they emerged from the concentration camps and prisons.

My memories are misty of the actual ceremony in which the People's

Council constituted itself as the Provisional People's Chamber of the German Democratic Republic and set calmly about the task of setting up a new state. Probably this is because I was working for a news agency; this meant that every few minutes I had to hurry out of the hall and try to get to one of the few phones available to report on the latest development. I do remember, however, that Reuters News Agency sent out page after page of news on the story; and that next day, in London at least, most of the newspapers paid little attention, or printed scornful messages from Bonn, which had just become the West German capital.

To be quite fair, I should mention an outstanding exception to the general silence, misinformation, and sheer ignorance in the days and weeks following the establishment of the GDR. On October 15 1949 the London *Times* stated in an editorial:

'While, therefore, the western Powers need to feel no particular alarm at the birth of the East German Republic, so long as they can avoid a new conflict over Berlin, it would be mistake to believe that the new regime has no substance . . . Instead of pretending that it does not exist it is wiser to recognise it for what it is – one more "People's Democracy" . . . imbued with a revolutionary toughness and persistence which may in the end produce results . . . '

So there was somebody sitting at the editorial desk in Printing House Square, London, in October 1949 whose crystal ball was surprisingly unclouded, although for more than twenty years after 1949 the western powers continued to turn Nelson's blind eye. The German Democratic Republic really did exist, and I went to live and work there.

27

Behind the Curtain

The time has come to pick up the story where it stopped at the end of the first chapter. The date: 12 June 1950. I was in the course of resigning rather dramatically from my post with Reuters News Agency and starting a new life behind the 'Iron Curtain'.

Since it was some bright young nazi in Josef Goebbels's Propaganda Ministry who thought up the catchy name 'Iron Curtain' in February 1945, it was perhaps fitting that my press conference in East Berlin was held in Goebbels's former ministry, in the very room where the Propaganda Minister used to address the nazi press.

Now, in June 1950, the ministry building had been taken over by the Government Information Office of the newly founded German Democratic Republic. Journalists stationed in East and West Berlin had been invited to a press conference on an undisclosed subject, and the room was packed.

I filed in with the rest, and took my seat among my colleagues. Gerhart Eisler, veteran Communist and now head of the Information Office, who had made an adventurous escape from McCarthy persecution in the USA only a few months earlier, announced that a western correspondent had asked for the opportunity to make a public statement. Necks were craned and eyes popped as I rose, shambled rather self-consciously to the speaker's desk, and read out a statement in my slightly mangled German. Re-reading the statement today, I cannot regard it as one of my more memorable bits of writing, but a few extracts will give a general idea of what I had to say:

I stand here because I do not wish to serve the warmongers any longer. As a western journalist, chief correspondent in Berlin for Reuters News Agency, I have gradually been becoming, against my will, a tool of the American-controlled war machine . . .

Everyone of you knows, or should know, that Anglo-American occupation policy is surely but slowly aimed at making West Germany a jumping-off ground for a new war.

To back up this statement I recalled that only a few weeks earlier General Keightley, Commander of the British Army of the Rhine, talking to a small group of correspondents, including myself, at the British Press Club in West Berlin, had stated that he had discussed the whole question with Field-Marshal Montgomery, and he agreed completely that a new German army should be raised as quickly as possible.

For the record I should note that General Keightley immediately issued a firm *démenti*. I stuck by my story, and he stuck by his: any discussion of the point nearly forty years later is obviously superfluous. In 1950 everybody was hotly denying the possibilty of ever again giving Germans arms; only a few months later the raising of a new West German army became a declared aim of US and British policy.

A large part of the remainder of my statement was devoted to practical examples of how the political scene in Berlin and the young German Democratic Republic was being distorted in the British and American press. I concluded:

I simply cannot consent to take part any longer in the warmongering which threatens not only the Soviet Union and the People's Democracies, but which also is well on the way to converting my motherland, Britain, into a powerless American colony.

My statement was followed by a flood of questions, of which I find I have kept no record, but they were mostly concerned with whether I was seeking asylum in the GDR (the answer was no, just moving there for the time being) and what my future job would be (answer: no idea). I also took the opportunity to assure my colleagues that my step had not been influenced by 'Russian gold or mysterious central Asiatic truth drugs'.

I was plagued at the time by the idea that some western journalists might suggest that I had run away because I was in financial difficulties – and in fact suggestions of this sort did trickle around the press for a while. In the middle of the press conference I suddenly recalled that in setting my affairs in order before I left West Berlin I had neglected one item. As head of the Reuters office in West Berlin, I naturally held the keys to the office safe, which always contained a considerable sum of money for sudden emergencies. So when a few British colleagues gathered around as the press conference ended, I picked out the man I knew best, William Hamsher of the *Daily Express*, and with plenty of western witnesses around I demonstratively handed over to him the safe keys and the keys of the Reuters office.

It was perhaps well that I had done so. For about one hour later, in Gerhart Eisler's office, a long-distance call came in from a Reuters executive in London. 'Is that John Peet?' asked a well-known voice. 'What have you done with the safe keys?' I told him, and he rang off. That was all he wanted to know.

It seems only fair at this point to offer an unsolicited testimonial to Reuters' head office, which behaved extremely correctly despite the trouble I gave them. A few hours after my announcement, Reuters issued a calm and very British statement. I have to re-translate it from the German, since the original is not available:

> Reuters headquarters in London has the following statement on John Peet's action: Peet's action comes as a complete surprise. None of his British or American colleagues in West Germany had any knowledge of the fact that he held particular political views. His reports were always exact, impartial and irreproachable.

A few weeks later Reuters sent me a cheque with a covering letter: this covered my salary up to the moment I left, plus repayment of my contributions to the pension fund.

Quite naturally, my decision to go east got quite a lot of press coverage, most of it predictable. I think the story I liked best was that printed by *Time* magazine on 26 June 1950:

D'ye Ken John Peet?

To his friends and acquaintances, shy, scarecrow-thin John Peet was not easy to ken. At 34, he had gone through an odd succession of careers: enlisted man in Britain's crack Brigade of Guards, English teacher in Prague, private in the Spanish Civil War's international brigade, policeman in Palestine, chief Berlin correspondent for Reuters news agency. Some people considered Peet insecure, haunted and unhappy; others regarded him as witty, well-informed and likeable. Allied officials in Berlin had privately marked him down as a Communist or at least a fellow traveller, who passed information to the East Germans in exchange for news beats, but his Reuters bosses considered Peet a non-political man who filed factual stories and never picked sides.

Last week Newsman Peet picked sides. At a press conference staged by Communist propagandist Gerhart Eisler in the Soviet sector of Berlin, Peet charged the Western Allies and their press with 'distortions' and 'warmongering'. Then he asked the Communist government of East Germany to let him stay.

In Britain, the defection was Page One news. Even so, one news agency threw away a good eyewitness account of the press conference. Under the circumstances, explained Reuters, that seemed the best thing to do: it had been filed by John Peet.

For a story in *Time* magazine it was remarkably accurate, though I would query the suggestion that I passed information in exchange for news beats. I got quite a number of news beats because I had a better understanding of what was going on in the newly founded German Democratic Republic, and went to see for myself instead of depending on 'news' leaked by western cold-war sources.

Looking up the old *Time* story for this book, I noticed for the first time the news item in the adjacent column. Somebody had polled US newspapers from coast to coast, asking what was the headline they would most like to print. *Time* reported the result: 'By far the majority – four out of five – wanted most of all to see an end to war, hot or cold.' And the magazine picked out this headline suggested by the *Los Angeles Times*.

ATOM BOMB OUTLAWED:
NATIONS OF WORLD BAN
WAR IN ANY FORM

I couldn't agree more.

One of these cold-war news sources tried to cloud the issue very massively a couple of days after my press conference. The long-deceased West Berlin Christian Democratic newspaper *Der Tag* reported breathlessly that I was an atom spy – a fairly new species at that time. Under screaming headlines the paper said that western intelligence officers were investigating reports that I had been in contact with Klaus Fuchs and Harry Gold, who had recently been arrested in Britain and the United States on atom-spy charges. The newspaper story continued:

'These investigations have shown that Peet was in contact with the atom spy ring during his activities as correspondent in Warsaw. It is assumed that Peet had become aware that these contacts were known, and that he therefore sought security in East Berlin.'

The British authorities in West Berlin promptly issued a carefully worded statement saying: 'An official British spokesman declared that the British security authorities knew nothing about these reports, and he regarded them as ridiculous.'

It was not until many months later that I learned from old friends in the press where the atom-spy story came from, and how it had been killed dead, so dead that it has never emerged since. When the story broke, Reuters' headquarters decided that this was the last straw. An important Reuters man was rushed to West Berlin to investigate, and he immediately brought great pressure to bear on *Der Tag*, threatening to have it closed down by the British military authorities.

The editor buckled, and disclosed that he had received the information from an American prominent on the cultural side of the activities of the US authorities in West Berlin. Reuters' man from London hurried over to US headquarters, and used the thumbscrews again, though I have never been able to discover just what sort of pressure he brought to bear. The American admitted that he had invented the whole thing. 'I thought we should lay some counter-mines,' he explained, and reluctantly agreed to withdraw the story.

It is probably unnecessary to note that I was never an atom spy. But if the American had ever known about the friendship between my father and the father of Klaus Fuchs, mentioned earlier, he could have strengthened his invention with some 'guilt by association'.

There was rather a satisfactory little footnote to the whole story. Some twenty years later I was invited to dinner at the Garrick Club in London by two British journalist colleagues, both of whom were widely known as having been engaged in British cloak-and-dagger work in the Second World War. While we were quietly dining, gossiping about old friends in the small world of foreign correspondents, the man who had invented the atom-spy story walked into the dining room with a leading British literary figure. Seeing me in those rather unlikely surroundings, he started; seeing my hosts, he did a classic double take, and you could imagine the little wheel whizzing in his head. Here was Peet dining with two men who were, or had been, associated with British Intelligence; everybody knows from the novels that British Intelligence did a large part of its business in the better London clubs; therefore Peet had obviously been a British agent all the time; or was he just being recruited? I hope it spoiled his dinner.

28

Settling In

Today it seems rather odd, but as far as I can recall I had taken no thought for the morrow when I arranged to move east. I think my mentor, who had master-minded the switch, had made some casual remark about there being plenty of openings for me in the German Democratic Republic, but that was all.

For the first few weeks I had no worries. I was put up in a comfortable government guest house in the centre of Berlin, and left in the main to shift for myself. Several correspondents from West Berlin turned up for interviews, most of which tailed off inconclusively after they suggested that I tell them, off the record of course, whether money difficulties or girl troubles had moved me to cross the curtain.

I bashed out a series of articles for *Neues Deutschland*, the leading GDR newspaper, on my experiences as a western correspondent in post-war Germany, and the danger of West German re-armament. The articles were reprinted in *Ce Soir*, the left-wing Paris evening paper, but turned down by the London *Daily Worker*, which stated that British libel laws would make publication impossible.

Then the German Peace Committee, the local affiliate of the World Peace Council, discovered that I was an attractive speaker at peace rallies, despite (or possibly because of) my fluent but fractured German. So I toured the country for several months, addressing schoolchildren, factory workers, earnest church study groups and practically everybody on the dangers of a new war and of West German re-armament and in particular the possible nuclear holocaust. It was the time of the now forgotten

189

Stockholm Appeal, the world-wide petition organised by the World Peace Council calling for the total renunciation of the atom bomb.

There were ready ears, for this was only five years after the end of the Second World War, and practically everybody could recall the war only too vividly. Some local notables in the towns and villages where I spoke were visibly worried by some passages of my lectures or speeches, because I made a considerable effort to avoid the tired clichés of the speakers' notes provided by the headquarers of the Peace Council and instead tried to speak in a language which people could listen to, even throwing in what I hoped were moderately funny anecdotes.

After the first few dozen meetings, when monotony began to set in, I started deliberately to pull the legs of some of the local worthies on the platform.

'To support the peace movement does not mean you have to agree with everything in the German Democratic Republic,' I said, an unorthodox and unexpected statement which made everybody sit up, particularly the platform party.

'I myself find several things hard to take,' I continued, watching the chairman starting to squirm, wondering what horrible heresy this odd foreigner was going to pronounce; 'for instance, I find the cigarettes here terrible.'

Gasps of relief on the platform, laughter and applause. It may not have been brilliant as oratory, but it was apparently highly memorable. Even today I meet middle-aged people who say, 'I remember you. When you lectured in Neustadt [or wherever it was] – it must have been more than thirty years ago – you said something I still remember.' At that point I interrupt them. 'Yes, I said GDR cigarettes were terrible.' When they express surprise that I still recall a little incident at Neustadt, I have to disillusion them: I said it everywhere.

The whole lecture-tour period is a bit of a blur, for addressing three or four gatherings daily inevitably means that you repeat yourself over and over again, and only some unexpected challenges in question periods at the end of a lecture remain sharply in my mind. At a factory peace rally in one of the halls of a big machine-shop in Magdeburg – formerly a Krupp factory, now nationalised – a worker asked me to prove that I was (a) really English and (b) not a British spy. I handed him my British passport and assured him I would do my best to answer the second part of the question if he could first prove that he was not a West German spy.

In the meantime I had moved from the government guest house to a tiny flat in the East Berlin suburbs, making myself as comfortable as possible in the rather straitened conditions of the severely rationed GDR. The things which worried me most were the lack of coffee (almost impossible to obtain) and the rather nauseous cigarettes, made of home-grown tobacco. There was no lack of company, for I had both old friends and acquaintances, mainly in the cultural field, such as Arnold Zweig and Bertolt Brecht, and a number of new friends, several of them German anti-fascists who had also fought in Spain.

In January 1951 there was a renewed flurry of odd stories in the West Berlin and West German press about 'the case of John Peet'. I had gone down with a nasty case of flu, and since there was nobody to look after me in my one-man flat, I was carted off to the hospital at Buch, a Berlin suburb. The hospital had once been a mental home, but for many years had served as a general hospital.

On 18 January 1951 the West Berlin evening paper *Depesche* had a minor sensation: 'John Peet in Lunatic Asylum'. The story told how I had been confined in the mental hopital at Buch. 'A male nurse from Buch who has fled to the West reports that Russian doctors have recommended that Peet be transferred immediately to the special hospital in the Crimea.'

The right-wing West German daily *Die Welt* elaborated in a leading article the next day:

John Peet, former Reuters correspondent in Berlin, has only been able to play the role of a showpiece in the 'peace camp' for less than half a year. The role has ended sadly: in a lunatic asylum. We do not yet know whether the atmosphere of the Crimea will cure him . . . Peet was dragged from lecture hall to lecture hall to blacken the West, to play and replay his gramophone record until it got a crack . . . It was all too much. His guardians had no mercy on him: they proved, to him too, that the word 'humanitarianism' was not included in their vocabulary. Peet has become a victim of Eisler's propaganda machine. Only one question is still open: Was Peet's change of front a sign of his mental illness, or have his activities for Eisler undermined his mental health?

One can never really catch up with a story like that. A few hours after the story first broke, a British correspondent from West Berlin visited me in the perfectly normal hospital ward, and found me sitting up in bed, well on the way to recovery, longing for a smoke and reading, if I recall rightly, one of the volumes of Stalin's collected works (some readers may see this as an indication of mental decay, but as a voracious reader I would even read Maggie Thatcher's collected works if there was nothing else around). He reported very correctly that I was in a normal hospital and had no prospects of visiting the Crimea; but the nervous-breakdown story echoed around the West German press for months.

There were plenty of other oddities like this at that time, and in years to come; but one less imaginative article on the Peet case ensured me the tiniest conceivable niche in contemporary literary history.

About 1970 a Lithuanian journalist colleague here in Berlin surprised me with the news that I was mentioned in the Collected Correspondence of Thomas Mann. Ever eager to bask in the very slightest ray of reflected glory, I hurried to the library, and after quite a search discovered that my Lithuanian colleague had been almost right. On 1 November 1950 Thomas (*Magic Mountain*) Mann had written to Hermann (*Steppenwolf*) Hesse, explaining that his daughter Erika Mann was having a hard time, for her nonconformism had made it impossible for her to work in the US media. Hesse would be glad to know that an article which he (Hesse) had recommended had been published in Swedish and Dutch papers.

Not a mention of John Peet, but I finally ran myself down in the footnotes at the end of the volume:

> This article, entitled 'The Case of John Peet', was published in the big Danish and Swedish weeklies *Information* and *VI*, and the Dutch daily *Vrij Nederland*. Basing itself on the available material, the article sought to explain what could have moved the chief of Reuters agency in Berlin to abandon his excellent position, to say 'adieu' to the 'Free World' and 'take off' for the East.

Then I remembered. In September 1950, a month or two after I moved to the GDR, Erika Mann had talked with me for about four hours, and later sent me the published version of her article. Since it was in Dutch, a language with which I have little acquaintance, I have never really discovered what she wrote, though one sentence – 'Arme wanhopige John Peet, deserteur uit braafheid' – looks as though it may mean 'Poor deluded John Peet, deserter out of uprightness', followed by 'de dulvel met Beelzebub to verdrijven', which is obviously 'to cast out the devil by Beelzebub'.

During 1951 I continued to work spasmodically for the Peace Committee, but a lot of my time was occupied with translation into English. The obviously inexperienced men and women who were running the GDR were becoming painfully aware that the new state was getting an almost universally bad press in the western world, and cast around for ways and means of presenting the GDR. One of the methods selected was the publication of a rather lavish four-colour monthly, in *Life* magazine format, entitled *GDR in Construction*, for circulation abroad. It was published in English and French and several other languages, and I was naturally hauled in to help in translation.

I did not wish to be overly critical of this first effort in the field, but I could not help feeling that this magazine was not exactly the right thing. It was planned, written and produced by journalists who had no knwledge or understanding of western mentality; it presented the still rather rickety young GDR in only the most cloying of sugary pictures; and it was far too expensively printed to be credible as a give-away journal.

In addition to all these defects, it was soon apparent that little or no thought had been devoted to how the magazine should be distributed in western countries. When thousands of copies of the first English-language edition were already cluttering up the storeroom of the GDR Information Office, I was approached one day by an earnest elderly comrade who had worked for many years in the central office of the Communist International in Moscow. He asked me agitatedly whether I happened to have the addresses of progressive bookshops or magazine distributors in Britain or the USA.

I suggested that for a start he should look up the lists of foreign distributors printed in various propaganda magazines published in the Soviet Union, Poland and other socialist countries, and he conceded that this might be a good idea.

'And what about individuals who might be interested?' he asked. 'We've found an old mailing list, but we are afraid it might be out of date. Perhaps you could take a look.'

The list was undated, crumpled and obviously very old indeed; it may well have come from the files of the pre-Hitler German Communist Party, which had been responsible at that time for the world-wide distribution of Comintern publications such as the weekly *International Press Correspondence*.

I ran my eye quickly over the list, and in the midst of the US addresses was caught up short. There was a name which rang a bell: Jay Lovestone. I did not know very much about the history of the US Communist Party, but I did remember that Jay Lovestone was one of their demon figures – a renegade, an ally of the class enemy, a minion of reaction, a sort of vest-pocket Trotsky. When I told the earnest comrade what I recalled, he blanched; and this particular list of addresses was never mentioned again.

(Looking up Jay Lovestone in histories of the American left, I find it hard to determine exactly what his offence had been. Apparently he had been read out of the party by Stalin personally at a meeting of the American Commission of the Comintern in 1929. One of his crimes had been to criticise Comintern leader Nikolai Bucharin when he had been a Good Thing, and then support him when he suddenly became a Bad Thing).

In conversations with Gerhart Eisler, the intelligent, energetic, but irascible head of the Government Information Office, I voiced my misgivings about the efficiency of publicity work for the GDR in the western world. Apart from the lavish four-colour monthly, various GDR bodies were already producing a small stream of pamphlets and books in English. There was, for instance, a 'White Book' on the plans for West German rearmament and remilitarisation, which I had been asked to translate.

In the course of this translation, I told Eisler, I had discovered that it was a curious mixture of well-documented and convincing information on the subject, and vague and unsourced reports, often prefaced with some phrase such as 'As is well known . . .' In a number of cases direct quotes were given from 'American newspapers' without any indication of the date or the name of the paper. I cannot be sure whether those notorious 'hyenas of Wall Street' figured in the 'White Book', for I have mislaid my copy, but that was certainly the tone of some of the comment.

At this discussion with Eisler, and at many subsequent arguments with GDR politicians and journalists about external publicity and propaganda, I found it quite useful to brandish a very relevant quotation which I had unearthed in the multi-volume collected works of Lenin (browsing through collected works is sometimes useful). In a speech to the Fourth Congress of the Communist International on 13 November 1922, Lenin pointed out that many people found it impossible to read long screeds, however 'correct' they might be:

In 1921, at the Third Comintern Congress, we adopted a resolution on the organisation of the Communist Parties and the methods and content of their work. The resolution is excellent, but it is Russian through and through . . . That is its good side, but also its bad side, because I am convinced that practically no foreigner can read it through. Firstly, it is too long, it has 50 paragraphs or more. Foreigners cannot usually read things like that. Secondly, even if they do read it, not a single foreigner would understand it, because it is too Russian. I do not mean because it is written in Russian – it has been excellently translated into all languages – but because it is permeated with a Russian spirit . . . As I said, the resolution is excellent,

Fourth Estate (Publishers) Ltd.
Classic House
113 Westbourne Grove
London W2 4UP
Telephone: 01-727 8993

Telex: 29940 Donleo G

The author's have then
has asked me to send
you a copy of the
enclosed).

Jane

Charteris

WITH COMPLIMENTS

FOURTH
ESTATE

4th

Winners
of the First
Sunday Times
Small Publishers Award
1988

and I subscribe to all its 50 paragraphs. But we have not understood how to present our Russian experiences to foreigners.

Now, Eisler was a veteran communist propagandist with international experience. He had worked as Comintern representative in Shanghai in 1929–31, escaped to the United States from nazi Europe in 1940 and made world headlines in 1949 when he smuggled himself out of New York aboard a Polish boat in 1949 after being harried by the Un-American Activities Committee and sentenced for 'contempt of Congress'. He now agreed with a number of my criticisms.

'So don't just criticise,' he said. 'Do something about it. You could publish a paper, for instance.'

I went away and mulled over the idea, and gradually the idea began to take shape. The paper should be small, cheap and unassuming: no four-colour job on art paper, not in any way an official GDR publication, but my personal report on what was going on both in the GDR and in West Germany, written in a language and presented in a form familiar to ordinary people in Britain, the USA and other English-speaking countires.

Obviously any attempt to distribute such a paper through commerical channels was hopeless; the only way to achieve wide dissemination was by direct mail. For psychological reasons it should not be too obviously a give-away sheet; from the very first issue we should appeal for subscriptions.

I provided Eisler with a dummy issue, and outlined my ideas. He was enthusiastic. He presumably submitted the plan to the appropriate section of the ruling Socialist Unity Party, and got the go-ahead.

Funds were quickly made available. I was provided with a tiny office and a secretary who had been an emigrée in Britain and had fair English, and we were ready to go. So *Democratic German Report* was born, the small eight-page paper which I published in Berlin every two weeks from January 1952 until December 1975. Since I researched and wrote or translated most of the matter myself, it was a fairly full-time job.

If I remember rightly, our first print was 1,000 copies, which seemed a lot at the time, for our mailing list was pitifully thin. It consisted at the start of addresses of my own friends and acquaintances in Britain and other parts of the western world, newspaper addresses gleaned from *Durrants Press Guide* and a few odds and ends gleaned from GDR citizens I knew who had spent the nazi years in the West.

In the first issue I published a short note: 'Send us the names and addresses of friends who would be interested in the paper, and we shall be delighted to give them a trial subscription.'

The response astonished me. A few people promptly asked to be taken off the mailing list, including Roger Baldwin of the American Civil Liberties Union, and a teacher at Roedean, the exclusive British boarding school for girls, who wrote: 'Your paper is not subtle enough to deceive English people.' But hundreds of letters came in with lists of names for our mailing list.

To get ahead of the story a bit, our circulation slowly rose to a peak of some 30,000. Of course, it is no trick to get a big circulation if the paper is a give-away and you can pay the printer and the postage: you can mail it to everybody in the London phone book. But we tried to be more discriminating, concentrating on trade unions, educationalists and politically interested people. It is impossible to assess how many of the 30,000 people who were on our list read the paper regularly, and how many simply dropped it into the waste-basket as just another piece of junk mail. Even so, various checks, particularly answers to questionnaires, indicated that at least half of the copies were actually read, at least some of the time.

29

Parrot in a Proletarian Cage

So what did I put into this little newspaper? At the start I had to devote prime attention to elementary facts, like where the German Democratic Republic lay, how and why it had come into existence, what its policies were and where it was going. For ignorance about this new German state was almost total throughout the western world, and most of the information available was very distorted. For most people in the English-speaking world, the GDR was a dim grey area somewhere off in eastern Europe, called the 'Soviet Zone'; many of them probably knew more about Albania.

Secondly, the growing pressure for remilitarisation in West Germany, and the steadily increasing numbers of old nazis with pretty bloody records who reappeared in all branches of the West German administration, gave me a lot of copy.

A third theme which grew increasingly important over the years, as the GDR emerged from the early period of just getting back on its feet and became one of the important industrial states of Europe, was to expose the idiocy of the official West German policy of pretending that the GDR did not exist at all, and insisting that everybody else closed their eyes firmly too.

This may look a little heavy; but since I spent the next quarter of a century interpreting the development of the two German states from the standpoint of a critical friend of the GDR, a bit of weight seems inevitable. Nevertheless I tried to keep *Democratic German Report* as readable as I knew how. From the very first issue *Democratic German Report* (identified as *German Report* from now on) made a point of drawing attention to misleading, muddle-headed or simply crazy reports about the GDR in the western press. In our first number we noted that West German newspapers had once again claimed that Christmas celebrations had been banned in the GDR, although a short visit to East Berlin or a glance at the radio programmes would have revealed that there was a big Christmas Fair in the middle of the city, the GDR radio was deafening listeners with carol programmes, and all the churches were running regular Christmas services. The 'banned Christmas' story became one of our boring hardy annuals, and it came as a relief when the London *Observer* a few years later rang a change on the story and announced that Christmas celebrations were now permitted.

Also in our first issue we asked readers for cuttings from their local papers with odd stories about the GDR. They responded with a will, and over the years we were able to stick a pin in weird reports appearing in newspapers from Phoenix, Arizona, to Christchurch, New Zealand.

And now allow me to present you with a rag-bag of quotations from *German Report* over the years, illustrating, among other things, some of the guff which was getting printed in so many countries:

A friend in England has sent me a cutting (unfortunately without date or source) apparently from a recent issue of one of Lord Kemsley's chain of papers. According to this account 'Military intelligence officers have been sent to Berlin to investigate a Communist fortnightly news-sheet *Democratic German Report* which is being sent to troops stationed in Germany and trade union leaders in Britain. They have discovered that it is . . . being produced by a Briton, John Peet, who went to live in East Berlin in June 1950. The investigators have discovered that Frau Zaisser, wife of the chief of secret police, has ordered Peet to write a book portraying 'appalling conditions' in Britain. Peet was summoned to secret police HQ and told he would either write the book or be arrested for espionage.'

I must congratulate the military intelligence officers on 'discovering' that I produce *German Report*. They must have read the small print at the bottom of this page, which has appeared there from the very first number.

The rest of the story is of course sheer invention. I do not know Frau Zaisser, have never been near 'secret police HQ' and do not know if there is such a place, have no intention of writing a book about Britain or anywhere else, and have not been arrested for espionage.

German Report, 5 June 1952

Honorary title for 'Phoniest Story of the Month' goes to Dennis Martin, Bonn correspondent of the London *Daily Express*, for the oustandingly imaginative paragraph in that paper on September 1st: 'Official figures in

West Germany tonight show that more than 16,000 people have fled from the Soviet Zone to Berlin in August alone – 11,000 by air.'

Now there is simply no air service from any part of the East German Republic to Berlin, with the sole exception of a Leipzig–Berlin shuttle service during the Leipzig Fair, running for a few days once a year.

German Report, 12 September 1952

A certain Mr Hy Gardner writes a regular column in the *New York Herald Tribune* called 'Coast to Coast'. Most of his material is tittle-tattle about show people, but every now and then Mr Gardner throws in little bits of 'inside information from behind the Iron Curtain'. Here in its entirety is such an item from the June 9 issue of the *New York Herald Tribune,* Paris edition: 'The German Communist Party is preparing publication of a new bible. Theme of the Red Bible will be that Jesus was poor, had no money, no property. Goal of the distorted version to convert religious peasants to the cause of Communism. (Aside to Casey – please file this in the How-Low-Can-You-Get Dept.!)'

We shall file Mr Gardner in our own 'How-High-Can-You-Get Department', but we can't help wondering what sort of a Bible Mr Gardner uses.

German Report, 25 June 1954

The story to end all stories about East Berlin was published in the Nottingham *Guardian Journal*. John H. Izbicki, a student who has just graduated from Nottingham University, described a visit to the new blocks of apartments being built on the Stalin Allee in East Berlin, and reported: 'Should the visitor venture to walk up one of the few sidestreets and look at the back of the Stalin Allee he will find – nothing. Absolutely nothing. There are only outer walls housing large shops. It is just like a stage setting.'

It's a funny thing, but only yesterday I was drinking tea in one of those 'stage-setting' apartments on the fifth floor of one of those outer walls, and it all looked solid enough to me. And it looks solid enough to all the 10,000 people who live in these apartments which, according to the Nottingham newspaper, are non-existent.

I have written to the Nottingham *Guardian Journal* offering to pay all Mr Izbicki's expenses if he will come to Berlin again to show me those phantom houses; I shall report in a later issue on the reaction.

German Report, 1 October 1954

Now, in very many cases where I slapped down colleagues, mainly British or American, who made fools of themselves in reports on the GDR, I offered them equal space for a reply; the challenge was otherwise never, as far as I recall, taken up. But in this case I got an adequate reaction, which I noted in the next issue:

I should like to take this opportunity of extending a small bouquet to the Nottingham *Guardian Journal* in England. In the last number of *German Report* we commented on a fabulous article . . .

In its issue dated September 30th the newspaper published a letter from me challenging the writer to come to Berlin again and show me the empty outer walls . . .

We are glad to note this effort on the part of this newspaper to keep the record straight. We hope the example will spread.

German Report, 15 October 1954

But Mr Izbicki never showed up; he is now, I believe, getting bylines on a London daily.

I had my favourite correspondents, generally from British 'quality' papers. For a while my top butt was Mr Terence Prittie of the *Manchester Guardian*. I should perhaps emphasise that I had nothing personal against Mr Prittie; but he was an easy target because he was so reliably inaccurate. Perhaps it is necessary to explain that in my tiny guerrilla war against the picture of the GDR as presented in the western press I tried to concentrate upon errors of fact, and not differences of opinion.

And it was here that Mr Prittie was a gift from the heavens. He consistently muddled up the names and positions of leading GDR personalities, got figures wrong and so on, all of them offences which would have got me promptly sacked from the *Bromley and West Kent Mercury* back in the 1930s. Reading today through some of my unkind notes on Prittie, I feel I was perhaps nit-picking; but let me demonstrate at a little greater length one of his howlers.

In 1964, after he had left the German journalistic beat, he published a book on the German wartime resistance entitled *Germans against Hitler*. I do not think it is a particularly good book, but that is not the point. I reviewed the book in *German Report* on 10 July 1964, stating: 'Mr Prittie's astonishing faculty for getting things wrong, even when he is simply copying from another book, can best be shown from one paragraph on p. 206,' and then listing a number of slipshod numerical errors he made in quoting from the other book, which was a GDR volume on the resistance. But his worst error was still to come. Prittie had written:

The official Communist *History of the German Anti-Fascist Resistance Movement* commented, with utterly undisguised and possibly involuntary cynicism: 'As a result of the entry into the war of the Soviet Union, they (the

German Communists) became convinced that it was necessary to restart their Communist work.'

As I pointed out in my review: 'Reference to the work quoted by Mr Prittie shows that this is not a comment, cynical or otherwise, made by the "official Communist history", but a direct and clearly marked quotation from an official nazi court indictment.'

Perhaps more than enough on the subject, but one delightfully obscure sentence in an article by Mr Prittie on price reductions in the GDR still sets me pondering:

The Bonn correspondent of the *Manchester Guardian*, Terence Prittie, stated at one point in his usually badly-informed article: 'The rulers of Eastern Germany do not necessarily believe in the principle of one parrot per proletarian cage.' The rest of the article, which has no mention of parrots, proletarians, or cages, gives no clue as to what he might possibly have meant.

German Report, 13 November 1953

Since we were so avidly searching for motes, we had to watch out for our own beams particularly vigilantly, and correct them as loudly as possible. Inevitably there were a number, as when we mistakenly pinned a nazi post on a Dr Hans Schirmer, who had just been appointed West German Ambassador to Australia. The post had really been occupied by another Schirmer, a nazi official with exactly the same name. But here is another, more important case:

In the course of twenty years of mainly political reporting on the state of the two German states, *German Report* has naturally made its fair share of mistakes, but most have not been of great importance. However, on October 4 1963, we pulled a memorable boner, with the front-page headline 'New Bonn Army Boss NOT a War Criminal', followed by a story which started as follows:

'The West German Government surprised the world at the end of September by appointing for the first time a Bundeswehr Commander in Chief who is not known to be a war criminal. The new C-in-C is General Heinrich Trettner. Like all other top Bundeswehr officers, he served Hitler truly throughout the Second World War, but unlike his two predecessors, war crimes charges have never been levelled against him.'

Six months later we had to eat our words. On March 20 1964, under the headline 'It Was Too Good to be True', we wrote:

'This statement must now be retracted. Further research into the nazi files has shown that General Trettner, who commands all West German forces today:

'1. Took part in the criminal air raid on the open town of Guernica in Spain in 1937.

'2. Personally ordered the bombing of Rotterdam, Holland, in May 1940 after a cease-fire had been arranged.'

German Report, 12 January 1972.

As far as I have been able to ascertain, *German Report* was only officially banned in one country – South Africa, on 6 February 1953. We dealt with this banning, a resultant prison sentence and some wise judges at some length:

A friend in South Africa has sent us a copy of the South African government's *Gazette Extraordinary* dated August 17 (1956) with a full list of the publications which it is forbidden to import into the country. The full list of 2,300 books and periodicals which are banned as being 'indecent, objectionable or obscene' makes weird reading.

The reason for the banning of some of these publications is fairly clear, though it may be narrow-minded: I refer to such works as *The Awful Disclosures of Maria Monk*, *The Blonde on the Street Corner* and *The Female Body Beautiful*.

Mixed up with such books, however, there appear the titles of all sorts of other publications which I cannot really believe constitute any serious danger to the morals of South Africans. Here are a few samples: *Anti-Duehring* by Friedrich Engels, *Agrarian Policy of Social Democracy in 1905* by Lenin, and a volume on the historic buildings of Czechoslovakia. In this section there is one title which really intrigues me: *Advertising Works of J. Stalin*. I knew that he wrote about all sorts of subjects – but advertising?

After that it is no surprise to find that *German Report* is banned, too, along with *Czechoslovak Life*, *China Reconstructs*, and dozens of other periodicals from the People's Democracies.

Of course it is all too easy to regard a list like this as merely comic: but it can be the very reverse for people in South Africa who can be fined £1,000 and sent to prison for five years for just having in their possession one of the books or periodicals listed.

I am glad to learn from *Saamtrek*, South African trade union weekly, that some judges in the South African Supreme Court have kept cool heads in the atmosphere of book-burning. The paper reported on August 31 that a South

African was recently sentenced to a prison term for the simple possession of a copy of *German Report*. He appealed the case, and the supreme Court quashed the verdict, ruling that the law only forbids *German Report* if it is imported into South Africa. The fact that *German Report* states at the bottom of the back page 'Printed in Germany' was not sufficient evidence that the copy seized was actually printed in Germany, and then imported into South Africa. It might have been printed in South Africa, the court ruled.

And far be it from me to argue with the decision of the august Supreme Court.

German Report, 12 October 1956

In the United States there was an indirect move to scare off readers of *German Report* and similar publications from other socialist countries. Subscribers received a card from the US Post Office, stating:

This office is holding unsealed mail matter addressed to you from a foreign country. Under Public Law 87-793, the Customs Bureau of the Treasury Department has determined this mail to be Communist political propaganda. It cannot be delivered to you unless you have subscribed to it, or otherwise want it. Please check the appropriate box on this card and return. If your reply is not received by the date indicated, it will be assumed that you do not want to receive the publication(s) listed or any similar publications

German Report reprinted this card in its issue of 11 December 1964, plus copies of two letters addressed to the US Post Office, one from the lawyers of Mrs Jessica Treuhaft (the Hon. Jessica Mitford, author of *Hons and Rebels*) and a rather more heated one from Mrs Madalyn Murray (militant US atheist who had just won a Supreme Court ban on school prayer). The first letter said:

Our client, Mrs Jessica Treuhaft, asks us to advise you that she objects to censorship in any form, and that she strongly protests your action in reading mail directed to her to determine whether it is 'communist political propaganda'. She needs no such Big Brother protection.

The second exploded:

Just who in hell do you think you are that you dare to send me this POD Form 2153-X? The job of the post office is to deliver mail and not to censor what I read.

The publication you list, the *Democratic German Report*, you say, has been determined by you to be Communist political propaganda. Well now, isn't that frightening? If I want to read Communist political propaganda that is my business and not yours.

I not only subscribe to this, but now that I know you are sticking your fat face into my reading habits I intend to increase my subscription to 10 a month in order to present copies of this to all my friends . . .

Your stupid form is herewith filled to indicate that I want the publication *Democratic German Report* and that now I will see how many other such publications I can get my hands on. Censorship indeed! Why don't you go work for Goldwater?

Mrs Murray promptly got her ten extra copies.

On 24 May 1965 the US Supreme Court ruled that it was unconstitutional for the US Post Office to hold up delivery of mail from the socialist countries.

Probably every journalist likes to reminisce nostalgically about the scoops he landed, and in a vague sort of way I thought that I could recall quite a lot of scoops in *German Report*. When I came to plough through the twenty-four volumes of the paper it turned out that most of these apparent scoops did not really stand the test. In my definition, a genuine scoop is a story of some importance which has never been published anywhere before; and most of our *German Report* scooplets, though totally new and of some interest to readers in English-speaking countries, did not measure up to this standard.

They ranged, in fact, from stories (mainly about old nazis in positions of importance in West Germany) which had already been published in both important papers and obscure journals in the two German states but ignored by the western press, to those which were buried away in published but seldom-read documents like the transcripts of trials of nazi criminals in the early post-war years.

But one story does appear to have been a 24-carat genuine scoop, though it reached us just forty years late. We published it on the first page on 24 April 1974 under the noisy headline: 'What's Good for Adolf Hitler is Good for General Motors':

Soon after Hitler came to power, he gave an assurance to General Motors, the huge US firm, that if they would play ball with him, he would see that General Motors 'gets a square deal'.

The understanding mainly affected Opel AG, at that time the largest producer of road vehicles in Germany; Opel was owned 100% by General

Motors. The deal was made in 1934, and in the following years Opel played a major part in arming and equipping the new nazi Wehrmacht.

German Report is today able to publish exclusively some details of this momentous deal. On April 30 1934, a three-man party of the top brass of General Motors, headed by Vice-President James D. Mooney, arrived in Berlin by plane for talks with Hitler. On May 3 1934 one of the members of the party recorded his impressions in a private letter. Chance (and the international network of journalists who don't like nazis) has now brought this letter into our hands . . .

Our account gave quotes from this private letter, describing rather breathlessly how the General Motors party were the only foreigners on the platform as Hitler addressed a May Day parade, and then went on:

And then the letter-writer comes to a short account of the meeting with Hitler:

'On Wednesday, Jim went to call on Hitler, and they had a regular round-table discussion on the motor-car industry in Germany, and the important part played by Opel. Hitler . . . said that if Opel will co-operate with him, he will see that we always get a square deal. Jim (Vice-President James D. Mooney) found him very human, very affable, quite a sense of humour and a clear picture of what it is all about.'

Since the exclusive story was forty years old when we published it, we were glad to be able to update it neatly with a quotation from a study submitted two months earlier, in February 1974, to the US Senate Anti-Trust and Anti-Monopoly Sub-Committee, stating: 'The General Motors plant in Germany built thousands of bombers and jet-fighter-propulsion systems for the Luftwaffe at the same time its American plants produced aircrft engines for the US Army Air Corps.'

I particularly like to recall some of the more flippant angles of editorial work. In a special issue marking our twentieth anniversary on 12 January 1972 I reminisced:

On a self-critical note, perhaps the time has come for me to admit that I have a weakness for trick headlines of various sorts, with or without apt alliteration's artful aid. To show you what I mean I should perhaps recall 'Yank Tank "Brink" Prank' on November 10 1961, and 'British Abet Bonn Border Bother Bid' on October 28 1966. Then there was 'USA Gets Proper Charlie' above a story about US libraries ordering the 50-volume definitive edition of the works of Karl Marx and Friedrich Engels; but that is enough, or even too much. I could just mention in passing two headlines in Latin: I had to abandon plans for a headline in Yiddish because the printers had no Hebrew letters. Our sole excursion into Welsh was confined to a cartoon caption which read:

'Dychwelwch – filwyr gorllewin yr Almaen!'

And if you want to know what that means, you will either have to ask a Welshman or look it up in *German Report* for September 1 1961 in which we gave an English translation.

The headline quoted above about the Yank Tank Prank caused a minor and successful revolt among my tiny editorial staff. For my first version was 'Yank Tank Prank Stank', and they felt that that was not up to our usual standards; a pity, but they were probably right.

This particular headline appeared over a story about a long-forgotten incident in autumn 1961 soon after the Berlin Wall had been erected by the GDR authorities. In a show of force the US Command in West Berlin staged US Military Police sallies through Checkpoint Charlie, the border crossing point for foreign nationals, and deployed a number of tanks with their guns pointing into the territory of the German Democratic Republic. A full explanation of the prank would take many pages; let me limit myself to my personal observations at the time, as published in *German Report* on 10 November 1961:

One day last week, only a couple of hundred yards from my office in the Friedrichstrasse, Berlin, I thought for a moment that I was going to get impaled on the sharp end of an American bayonet.

It all happened in the course of the extraordinary 'demonstration of force' indulged in by the Americans in the centre of Berlin, which we report fully on another page. I was standing a few yards inside East Berlin with a number of other journalists, flanked on one side by a man from TASS and on the other by a man from AP, when an American Military Police jeep swerved at full speed across the border of the German Democratic Republic. The jeep slowed, and four hefty American MPs, in camouflage uniform with fixed bayonets, leaped out and nearly ran us through.

Then they solemnly formed up on both sides of a small grey Volkswagen with three civilians in it, trotted about 50 yards into East Berlin, and then turned round and returned to West Berlin. It would all have been very comic, and in fact one American spectator called it the 'Friedrichstrasse Follies of 1961', if it had not been so dangerous.

After all, whatever the rights and wrongs of the conflict might be, here were armed American troops invading a small part of the German Democratic Republic. There was no possible excuse for their action: they were not saving the lives of threatened American nationals, going to the aid of a damsel in distress, or intervening to quell a riot. The only possible explanation could be that they were hoping to provoke one of the GDR frontier guards to strike the first blow or fire the first shot. I must say I admired the coolness and level-headedness of the GDR police who watched the American comic opera with polite smiles.

Let me say something about the rights and wrongs of the case, because they have been very poorly reported in the western press. Since August 13 1961, the previous 'invisible frontier' along the border between West Berlin and East Berlin has become a full-blown state frontier. There are the normal frontier crossing points, at which anyone wishing to enter or leave the GDR must show his passport.

Owing to the unclarified situation of the western occupation troops in West Berlin, and in order to avoid any possibility of a clash, the Government of the German Democratic Republic decreed that until the question of western troops in Berlin is properly settled, members of the western forces in uniform could pass the frontier into East Berlin freely. Occupation officials in civilian clothes must show their documents, to prove that they are in fact what they claim to be, but may also pass freely.

The British have always complied with this requirement, but the Americans, seeking a cause for conflict, refused to show identity documents, and then whistled up a show of armed force to crash the frontier.

Just imagine what would happen if a bunch of Russians came down the gangway at Idlewild Airport, New York, and brushed aside US Immigration officials, declaring loftily: 'We are Soviet diplomats: we don't need to show our passports.' And just imagine further that when they were turned back by US Immigration, they disembarked a platoon of Soviet infantry with fixed bayonets who escorted them through. Imagination boggles: but that is a pretty fair parallel to what happened in Friedrichstrasse, Berlin.

Just to tie up the odd ends of the odd story: a few minutes after the US sally of which I gave an eyewitness account, ten Soviet tanks, acting in accordance with the Warsaw Pact guarantee of the GDR frontier, lumbered into position on the East Berlin side of Checkpoint Charlie. The London *Times* commented on 28 October, the next day: 'It is hard to imagine this sort of thing going on, say, for months without a serious clash. It would be like playing last across, or seeing who can lean farthest out of the carriage window.'

A minimum of good sense prevailed at last, the US and Soviet tanks were withdrawn, the mini-invasions ceased, and US officials in civilian clothes started showing their papers, through tightly-closed car windows, to the GDR frontier guards. A US spokesman in West Berlin explained rather convolutedly that they were not really submitting their documents for scrutiny to persons not entitled to inspect them (that is, officials of the non-existent GDR); they were just proving, by showing their documents, that they were persons who did not have to show their documents.

In a subsequent chapter I shall be dealing more fully with the extraordinary song and dance, which lasted for more than twenty years, resulting from general western compliance with the West Germany article of faith that there never had been and never would be a German Democratic Republic.

Finally let me disinter one of the few occasions when I took a side-swipe at something I had spotted in a GDR newspaper:

> Mixed metaphors and clotted similes have always been a pitfall for writers and public speakers: many readers undoubtedly know the classic: 'I smell a rat; I see him forming in the air and darkening the sky; but I'll nip him in the bud' – attributed to the eighteenth-century Irish MP Sir Boyle Roche.
>
> As a keen hunter of such felicitous turns of phrase I was delighted to find the following in a political speech quoted in the GDR newspaper *Neues Deutschland* recently. The speaker was referring to some figures with whom he obviously disagreed: 'They play upon the piano of convergence-theory and alienation-theory, whilst, as skilled manipulators, they brew in their witches' kitchen magical potions . . . Clearing aside the barricades of Marxism-Leninism they hurry over the bridge constructed by the West German monopoly capitalists to the hard-currency-laden breasts of the strategists of psychological warfare.'
>
> *German Report*, 13 November 1968

30

Bashing the Brownshirts

While I was publishing *German Report* I often felt smug when readers' letters and visitors to Berlin assured me that the paper was far brighter and more interesting than similar journals from other socialist countries. Adding to my smugness was the fact that on several occasions weighty West German periodicals grumbled that English-language publicity put out by Bonn was dull and pedestrian compared to the lively journalism of *German Report*. Looking back from today with perhaps more sense of proportion, it is clear that this was due more to outside factors than to any particularly brilliant journalism on my part.

First of all, the editors of similar publications in most other socialist countries were, by the nature of things, mainly confined to boosting the achievements of socialist construction in Czechoslovakia or wherever, and a solid diet of plan fulfilments and model nursery schools can make stodgy reading. *German Report*, on the other hand, had both East and West Germany as its field, and could get very good and often sensational mileage out of juicy scandals in West Germany, old nazis back in responsible positions there and similar subjects.

Secondly, the GDR authorities, either by intention or inattention, interfered minimally with the way I ran the paper. At not very frequent intervals some GDR official, generally from the Foreign Ministry, would give me some very mild and generally useful guidance on trends and useful lines of argument – a rough parallel might be the briefings which the British Foreign Office gives regularly to the diplomatic correspondents of leading British media.

I can recall only one instance in all my twenty-four years of editorship when I was rapped over the knuckles, and this was lightly. At the time – it must have been the early 1960s – the main GDR newspaper *Neues Deutschland*, the organ of the Central Committee of the Socialist Unity Party, published a 'humour' page in its weekend edition. Wishing to use a moderately funny joke from this page, I prefaced it with the unkind but possibly true remark that this was probably the saddest humour page in the world. Soon after the paragraph appeared I was summoned to the office of the head of the Government Press Office, who reprimanded me crossly for slandering the Party newspaper: I should immediately send a polite letter to the editor expressing my regret. I assured him that I would think it over, and that was the last I ever heard of it. I am still thinking it over today.

But let me say more about *German Report*'s campaign of bashing old nazis back in positions of importance in West Germany. Up until the foundation of the West German state in 1949, men who had played an active part in running the nazi regime had generally kept a low profile in the three western occupation zones; but almost as soon as the Bonn state was born they began surfacing again, often in very high positions in government, the judiciary and the police forces. At the same time a number of political figures from all the main parties who had actually been at odds with the nazi regime for some reason now sensed a change in the atmosphere and tried to make people forget their anti-nazi past.

On 10 October 1952 *German Report* produced a few examples of this by comparing the past record of West German MPs as presented by themselves, first in the *Parliamentary Handbook* for 1949 and then in the 1952 issue. In 1949 Thomas Dehler, Free Democrat, had stated in his autobiographical note: 'From 1933 to 1942 member of an opposition group against Hitler . . . Arrested in 1938 and sent to forced labour in 1944.' For the 1952 *Handbook* he had decided that these details were no longer timely, and struck them out.

It was the same with a number of Christian Democrats, Free Democrats and Social Democrats who had recorded in 1949 that they had been 'arrested', 'sent to concentration camp' or 'politically persecuted' by the nazis: by 1952 these episodes had slipped their memories.

Details like this were presented by *German Report* more in sorrow than in anger, but one year later we were able to present details of the past histories of many of the members of Chancellor Adenauer's 1953 cabinet. The details were inevitably rather sketchy in places, since proper research into the old nazi files had not yet been organised. However, we were able to show, without any serious contradiction then or later, that, for instance, the Minister of Justice and the Minister for Expellees had been members of the nazi stormtroops; the Minister without Portfolio had been a *Haupt-sturmfuhrer* (major) in the SS; and the Housing Minister had been an SS instructor on racial questions and had been active in 'aryanising' Jewish property.

Our prize exhibit was certainly Hans Globke, State Secretary and personal assistant to Chancellor Adenauer, who had been head of the department for racial questions in the nazi Ministry of the Interior. He was finally sacked ten years later after fuller details of his career in the nazi period had emerged, and he had become a serious embarrassment to the West German Government. Journalistically I was sorry to see him go, for new documents on the Globke case were constantly coming to light, and he was always good for a story in a dull week.

In subsquent issues we published, as a contrast, details of the careers of the members of the government of the GDR, all of whom had firm and public anti-nazi records; but for quite a while the occasional reports which did appear in the British or American press about old nazis back at the top in Bonn generally ended with a not very specific charge that there were just as many old nazis in leading positions in the German Democratic Republic.

In one case I tried, unsuccessfully, to get such a charge withdrawn. Let me present a summary of the correspondence which ensued:

> On January 5 (1954) the Foreign Affairs Committee of the Board of Deputies of British Jews passed a resolution deprecating the growth of neo-fascism in West Germany. In the same resolution it was stated 'in East Germany a similar position obtains, in that several well-known nazis are Ministers in the East German Government'.
>
> On February 15 I wrote to the Foreign Affairs Committee pointing out that not a single member of the government in East Germany had been a nazi, that every minister had a good anti-nazi record, and asking for withdrawal of a statement which was clearly libellous.
>
> *German Report* 19 March 1954

Below this introduction we published a polite reply from Mr A. G. Brotman, Secretary of the Board of Deputies of British Jews, which stated in part:

> Our information – both in regard to East and West Germany – was given on the basis of information from sources which we know to be reliable. We had, and still have, no reason to doubt the accuracy of this information, but we have to recognise that there are possibilities of error in some of the details we

have received about these former nazis. In the circumstances we feel it would be inadvisable to publish names and other details.

I replied, in the same issue, urging him once again to make a public retraction of the statement.

The correspondence meandered on for another month, with Mr Brotman dragging in several side issues such as the wording of Soviet proposals for a peace treaty with Germany, and the theoretical possibility that all the ministers in a possible future All-German government might be old nazis, but avoiding the question of the alleged old nazis in the East German Government. I replied, stating:

These are undoubtedly points of public interest and concern: I shall be glad to give you space to set forth your reasoned views on the subject. But let us first settle the matter under discussion: does the Board of Deputies stand by its statement that there are 'well-known nazis in the East German Government'? If so, then please produce the evidence. If not, then a public retraction is urgently needed.

By this time, I think both of us were wearying of the correspondence, and it ceased. There was never a retraction.

Over the following years, until biological attrition set in, and most old nazis in high posts in West Germany reached retiring age and faded from the picture, *German Report*, basing itself mainly on painstaking work on the surviving nazi archives by GDR researchers, kept up the campaign. In early years the West German authorities tended to ignore the charges; later Bonn spokesmen usually brushed them aside with angry statements that the GDR charges were simply 'Soviet-Zonal propaganda attempts to embarrass the West German Government'; but I cannot recall a single case where such information drawn from the old nazi files was shown to be false. Finally, under the pressure of public opinion both in the world at large, and in West Germany itself, very many of the named old nazis had to be withdrawn from circulation and sent into retirement.

Just to round out the story, it is interesting to compare the West German foot-dragging with the very prompt action taken by the GDR authorities when in just two cases – compared to the several thousands of cases presented by the GDR – old nazis were in fact uncovered high up in the GDR establishment.

I dealt with the first case in *German Report* dated 19 June 1959, and I would like to quote fairly fully, since it fills in the background:

In March 1959 the West Berlin 'Investigating Committee of Free Jurists' published a pamphlet entitled *Former National Socialists in Pankow's Service* [Pankow was the derogatory name for the GDR Government invented by West German propagandists] listing 150 persons described as former nazis today serving in high positions in the German Democratic Republic. This pamphlet formed the basis for various articles in the British and American press.

Now at this point we have to go back in history a little way. During the reign of Hitler, the nazi Party had a total of over ten million members, and naturally quite a lot of these ex-members live today in the GDR. Immediately after the war all old nazis were removed from posts of responsibility, and any who could be shown to be guilty of crimes were punished.

It was obviously impossible, however, to turn some one-sixth of the population into permanent second-class citizens, and gradually the restrictions on the employment of ex-nazis were relaxed. It should not cause any surprise that quite a considerable number of them gradually came to realise the mistake they had made in the past, and decided to play their part in building up the GDR . . .

These men and women, with the exception of course of persons who had been guilty of war crimes, were judged by their deeds, and many of them have developed today into useful members of society.

But let us get back to the West Berlin pamphlet. It claims that the 150 ex-nazis listed hold key posts today in the GDR; but a little investigation shows that these 'key posts' are often nothing of the sort. They include, for instance, a professor of botany and a professor of theology at Greifswald University, a professor of pathology at Magdeburg, a scientific adviser to the Zeiss factory . . . and no fewer than 35 persons whose only claim to prominence is that they serve on town or district councils in various parts of the country. Since there are a total of 80,000 members on the various local councils, these ex-nazis do not present a very formidable contingent . . .

In the GDR the overwhelming majority of people who are really in key posts today – cabinet members, generals in the People's Army, police officers, etc. – are men who have really outstanding records in the resistance movement . . . Such men and women would not, and do not, work side by side with former nazi Party members unless they are certain that they have genuinely changed their views . . .

There is one exception, however. This is the case of Ernst Grossmann, a member of the Central Committee of the Socialist Unity Party of the GDR. The West Berlin pamphlet shows a photograph of Herr Grossmann in the uniform of the SS, and his case was made much of in reports in the British and American press. Now the fact of the matter is that prior to the publication of the pamphlet it was unknown in the GDR that he had been a member of the SS. Immediately after the pamphlet appeared a full investigation was made, and the results were made known on June 7th, when the official Socialist Unity Party paper *Neues Deutschland* published the following notice; 'Ernst Grossmann has been strongly censured for making false statements about his past record, and has been expelled from the Central Committee of the Socialist Unity Party.'

And if the West German authorities would take similar action to remove the thousands of men with far worse records serving in far more sensitive posts in the West German administration, there would be more hope of a bright future for Germany.

The second case, four years later, can be dealt with more briefly. On 9 February 1963 the GDR authorities announced that Professor Karl-Heinz Bartsch, who had just been appointed chairman of the agricultural commission with the rank of minister, had been summarily removed and expelled from the Central Committee of the Socialist Unity Party because he had concealed the fact that he had been a member of the Waffen-SS. The case of Professor Bartsch had also come to light as the result of details of his record published in West Germany, and we noted in *German Report* on 22 February 1963:

> It is important to note that the West German authorities can immediately check on anyone's past nazi affiliations, since the full records of the nazi Party and its ancillary organisations are held in the US Documents Centre in West Berlin. These complete indexed records are available to the West German authorities; they are barred to the GDR authorities, which have to rely on the fragmentary nazi records in their hands. The case of Professor Bartsch shows that it may be possible for a minor nazi who has managed to conceal his past record to attain a position of some importance in the GDR; the situation cannot be compared with that ruling in West Germany.

To wind up the story of the old nazis, let me just quote a few paragraphs from a book review published in *German Report*:

> I have just been reading, simultaneously, two new books dealing with the hunt for old nazis. One is frankly fiction: *The Odessa File* by Frederick Forsyth; the other claims to be fact: *The Bormann File* by Ladislas Farago.
>
> The odd thing is that the fictional work, *The Odessa File*, a crisp though rather plastic thriller, is thoroughly factual and well researched about the 'Odessa' nazi old-boy network which looked after SS officers on the run after the Second World War, and still looks after them to some extent today. The other book, *The Bormann File*, which masquerades as a piece of

documentary contemporary history, is quite the opposite: it is a collage of old rumours dredged from newspaper libraries and fleshed out with some rather marginal documents . . .

But let me get back to the realistic book . . . Mr Forsyth served a term in Reuters News Agency offices in both German states, so the background for his second book was obvious – nasty old nazis . . .

What I found interesting was not so much the story as the way the author had reinforced his fiction with well-researched fact. His particular trick is to write real people into his stories . . . and in *The Odessa File*, he has done this so successfully that at one point I found myself looking up my own reference files to discover whether one of the main SS characters was fictional or not.

If you are a long-time reader of *German Report*, the title should not puzzle you: Odessa is the name, formed from the German initials, of the 'Organisation of Former Members of the SS', a shadowy body which helped SS men on the run immediately after the war. Odessa came into the news again in the early 1960s, when key SS men who had been belatedly arrested in West Germany either escaped from prison with great ease, fell out of seventh-storey windows, or committed suicide in various unlikely ways.

During this period Mr Forsyth was the Reuters correspondent in East Berlin, and I would hazard a guess that he first learned about Odessa from this paper, which plopped through his letter-box every two weeks.

But let us leave Forsyth's factual fiction, and devote some attention to Farago's fantasy facts . . .

Martin Bormann may in fact be alive and well in Argentina as Mr Farago claims, but he has failed, at great length, to prove it.

I am equally unable to prove my contention that Martin Bormann is buried in my front garden here in the centre of Berlin.

I have made this claim before, but since my story is about as water-tight as Mr Farago's, let me repeat it.

Martin Bormann, Hitler's personal assistant, and the only really top nazi whose fate is unknown, was seen by many witnesses in Hitler's bunker in Berlin at the end of April 1945 as the battle of Berlin climaxed.

During the night of May 1st, Bormann and others tried to break through the Soviet military ring round Hitler's Chancellery and bunker. They got as far as the Weidendamm Bridge across the Spree River, where they came under Soviet artillery fire. One of the survivors of the party states he saw Bormann lying dead there.

When the battle of Berlin ended a few hours later, the overriding priority was to get the corpses off the street and buried. That is where my front garden comes in: it is only about 100 yards away from the spot where Bormann may have been killed, and was the obvious spot for emergency burials, since most of the surrounding area was covered with rubble, but this patch was open. Even today a bit of strenuous digging in the garden is liable to turn up rusted remains of rifles and steel helmets – and bones.

But to downgrade the Peet Private Theory a bit, I should point out that several other witnesses saw Bormann lying dead in various other parts of Berlin on the same day.

German Report, 27 December 1972

Today, many years later, I think I should add a couple of 'now-it-can-be-told' notes.

Note One: It was not simply a guess of mine that Freddy Forsyth learned of the existence of 'Odessa' from the pages of *German Report*. He told me so himself when he visited my office while he was writing the book to glean some of his 'well-researched facts' from our files, but asked me to keep this under my hat since he felt that any association with a notorious Red rag like mine would be the kiss of death for his book. After the passage of time and his present-day millionaire status I do not feel this revelation can do him any harm.

Note Two: In the meantime it seems fairly soundly established that Bormann was killed miles away from my front garden, and I relinquish unreservedly all claims, particularly since I have long since moved and no longer have a garden. But there was an intriguing further bit of rather far-fetched support for my 'Bormann-in-my-garden' theory. In those days one of the flats whose windows looked out on my garden was occupied by a matron of unimpeachable integrity who had had the misfortune to catch the eye of Martin Bormann when she was young.

Another of our main themes, which lent itself to both heavy and light coverage, was the official West German policy of pretending, for over twenty years, that the GDR was not there at all, and would go away if it were only ignored firmly enough. Clapping their telescopes firmly to their blind eyes, the Bonn Government declared that the German Reich still continued to exist within the frontiers of 1937, that is, before Hitler proceeded to enlarge it by taking over and incorporating Austria and large portions of Czechoslovakia and Poland, and that the Federal Republic of Germany was the only legitimate government of the whole area.

This meant that it laid claim not only to the GDR, but also to the western third of Poland and the northern half of East Prussia which had been incorporated into the Soviet Union under the terms of the Potsdam Agreement concluded by Britain, the USA and the Soviet Union in August 1945.

If this had all remained a lawyer's quibble – like, let us say, the ancient claim of English sovereigns to rule France long after they had ceased to do so – it might not have mattered so much; but they apparently really meant it. West Germany threatened to break off diplomatic relations with any state which dared to recognise the non-existent German Democratic Republic and in fact took this step in a number of cases; and it internally went to extreme lengths to censor the GDR off the map of Europe and to pretend that large areas of eastern Europe belonged to Germany. An official West German Government ordinance ordered map-makers to refrain from marking the border between West Germany and East Germany, and further east large chunks of Poland and part of the Soviet Union had to be clearly marked 'temporarily under Polish [or Soviet] occupation'.

Attempts were made to extend this censorship to other countries:

The West German Embassy in London is endeavouring to get the Oxford University Press to alter its newly published atlas of the world, West German Foreign Minister Heinrich Brentano announced in the Bonn Parliament on June 6.
He stated that the West German authorities objected to the atlas because it showed East Germany as an independent state, the Oder–Neisse line as a permanent frontier, and the 'German eastern territories' as a permanent part of Poland.
Unreliable reports state that British Foreign Minister Harold Macmillan will shortly ask West German map-makers to change their maps so as to show the United States as a British colony.
German Report, 22 June 1956

In 1960 the West German map war got even more heated with threats to take legal action against the Times Publishing Company if it went ahead with its plans to publish an edition of its atlas in West Germany. *The Times* had committed the same crime: showing the European frontiers where they really were, instead of where Bonn considered they should be:

What makes the crime of the *Times Atlas* even more heinous in the eyes of Bonn is that it actually dares to give the various towns and villages in the western parts of Poland the names by which they are known today to their inhabitants; these towns and villages should be marked with their German names, even if no Germans live there, the West Germans claim.
German Report, 23 December 1960

The Times Publishing Company and the Oxford University Press ignored Bonn and continued to show Europe as it is, but the British military authorities, apparently under West German pressure, went along with the map war. In 1965 *German Report* decided to get in on the act:

> Bonn propaganda for the conquest of large parts of eastern Europe is officially supplied by the British Army to British troops serving in West Germany and West Berlin.
>
> The small map reproduced above [in the original issue of the paper] which implies that large parts of Poland and a section of the Soviet Union really belong to Germany is handed out every week to the British Rhine Army . . .
>
> The entire map shows Germany within the frontiers of 1937, the area which is officially claimed by the West German authorities to constitute Germany today.
>
> The map is printed regularly every week as part of the title of an eight-page propaganda sheet called *Focus on Germany* published by the West German Government press office and supplied gratis to the British military authorities. They insert it in every issue of the weekly official news-sheets published by the British Army of the Rhine . . .
>
> It would be interesting to know whether Mr Dennis Healey, Minister of Defence in the British Labour Government, is aware of the fact that this West German propaganda for a revision of the frontiers of Europe is being officially distributed to the British troops.
>
> *German Report*, 5 February 1965

Reaction to our story was fairly swift, and a few weeks later we could crow 'Thank You, Mr Healey' in a headline:

> Mr Arthur Lewis, Labour MP for West Ham North, decided to find out whether Defence Minister Healey did know and put down a parliamentary question.
>
> On March 1st, Mr Healey gave his reply. He claimed that the contents of the Bonn sheet were 'innocuous and of a non-controversial nature' but he added that the HQ of the British Army of the Rhine had been instructed to delete the map from future editions.
>
> Thank you, Mr Healey, for the prompt attention which you have given to this matter.
>
> Postscript: An official spokesman in Bonn, commenting on the case, laid great stress on the fact that the map in question 'is only about nine square centimetres in area', but proceeded to claim that the frontiers of the German Reich of 1937 as shown on this little map 'have been given recognition under international law in various treaties concluded with the Allies in the Federal Republic'. He failed to specify any such treaties, and research by *German Report* has failed to bring any to light.
>
> *German Report*, 19 March 1965

But we had crowed too soon. Bonn apparently kicked Mr Healey, and he did an about face in the House of Commons on 15 March:

Mr Healey said that his earlier reply had been 'based on misunderstanding', and added: 'I have since found that the map shows the 1937, rather than the 1939, frontiers of Germany. Had it been the 1939 frontiers it would have been most objectionable. But the 1937 frontiers are a different matter. I have therefore decided that there are no grounds for removing this map from future editions of *Focus on Germany*, and I have rescinded the orders for its deletion.'

German Report, 2 April 1965

To wind up this collection of the oddities arising from Bonn's determined attempt to send the German Democratic Republic to Coventry and keep it there, to cling to long-lost frontiers and to pressure its allies to do the same, let me give a small selection of further specimens:

I have just come across a thoroughly remarkable document issued by the consular department of the British Foreign Office. This document, dated December 1968 . . . is distributed to British citizens who enquire at the British Foreign Office about the possibilities of visiting the GDR. Perhaps we can ignore the curious old-fashioned style in which this document refers throughout to the 'Soviet Zone of Germany' when it means the German Democratic Republic. But there are one or two passages early in the document which do raise the eyebrows. The memorandum starts off by saying:
    'The Soviet authorities, whom Her Majesty's Government continue to hold legally responsible, no longer issue permits to travel into or through the Soviet Zone of Germany . . . ' No longer is good: in fact the Soviet authorities have not issued permits of this sort for some twenty years now. It is the next sentence, however, which I find particularly amusing: 'It is understood, however, that visas may be obtained from East German authorities.'
    It is this cautious phrase 'it is understood' which I find sweet: many thousands of British citizens visit the GDR or travel through the GDR every year, and they all obtain visas from the GDR authorities. But in order to retain its careful virginity, the Foreign Office can only say 'It is understood'.

German Report, 8 April 1970

Probably no subject has been mentioned so often in this column over the past 19 years as the repeated rather childish attempts to down-grade the German Democratic Republic by thinking up other names for it: 'Soviet Zone', 'Middle Germany', 'Pankow', 'so-called GDR' and so on.
    On the whole, this fruitless attempt to apply black magic in the field of

international relations has gone into a decline, so I was rather surprised to find that the British Post Office has invented a new variant. In the current GPO International Telex Directory, telex subscribers in the Federal Republic of Germany are listed under 'West Germany', and those in the GDR under 'Germany – Remainder'.

German Report, 6 September 1971

United States citizens who state on their passport applications that they intend to visit the German Democratic Republic receive from the State Department a remarkable four-page document warning them to watch out . . . It is issued by the Passport Office, US Department of State, Washington, DC . . . and is numbered M-249 3-71 . . .

Here are a few verbatim extracts from the original . . . and my comments, printed in italics:

'Although the United States Government does not encourage travel by American citizens to or through East Germany, it does not place any restrictions on such travel. American travellers contemplating such travel are, however, strongly advised to get in touch with a United States consular office in Germany . . . in order to get the latest information on conditions there, and to leave a record . . . of their home addresses in the United States.'

Or in clear text: *no restrictions are placed on your travel, but the US consulate would like to register the names and address of people who do things that the United States Government does not encourage them to do.*

'Travellers are reminded . . . that East Germany is controlled by a Communist regime called the German Democratic Republic or GDR. The United States Government does not recognise the East German regime . . . American travellers in East Germany are therefore assuming a greater risk than is connected with travel to other Communist countries and must be prepared for the consequences in case of trouble.'

Or in clear text: *if you persist in ignoring our warnings it's your own silly fault and we hope they send you to the salt mines.*

'It is strongly recommended that American citizens enter and depart East Berlin at Checkpoint Charlie and register with the United States Military Police before entering and after exiting East Berlin . . . Do notify some reliable person in West Berlin where you are going in East Berlin and when you expect to return . . . If you do not return by an agreed time this person should immediately inform the consular section of the US Mission.'

And the US Mission presumably then whistles up the B-52s to bomb the GDR back to the stone age.

German Report, 26 January 1972

When the GDR and FRG formally signed their Basic Treaty at the end of last year, regulating their relations, I rather feared that this paper would finally be forced to stop sniggering about Bonn's terminological tintinnabulations.

For over 20 years official West German circles had been tripping over their own toes in efforts not to say the dread words 'German Democratic Republic' . . . Two high points were reached when West German Chancellor Kiesinger ruled that the GDR should be called first 'that phenomenon' and later 'the other side'.

But despite a treaty, things were soon back to normal. A Bonn spokesman announced on August 10 that as a result of the Basic Treaty with the GDR, notices near the GDR frontier which had hitherto said 'Warning: Zonal Frontier' should now be removed . . . The only difficulty, the spokesman said, was that while everyone agreed that the notices were outdated (23 years outdated, actually) nobody could agree on the wording of the notices which should replace them. To put up notices saying 'Frontier Ahead' might be interpreted as meaning that the line of division between the GDR and the FRG was a state frontier, and the Federal Constitutional Court had ruled that it was not a state frontier. (Why not notice boards saying: 'Warning: Phenomenon Ahead'?)

This whole situation can go on for years or even decades: we promise to keep you informed if anything actually happens.

German Report, 12 September 1973

But the promise in the last line was one which I have not been able to keep, though at the time of writing (1985) some leading West German publications still try to keep the GDR in quarantine by referring to it as the 'GDR' in inverted commas, and some conservative politicians proclaim, though today generally in rather more muted terms, that the western one-third of Poland is really their property.

The reason why I was unable to keep this promise made in September 1973 was that, just over two years later, *German Report* finally folded, after twenty-four years of publication. Announcing the close-down in the pages of the paper, I stated:

When *German Report* first appeared 24 years ago, in January 1952, the young German Democratic Republic was unrecognised and largely unknown in the western world.

German Report made it its task to help break down the 'cordon sanitaire' of silence, stupidity and slander, and to tell people in the English-speaking countries about the existence and development of the GDR; at the same time we drew attention to the dangers of a rebirth of German militarism and reaction in the Federal Republic of Germany.

Today the German Democratic Republic is an active member of the

United Nations, and maintains full diplomatic relations with nearly 120 countries in all parts of the globe.

In these circumstances, *German Report* has become redundant.

Apart from the changed situation of the German Democratic Republic in world affairs, which meant that *German Report* had to be much more careful not to tread undiplomatically on sensitive toes, I was, in fact, running out of steam. Though the paper appeared only every two weeks, I was researching and writing practically the whole thing, apart from making up the paper and reading proof. So, in a way, I was quite glad to see it die.

31

Peet's Progress

L ike many journalists, I am probably a rather superficial person,
with a wide range of not very profound knowledge, a certain knack
for writing readably but little interest in retrospection. That inevitably means that the following pages may tend to be superficial rather than
reflective. In addition, as anyone knows who has tried to do it, it is
extraordinarily difficult to recall exactly what one really thought and felt,
and the real motives for one's actions, twenty or thirty or fifty years ago.

Ever since the age of about fifteen I have felt myself aligned with
revolutionary socialism and, with some waverings and misgivings, to the
mainstream of 'orthodox Marxism-Leninism' as exemplified until 1945 by
the Soviet Union and the parties of the Comintern, and since then by the
'socialist countries'. Here, of course, the picture has become blurred ever
since the late 1940s, as this once-monolithic bloc shifted and changed as
the various schisms and heresies waxed and waned: Yugoslavia, China,
Albania and others, plus, a far-out sport, Pol Pot's Kampuchea.

Back in the bright days of my youth, the picture seemed very clear
indeed. On one side stood the retrograde forces of capitalism, which
controlled five-sixths of the surface of the globe and was quite obviously on
its last legs; and on the other side the young and revolutionary Soviet
Union, which was ushering in, at high speed, a new society and held out
the promise of a different and better way of life.

It had all been explained so very simply and plainly back in 1848 by Karl
Marx and Friedrich Engels. Bourgeois society had passed its prime and
produced, in their words, 'its own grave-diggers. Its fall and the victory of
the proletariat are equally inevitable.'

Since I and uncounted other middle-class converts to Marxism were clearly not proletarians (nor were Marx and Engels either), we took great comfort from another passage in the *Communist Manifesto*:

> in times when the class-struggle nears the decisive hour, the process of dissolution going on within the ruling class, in fact within the whole range of the old society, assumes such a violent, glaring character, that a small section of the ruling class cuts itself adrift, and joins the revolting class, the class that holds the future in its hands.

(Incidentally, reading the *Communist Manifesto* once again to verify these short quotations, I was struck anew by the simplicity and clarity of this extraordinary document, which has weathered far better than most political manifestos.)

So in the 1930s it was very obvious that 'historical inevitability' (one of those Marxist catch-phrases which in later years increasingly became an easy substitute for thought and analysis) was all on the side of the young Soviet Union. The wars of intervention, in which Britain, France, the USA and the other states had tried to stifle the young Soviet Union at birth, lay only fifteen years in the past; fascism, the last stage of monopoly capitalism, had taken over in Germany, Italy and Japan, and these states were being tacitly encouraged by the other imperialist states to finish the job. Thus the place for every clear-thinking person was in the ranks of the international Communist movement – or at least on the sidelines cheering it on.

Looking back from today, it is evident that my faith – and that of so many others – was an over-simplification, and held many utopian elements. To sum our vision up in one sentence: all that had to be done was to expropriate the expropriators, socialise the means of production, and man would become Good with a capital G. In some ways it resembled the faith of those Esperantists who believed that an international language could eliminate most, if not all, of the evils in the world, or of some vegetarians who believed that total abstention from meat might do the same.

How, then, did we handle the hostile reports from the Soviet Union published in the bourgeois press? Many of them could be discounted or ignored just because they were spread by the 'boss-press monopoly'; others were, or appeared to be at the time, demonstrably untrue.

But some events, like the Moscow trials of leading Bolsheviks in 1936–8, could not be dismissed so easily. My own reaction, as far as I can reconstruct it today, was three-pronged. Firstly, there was the all-purpose response that you cannot make an omelette without breaking eggs.

Secondly, there was the argument based on faith, but little else, that while Zinoviev and all the other Old Bolsheviks were quite probably not nazi or Japanese spies, they must be guilty of something. And thirdly, there was the excuse based on Lenin's polemical *Left-Wing Communism – An Infantile Disorder*, written in 1920, in which he displayed, with examples, that many elements who were not true Marxists had attached themselves to the revolutionary movement, but that when things got tough they had fallen by the wayside or become traitors to the cause.

In addition to these more or less specious arguments, it appeared clear to millions of people, in that period of growing threat of fascism and war, that the Soviet Union was the only hope, and that Stalin, we hoped and believed, knew what he was doing. Certainly most people in western countries had at that time no true conception of the gigantic scale of the Stalin purges; by chance I myself got a more or less inside glimpse, at least of the havoc they had wreaked among the leading cadres of the Soviet Party.

It happened like this. After the end of the Spanish War, some time in early 1939, Louis Fischer, the American radical journalist and veteran Moscow correspondent of the New York *Nation*, was passing through London on his way back to the United States, accompanied by his Russian wife and two children. Needing somebody to take the kids off his hands for a few days while he attended to business in London, Fischer applied for help to the International Brigades Association, the organisation of the Britons who had fought in Spain. He himself had close links with the International Brigades, for at an early stage of the war in Spain he had worked as supply officer at the Brigade base in Albacete.

I got the child-minding job, and for about a week busily took his two bright and friendly Moscow-educated sons, aged ten or twelve, round tourist London – the Tower, the Zoo and all the rest.

One day the boys were not ready when I called to pick them up at their hotel, and while I was waiting for Mrs Fischer to bring them from their room, my eye was caught by a double-page newspaper spread of photographs under the glass top of her dressing table. The captions were all in Russian, but I managed to work out that the portrait photos showed the members of the Central Committee of the Communist Party of the Soviet Union elected at the Seventeenth Party Congress in 1934 – the 'Congress of Victors' as it was called at that time. What puzzled me was that very many of the portraits were crossed out.

When Mrs Fischer returned to tell me the boys would be along shortly, I asked her about it.

She explained, almost in tears, 'That is what Stalin has done to our

225

Central Committee. Probably more of them have gone. I've only crossed out those I have heard about; a number of them were our friends. But probably there are more.'

Some twenty years later, in the late 1950s, Louis Fischer, who had long broken his Moscow connections, dropped in to see me at my little office in East Berlin, and I recalled the episode.

'I told my wife she shouldn't keep that page on display, even in London,' he said, 'but there's no harm in talking about it now. We tried to keep a check at the time, but it was only after the Twentieth Congress in 1956 that we learned authoritatively that a good many more had in fact gone than those my wife had crossed off.'

(Figures revealed in 1956 showed that of the seventy-one leading Communists, many of them veteran Bolsheviks, who were elected to the Central Committee in 1934, only sixteen survived to be re-elected in 1939.)

Mr Fischer's evidence, direct from Moscow, of the extent of Stalin's purge right at the top must obviously have made a very deep impression on me, since it is one of my few really sharp memories from those far-off days. I can still see before me that rather grey sheet of Russian newsprint under the glass top of the toilet table, and can still hear Mrs Fischer's voice. But curiously enough I have no recollection of my reaction at the time, and I do not believe that I even mentioned the incident to anybody until many years later.

Trying to reconstruct my mental processes back in 1939 I can only conclude that I rationalised, as most of us do when our faith is being jeopardised by inconvenient facts: the Soviet Union, personified in Stalin, is the one rock in a world hell-bent for destruction; Stalin works in a mysterious way his wonders to perform; and anyway you can't make an omelette without breaking eggs.

There were other events which worried many fellow travellers – I suppose I must stick this label on myself – and not a few Communist Party members in the following period. There were, for instance, the astonishing Hitler–Stalin non-aggression pact in August 1939, the Soviet–Finnish War that winter, the 'plague on both your houses' attitude adopted by the world Communist movement in the first two years of the Second World War and others.

But as the Soviet Union won the respect of the world for its resistance to the nazi invaders, the doubts receded. After the end of the Second World War the socialist section of the world had expanded enormously, both in eastern and central Europe and in the Far East. There were obviously great difficulties in the new People's Democracies which were coming into existence, and the shortcomings and mistakes were many, but they could easily be brushed off as teething difficulties.

And by the late 1940s, only four years after the end of the Second World War, it began to look as though post-1918 events were coming up for a second showing. At that time the main capitalist countries had made frantic attempts to stifle the young Soviet Union at birth in the wars of intervention; and now in 1950 the United States, still the sole possessor of nuclear weapons, was plunging into the cold war, was urging the creation of a new West German Wehrmacht and was making no bones about the fact that the socialist states were the potential target.

Under these circumstances it seemed only logical for me to line up with the young German Democratic Republic, which against great odds appeared to be making a good start in constructing a new-style state on a socialist basis on German soil. So I crossed the dividing line.

The change-over from life as Reuters correspondent in West Berliin to that of a freelance journalist in the GDR, where life and work were organised on a very different basis, was not as much of a culture shock for me as might have been expected.

First of all, in the previous five years I had had considerable experience of a number of eastern European countries at various stages in their early war-battered transition from capitalism to socialism. Apart from my stay of several months in Warsaw in early 1947 I had paid several short visits to Czechoslovakia and Hungary for Reuters; since the summer of 1947 I had been working in the Reuters office in West Berlin, and had been a constant visitor to East Berlin, both professionally and privately. So I had at least some idea of what I was letting myself in for.

Secondly, I found myself in many ways in a privileged position in East Germany, though I do not think that I appreciated this fully at the time. When I list some of these privileges they may not seem all that important, but they have to be seen against the generally spartan standards of food, housing, transport and so on back in 1950, when the GDR was just taking its first rather uncertain steps out of the initial post-war chaos.

After only a few weeks in the GDR, for instance, I was given a small flat. It bore no comparison to the very good centrally heated flat I had had in West Berlin – a middle-class flat requisitioned for correspondents by the British military authorities – but it had a bath and a lavatory and proper glass in the windows, and the roof did not let the rain in. Altogether superior accommodation for East Berlin in 1950.

All food was sharply rationed in the GDR at the time, and ration cards came in a number of categories, ranging from 'heavy worker', which provided a fairly adequate amount of food, down to 'non-working dependants', which provided just about enough calories to stay alive on. As a 'working intellectual' I got one of the better categories of ration card. In addition, I had the privilege of being able to eat off-the-ration at a club for 'cultural workers'. Again it was a peg down from my West Berlin life, where the British forces NAAFI provided cheap cigarettes and drinks and many items of food, but I was much better off than the mass of the GDR population.

And in the field of transport I was infinitely better off than the ordinary man in the street, since I had the car I had brought with me from West Berlin. At that time there were almost no private cars on the road in the GDR; practically all the vehicles you saw were on official business or belonged to doctors or other essential services.

In addition, a rather more intangible privilege, I had 'freedom of information'. Western newspapers and periodicals were not available to the general population, but for my journalistic work I needed them, so the GDR Information Office provided me with a broad variety of West Berlin, West German, British and US periodicals.

I tended to find my friends and acquaintances among a relatively small section of the population, mainly anti-nazis who, emerging from the concentration camps and the underground, or returning from emigration, were now tackling the enormous task of getting things going in a new and different sort of German state.

There were the outstanding figures in the cultural world like Bertolt Brecht and Arnold Zweig, whom I already knew, the famous actor and singer Ernst Busch, Hanns Eisler the composer and many more, and of course many old comrades from the Spanish War, several of whom took me under their wing. On a less name-dropping level there were a number of veteran Communists who had spent their entire lives in the struggle against the state – first as rebels in the pre-Hitler Weimar Republic, and later in the resistance against Hitler – and who had quite naturally been given important jobs in an anti-fascist state. Some of them were finding it difficult to adjust to becoming pillars of society instead of Red moles.

I suppose that anybody occupying a relatively privileged position in a foreign society tends to be in that society but not really of it; and in my case this tendency was probably reinforced and prolonged when, in 1952, I contracted my penultimate marriage. Although this marriage lasted considerably longer than my two previous trial runs, I shall treat it briefly, since the details are of no wider concern.

My wife, a few years younger than myself, was very much an 'orphan of the storm' which the Second World War had brought to Europe. As a child she had been pushed around Europe with her parents, political refugees from Bulgaria. Her father disappeared in the 1930s; her brother was reported killed in the Spanish War; her mother was killed in an air raid on Warsaw. She herself had been sent as a slave labourer to nazi Germany, and then to concentration camp for anti-nazi activities. When the war ended, she had nowhere to go, and stayed in East Germany, working as a translator.

So we got married and had two children. As the children grew up we gradually drifted apart, and we got divorced a number of years ago. The relevance of this marriage to my theme is that, as the result of her harrowing experiences, she was very reluctant to have anything to do with Germans, particularly of the older generation, unless she knew that they had a clear anti-nazi record. Since relatively few people fell into this select category in her eyes, our circle of acquaintances tended to remain limited.

Readers may recall some fairly undramatic details in the chapter entitled 'Back in Blighty' about my recruitment as a Soviet spy. A full fourteen years after my first contact with the anonymous Soviet intelligence service, the relationship was suddenly resumed. Early in 1954 a Soviet citizen in East Berlin vaguely associated with the journalistic network suddenly produced the recognition signal which I had almost forgotten, and arranged a meeting with a superior official.

This renewed contact I found rather disturbing. First of all, I had become a fairly well-known figure in both the German Democratic Republic and West Berlin. Secondly, I held a moderately important and very exposed position as a public relations man (or paid propagandist if you prefer the phrase) for the GDR, and the slightest suspicion that I was doubling as a Soviet agent would be embarrassing for all parties. And – though I probably suppressed the thought at the time – I was not by then so completely convinced that the Soviet Union always did the best thing to achieve the best of all possible worlds.

But despite these reservations I kept the appointment. The cold war was at that time reaching new dimensions, West German rearmament was as good as settled, the USA was brandishing the atom bomb in which it still had great superiority; and with all its faults the Soviet Union appeared to be the only hope for mankind.

I tried to explain to the senior official the difficulty or impossibility of combining my public relations job with any form of intelligence work. He conceded that my position was somewhat difficult, but reminded me fairly tactfully that I had entered into a contract many years earlier and had an obligation to fulfil it. However, his service was ready to take my difficulties into consideration, and I would be free to turn down assignments which might get me into difficulties.

In the following weeks the subordinate agent who maintained contact came up with a series of preposterous suggestions, all of which I turned down.

First of all, he wanted to make the acquaintance of a particular western correspondent working in West Berlin. Nothing easier, I said, I meet this particular correspondent every week or two for lunch, and all he had to do was drop in by chance at the same restaurant. But this plan was much too simple. I should arrange a trip round the GDR with the western correspondent, stage an apparent car breakdown at a specified time and place, and my Soviet contact would suddenly appear as a friend in need. It all sounded far too complicated, so I refused to participate.

Next week's suggestion was far worse, a fancy-dress kidnap. Dressed as a British officer, I should drive to the British sector of Berlin with two apparent British sergeants to 'arrest' a German national suspected of spying in the GDR. I had no need to argue about this one: it was a very definite non-starter.

In the following weeks there were several other suggestions, none as outrageous as the kidnap plot, but all of them totally outside my conception of what I could sensibly do. I could, in a limited way, provide information about what western journalists knew or suspected about the plans of the western allies. So I transmitted a certain amount of West Berlin journalistic scuttlebutt, which Soviet intelligence could have obtained more easily and directly if Soviet correspondents had had more liberty to mix freely with their western counterparts.

But finally my contact man came up with a proposal which seemed interesting, simple and non-James-Bondish (though Bond had not yet been invented). The plan was that I should attend, perfectly normally, the top-grade Geneva Conference on the Far East, due to begin at the end of April 1954. This time I agreed without hesitation: it would be a nice break to get away from everyday life in the GDR, to join the international foreign correspondents' circus once again for a few days and meet a number of old friends.

In Geneva we all milled around at the press centre bar, at press conferences and at lavish receptions where you were liable to find yourself chatting with Chou En-lai at one moment and John Foster Dulles at the next. The journalists all had their favourite rumour to spread, but mixed up with the rumours there was a certain amount of fact, for instance the maximum and minimum positions likely to be taken by their respective government delegates.

(One day, incidentally, I found myself suddenly confronted by the opposition. An American journalist, apparently acting for the CIA, took me aside and informed me he had heard I was dissatisfied with life in the GDR and would like out. He had been authorised, he said, to promise me $20,000 cash down as soon as I took the step. I thanked him politely for the information about my cash value on the free market and left.)

At my next meeting with my Soviet contact, who had also come to Geneva, he said that he had been instructed to inform me of a new plan, a long-term plan. I should get on good terms with some of the female members of the various UN agencies stationed in Geneva; there would be expense money available to take them out to expensive restaurants and night clubs. He hinted broadly for quite a while until I interrupted to tell him that the seduction of prospective spies was definitely not my line, and I had to hurry back to Berlin to get on with my normal public relations job.

At a subsequent meeting in Berlin I told him I could see no future in any further collaboration. He made a rather mild attempt to convince me that I should continue with 'the work', but said he would consult his superiors. A few days later there was a curt phone call: 'No further meetings.'

For a long time I expected an attempt to resume the relationship. But I have now ceased to expect that telephone call. If it should come, I shall answer curtly, 'Wrong number,' and hang up.

32

Trials and Tribulations

L ong ago, when I left school and went to work for the first time, my
father, who rarely insisted on anything, said very firmly that the
time had now come for me to take out life insurance. 'Then you will
have something to depend on in your old age, or a nest egg for your
widow.'

I found the suggestion ridiculous. This was partly the normal reaction of
a teenager who could not imagine getting old or having a widow; but there
was another and more important factor in my case. I explained to my
father, I hope with patience, that long before I had reached retirement age
the whole world would be socialist, with cradle-to-grave social security,
and private life insurance would have been consigned to the dustbin of
history along with millionaires. I may even have suggested that money
would have been phased out too.

My father agreed I was painting a very pleasant picture of the future, but
he would pay the instalments for the first year himself, just in case. I
cannot remember what happened to the policy; I probably cashed it in as
soon as I could.

Today – though in the German Democratic Republic and other developed industrial countries, both socialist and non-socialist, there is a far
higher degree of lifelong social security than there was in the 1930s – my
happy vision has, of course, remained a dream.

After I had settled in the GDR in 1950, the first event which worried me seriously about the way things were going in the socialist countries was, once again, a political trial. This was not in the GDR, but in a neighbouring country, Czechoslovakia.

From 20 to 27 November 1952 fourteen members of the Czechoslovak Communist Party headed by Rudolf Slansky, who had been general secretary of the party only a few months earlier, went on trial for high treason, espionage and sabotage: eleven of the fourteen were sentenced to death and executed, and the other three got life.

The whole course of the trial, which was given full coverage in the GDR press, reminded me uncomfortably of the Moscow trials of the 1930s. The accused abjectly pleaded guilty to multiple crimes, without giving even halfway-believable explanations of how and why they had suddenly become traitors to a cause for which most of them had fought and suffered for many years. The evidence offered was, to say the least of it, very curious in places, and there were clear and unpleasant anti-Semitic tones in some of the court proceedings.

For a number of reasons the Slansky trial made a much greater impression on me than the earlier Moscow trials. Those had been in a far-off country, and the accused were only rather exotic names to me; the trial in Prague was just around the corner and in a country I knew quite well. Most important, several of the accused, and a number of others alleged to be involved, were people whom I knew personally, for instance Peter Smollett, mentioned earlier, who was named as a 'notorious British spy' together with Claud Cockburn of *The Week*.

A close study of the 'confessions' showed, in many cases, their inherent incredibility. There is really no need to labour the point at this late date; for during subsequent years the Czechoslovak authorities themselves declared that the trial had been a frame-up, and rehabilitated the accused, most of them posthumously.

But it is perhaps worth recalling that some of the prisoners apparently tried to signal the absurdity of the charges to the outside world. Vavro Hadju, for instance, told the court at great length how, when he was living as a political refugee in Britain, he had been summoned in summer 1941 to the police station in the little village of Wiveliscombe, where the local constable had promptly signed him on as a British spy who could serve as a Trotskyite agent in post-war Czechoslovakia.

At international conferences after the war, Vavro Hajdu testified, various high-ranking British politicians including Selwyn Lloyd had forced him to continue spying for Britain by waving the 'Wiveliscombe Document' under his nose. With the aid of a large-scale map I located Wiveliscombe in the heart of Somerset, happily poised between the hamlets of Huish Champflower and Langford Budville: it is rather difficult to imagine the village constable recruiting Czech Trotskyite spies there.

In Victorian days in Britain conventional churchmen who began to query precepts of the Christian faith from the Virgin Birth to the Thirty-Nine Articles were said to have 'doubts'. In the GDR in the 1950s when supporters of Marxism-Leninism began to worry about the gospel as interpreted by Stalin, or apparent inconsistencies between theory and practice, they were described as having 'stomach-aches'.

These stomach-aches became endemic in 1956 when, at the Twentieth Congress of the Communist Party of the Soviet Union, certain aspects of Stalin's rule were condemned publicly, and when far more extensive and bloody details were revealed in Khrushchev's 'secret speech'. This speech has never been published in the GDR to this day, though watered-down versions were handed on in 1956 at internal meetings of party members. When *Neues Deutschland*, the central party newspaper, could not avoid mentioning the speech, it referred to it as 'the alleged secret speech'. But the contents became very widely known indeed, both from western broadcasts and from copies smuggled into the country from West Berlin.

My first reaction to the downgrading of Stalin at the Soviet Party Congress was quixotic, and I report it rather reluctantly.

After the Congress was over, but before details of Khrushchev's secret speech had become known, Walter Ulbricht, the GDR Communist leader, returned from Moscow and gave a report to party activists. In this report he announced that Stalin could not be regarded as a classic of Marxism-Leninism. In previous years Ulbricht had insisted on every occasion that Stalin's works were practically the Holy Writ, and this sudden about-face annoyed me so much that I immediately hung up a large portrait of Stalin in my office. I kept it there for some days until sober reflection showed that Stalin was the guilty man, and Walter Ulbricht had really only made a rather clumsy attempt to dethrone him.

The general confusion among party members increased enormously when details of the secret speech finally leaked out. I learned about it in Copenhagen, where I bought a copy of the *New York Times* while changing planes on my way to an international journalists' congress in Helsinki. As a result I spent quite a lot of the congress translating excerpts into German and Spanish for various delegates who knew no English. A few Communist stalwarts, clinging to their faith in Stalin, felt that the whole thing was a wicked CIA plot; others were in tears.

(Incidentally, American sources still claim the acquisition of the text of the secret speech as a brilliant victory for the US intelligence agencies. It soon became an open secret among well-informed journalists that the real story was more mundane. In Warsaw a few hundred copies of the speech had been run off for the confidential information of leading officials. Someone in the printshop saw the chance of turning a quick penny, printed a few more and flogged them on the black market. A man from the US embassy walked down the street, bought a copy – allegedly for two dollars – and the intelligence coup was complete.)

Back in the GDR there was only one subject for discussion in politically interested circles that summer. After the first shock at the revelations that some things had been very wrong indeed in the Soviet Union since at least 1934 when Kirov was murdered in Leningrad, there came the second shock when it appeared that the GDR party leadership was pursuing a policy of business-almost-as-usual. Ordinary party members were pressing for an explanation of how such horrors had come to be perpetrated in the name of socialism, and asking what steps could be taken to prevent such things happening again.

The position adopted by the GDR party leadership at that time is summed up well in an uninformative passage published over twenty years later in the official *History of the Socialist Unity Party*:

> The 20th Party Congress discussed further steps to overcome the cult of the personality and its results. This had come into existence in connection with a series of concrete historical conditions, was expressed in an over-emphasis of the role and achievements of J. V. Stalin, and led to an infringement of the Leninist norms of Party life and the laws of the Soviet state.
>
> It is a proof of the strength and the revolutionary spirit of the Communist Party of the Soviet Union that it uncovered such phenomena, took a determined stand against the cult of the personality, which is alien to Marxism-Leninism and socialism, and took all steps to eradicate its results in all fields of Party work and governmental and ideological activity.

All of which was not a very satisfactory explanation for tens of thousands of party members, particularly young party members who had been brought up to believe that Stalin was the fount of all wisdom. The confusion in the minds of most politically interested people was well expressed in a short parable by the Polish writer Janusz Osenka which was printed in a GDR weekly in November 1956, at the height of the discussion on Stalinism, and which I reprinted on 9 November 1956 in *German Report*. The parable can be summarised as follows:

A schoolteacher always taught his pupils that twice two makes nine. When he retired, the other teachers decided that the pupils should in future be told that the result of the sum was seven, and after a while six, thus bringing them nearer the truth without upsetting them unduly.

The pupils reacted in various ways. Some just wrote the result of the moment and continued to think of sweets and football; others got together and asked their teacher for an explanation, but were put off with an excuse; yet others stuck to twice two makes nine, for they were too lazy to change.

The well-behaved children enthusiastically wrote down the latest result; the badly-behaved children covered the lavatory walls with shocking scribbles such as 'Twice two makes four'; the careerists, looking ahead, shouted loudly that twice two makes three, or even one. But even the smallest child could see that twice two makes four, since he could count it off on his fingers.

That is the end of this very striking parable, which I assume does not need to be explained. By chance its publication marked fairly precisely the end of the public discussion of Stalinism which had begun to surface in various periodicals in the GDR. The GDR authorities had decided, particularly after the bloody events in Hungary in October and November 1956, that any open discussion endangered the stability of the socialist system as a whole, and thus the peace of Europe. So the word went out that any *Fehlerdiskussion* (discussion of past mistakes) was potentially counter-revolutionary, and must be halted; any errors of the past should be overcome in the forward march for the construction of a Socialist society.

Now a leap forward to another crisis. About daybreak on 13 August 1961 my phone rang. It was the correspondent of *Unità*, the Italian Communist newspaper, with whom I often exchanged news tips and rumours.

'The big story has broken,' he said. 'Barbed wire is going up right across Berlin.'

So I got out my car, and we toured the city for most of the day, watching the unusual spectacle of a modern city being carved into two pieces. Everywhere along the old borough boundaries between East Berlin and West Berlin men of the GDR Army Pioneer Corps and the factory militia in their green-grey overalls were stringing barbed wire: later in the day concrete slabs some 12 feet high were erected at some points. The 'Berlin Wall', as it was called in the West, and the 'Anti-Fascist Protective Barrier', as it was called in the East, was under construction.

Since the old borough boundaries had been fixed many years or even generations previously, when nobody could have foreseen that they could become an international frontier, the border often had a complicated and confusing configuration. In some places it ran along the middle of the road, in others along the edge of the pavement and in a few particularly complicated sections along the house frontage.

One of the stretches over open ground at the eastern end of the Tiergarten Park provided a particularly puzzling scene, and led to a misleading photograph which went round the world in the next few days. For some obscure historical reason a narrow tongue of East Berlin territory some 10 yards wide jutted for about 50 yards into West Berlin, and this too was being shut off with barbed wire. At one point on the western side a small group of West Berliners had gathered to watch the barrier going up. An enterprising West Berlin photographer walked round to the other side of the tongue and got a good action shot: in the foreground GDR soldiers stringing barbed wire, and behind the wire a nondescript group of civilians watching in silence.

Soon the picture was on the wires, with the caption: 'Angry East Berliners watch themselves being fenced in.' It was a good picture, and widely reproduced. In fact, it showed West Berliners being fenced out; and right in the middle of the group stood my Italian colleague and myself.

Whole books have been written about the whys and wherefores of the Berlin Wall, and I shall not try to compete; but a few sentences on the GDR point of view may be helpful. The central point was this: by the year 1961 the GDR was faced with a serious crisis. The West German economy, for a whole number of reasons including big foreign credits which had primed the pump, had taken off like a rocket; the GDR economy, which had had a much more difficult start, was doing quite well, but not that well.

The imbalance between the boom atmosphere in West Germany, which could offer jobs for all and a profusion of consumer goods, naturally attracted a considerable number of GDR citizens. After all, it was Karl Marx himself who had pointed out that the worker usually endeavours to sell his labour power in the highest market to the highest bidder, and West Germany was certainly the highest bidder.

And there was little difficulty in getting there. There was an open frontier between East and West Berlin. All that a GDR citizen who wished to emigrate had to do was travel a couple of stops on the elevated railway to the nearest West Berlin station. Then he reported to the nearest refugee camp and after a few days, and interrogation by western intelligence services, he was put on a plane and flown to West Germany. There, particularly if he was a skilled worker, he got a well-paid job without much trouble.

It is perhaps worth recording that the great majority of those moving west were in fact emigrants looking for a better standard of living, and not 'refugees fleeing from Red oppression' as the western media usually put it. Responsible West German observers noted that not more than 5 per cent of those leaving the GDR made any serious claim to be political refugees.

It is also worth recalling that, at just about the same time, countries like Britain were complaining bitterly of the 'brain drain', as British scientists and other experts streamed off across the Atlantic to the lusher pastures of the United States. The GDR was experiencing not just a brain drain, but a muscles drain and a skills drain too.

West German agencies soon noted the way in which this drain, which steadily increased, was weakening the GDR, and decided to give a helping hand. Whole categories of GDR citizens with particular skills, ranging from doctors to print workers, were lured to join the rush with job contracts, guarantees of housing and special financial help.

We must remember that this drama was being played out against a background in which US Secretary of State John Foster Dulles was dreaming of 'rolling back' socialism out of eastern Europe, and the West German Bundeswehr, commanded by old Hitler generals, was becoming a serious factor. And this was a time too when the West German Government, with the support of all the mainline parties, was calling for a revision of the frontiers of Europe – specifically the incorporation into the Federal Republic of Germany of the GDR plus the western third of Poland and a slice of the Soviet Union.

By mid-1961 GDR citizens were moving to West Germany at a rate of over 300,000 a year, and the numbers were rising steadily. The calculation, in some circles at least, was that, if the trend continued, the GDR would eventually collapse, and the 'roll-back' could begin.

After the closing of the open frontier, the GDR economy, which had been sagging, soon began to pick up again, and it ultimately produced the relatively good standard of living of today. But that was not the only satisfactory result of a painful decision. Looking back from today it appears evident that this was the decisive step in clearing the way for a settlment of the 'German problem', which had been bedevilling many aspects of European and world politics since 1945. I believe you can trace a direct line from the Berlin Wall in 1961 to the complicated series of agreements and treaties concluded in the early 1970s. The status of West Berlin, which had been a bone of contention between the power blocs since at least 1949, was properly settled; the two German states established normal relations with each other; and the GDR, which had been regarded as non-existent by most of the non-socialist world, was finally received into the comity of nations.

The division of the old Germany into two separate and distinct states today looks as permanent as anything else in a world largely divided between two power blocs. As long as the balance of power rules the world scene, any reversal appears inconceivable.

In the weeks and days preceding the closing of the Berlin frontier, it became obvious that something fairly drastic was going to happen. Special correspondents from all over flooded into West Berlin, for another 'Berlin crisis' was clearly pending. Several of them, old acquaintances, tried to pick my brains, but I had no inside information, and a striking lack of good guesses.

On 12 August, the day before the closure, Flora Lewis of the *New York Times* dropped in to see me. I had known her for many years as a tough and well-informed observer. For quite a while we chewed over the situation, and discussed the splurge of rumours as to what might happen next. The whole of Berlin was going to be declared a free city, and the GDR Government would move to Leipzig, said one rumour; East Berlin would be given a special status, and people from other parts of the GDR would be kept out, said another; and there were plenty of other suggestions.

Finally Flora put the question: 'Look, John,' she said, 'we are old friends, and I promise not to use the story; this is just for background information. Is Ulbricht going to build a wall along the sector borders in Berlin?'

I could not really conceive of this happening, and I said flatly that he would not. About fourteen hours later, the wall went up, and in the flurry of events it occurred to me that Flora Lewis must have lost all faith in my abilities as a soothsayer.

But quite the contrary. When I met her again some months later it became clear in conversation that she was convinced that I knew all the secrets of the GDR. Otherwise, she thought, I would not have given her such a straight 'no' in reply to her question. I did not disillusion her.

33

But Where Is the Omelette?

When I first began to plan this volume rather vaguely a number of years ago, I discussed the subject with James Cameron, the British radical journalist whose autobiography *Point of Departure* helped to jog me to my typewriter.

'You've been a journalist all your life,' he said, 'and that is perhaps the worst preparation in the world for writing a book. We journalists spend our lives compressing as much information as possible into as few words as possible, particularly if the cable tolls are high.'

Despite James Cameron's friendly advice that I should acquire a more expansive style for my book, I shall not dwell long on 1968, the year of the Czechoslovak 'events'. For a short period many of us on the left saw in the Prague Spring a chance for a revival of our socialist dream instead of that form of socialism which had come into being with greater or lesser success in eastern Europe. The reformers of Prague were never given a chance to see whether their recipes would work. The other Warsaw Pact states, concerned at any possible change in the European balance, intervened.

In the 1930s, when party members or fellow travellers were upset or mystified by inexplicable events in the Soviet Union, they were often assuaged with the glib phrase that you could not make an omelette without breaking eggs. Sometimes this argument had a measure of validity. In face of the counter-revolutionary 'White Terror' in Russia after the 1917 Revolution, counter-measures, usually described as the 'Red Terror', may have been inevitable. But in later years the broken eggs became all too numerous, and the omelette failed to make a very satisfactory appearance.

So where is the omelette today? Here I would like to present my personal view, based on the thirty-five years I have spent in the German Democratic Republic, the only socialist state of which I have any intimate knowledge.

Let us start with the good news. Taking off on an uncertain basis soon after the Second World War, the GDR has developed today into a moderately prosperous and well-run state with a functioning socialist economy. According to how you interpret the statistics, it is one of the ten or twelve leading industrial nations of the world, and probably within the top twenty with regard to standards of living, something notoriously hard to measure.

From the very start, under the leadership of veteran Communists, who proved in the main to be people of personal integrity, energy and intelligence, it broke much more successfully than West Germany with the heritage of nazism and constructed a new society. In the field of social legislation it has often been among the world leaders, with sensible and liberal laws on such subjects as family planning (every woman has the right to free contraceptive devices and free and unquestioned abortion up to three months), long maternity leave on full pay and the non-criminal-isation of homosexuality.

Social mobility has been encouraged; in the early years of the GDR there was 'positive discrimination' in this field, with special facilities for work-ing-class children to go on to higher education, thus helping to redress the balance of the old class system.

Today, in 1985, there is no unemployment in the GDR, and every school-leaver gets trade training and a job; the future will show whether this proud record can be maintained.

But now I must turn to more negative aspects.

'Benevolent paternalism' may not sound so bad, but when it is all-embracing and inescapable it can become stifling. I do not think it is really unfair to compare society in the GDR in some ways with a Victorian family. Paterfamilias, himself strict and rather puritan, wishes only the best for his household; and he, very definitely and finally, knows what that best is. Many of his decisions are wise, but whether they are wise or not, the family has to conform without argument.

As I write, I can look out of the window of my comfortable flat in a modern block in the centre of East Berlin at the side wall, less than one hundred yards away, of the huge building which houses the Central Committee of the Socialist Unity Party of the GDR. All important decisions on the life of the country are arrived at here. As I mentioned above, I believe that many of these decisions are wise. But they are arrived at without any public discussion of the pros and cons, and without any proper channel for dissent to be registered.

And at least in the long run I fear that the results can only be negative. Since the vast majority of the population have the feeling that they cannot participate in the decision-making, they tend to withdraw and live their private lives. They march on May Day demonstrations and vote in the single-list parliamentary elections because it is the done thing, but without any particular enthusiasm. There are obviously all sorts of creeping dangers in such a conformist society; for instance, it is almost inevitably the mediocre, the conformists, who get ahead.

Karl Marx once said that his favourite motto was 'De omnibus dubitandum' – doubt everything. Today in the GDR the ruling motto would appear to be just the opposite: 'Father knows best.'

To round off my personal story, I should note that since 1978 I have been very happy with my fourth – and presumably last – wife, a GDR girl who does not even remember the Second World War. Since *German Report* closed down in 1975 I have been supplementing my old-age pension with all sorts of translation work, including a lot of time on the definitive English translation of the works of Karl Marx and Friedrich Engels.

But where is the omelette? I am still looking.